CHARMING
SMALL HOTEL
GUIDES

France

CHARMING
SMALL HOTEL
GUIDES

France

Edited by Andrew Duncan

DUNCAN PETERSEN

HUNTER
PUBLISHING INC

300 Raritan Center Parkway,
CN 94, Edison, N.J. 08818

Conceived, designed and produced by
Duncan Petersen Publishing Ltd,

Editor	Andrew Duncan
Revisions editor	Nicola Davies
Art director	Mel Petersen
Designers	Chris Foley and Beverley Stewart
Editorial director	Andrew Duncan

This edition published in the UK and Commonwealth 1997 by
Duncan Petersen Publishing Ltd,
31 Ceylon Road, London W14 OYP

Sales representation in the U.K. and Ireland by
World Leisure Marketing,
9 Downing Road,
West Meadows Industrial Estate
Derby DE21 6HA
Tel: 01332 343 332

Distributed by Grantham Book Services

ISBN 1 872576 65 6

A CIP catalogue record for this book is available
from the British Library

AND

Published in the USA 1997 by
Hunter Publishing Inc.,
300 Raritan Center Parkway, CN 94, Edison, N.J. 08818.
Tel (908) 225 1900 Fax (908) 417 0482

ISBN 1-55650-778-X

Typeset by Duncan Petersen Publishing Ltd
Printed by G. Canale & Co SpA, Turin

Contents

Introduction   6

Reporting to the guides   11

Hotel location maps   12

The North-West   20

Ile-de-France   45

The North-East   78

The West   90

The East   109

The South-West   131

Massif Central   157

The South   171

Corsica   215

Index of hotel names   216

Index of hotel locations   220

Readers' reports

Reports from readers are of enormous help to us in keeping up to date with the hotels in the guide – and other hotels that should be in it. The most helpful reporters are invited to join our Travellers' Panel, and to stay in listed hotels at little or no cost. More information on p11.

Introduction

This new edition
It's nine years now since we first set out to identify the hotels that help to make travelling in France such a special experience. Then, we were looking for the 300 most captivating auberges, châteaux, moulins and chalets in the land. After our recent major overhaul of the guide, we now have an expanded coverage of over 360 hotels, with photographs of more than 120. We've achieved this by organising the book differently, as explained on page 8.

In this new edition we have made further important changes to two parts of the book: Paris, and those sections covering the southern part of France. These arise from extensive new research done in 1996 for two forthcoming titles in the series: *Paris* and *Southern France*. Both will be available in 1997 and we are sure that enthusiasts will find them very useful complements to this book. They give an in-depth view which is impossible in a guide covering the whole country.

Charming and small
There really are relatively few *genuine* charming small hotels. Unlike other guides, we are particularly fussy about size, rarely straying over 20 bedrooms. If a hotel has more than that, it needs to have the *feel* of a much smaller place to be in this guide.

We attach more importance to size than other guides because we think that unless a hotel is small, it cannot give a genuinely personal welcome, or make you feel like an individual, rather than just a guest. For what we mean by a personal welcome, see below.

Unlike other guides, we often rule out places that have great qualities, but are nonetheless no more nor less than – hotels. Our hotels are all special in some way.

We think that we have a much clearer idea than other guides of what is special and what is not; and we think we apply these criteria more consistently than other guides because we are a small and personally managed company rather than a bureaucracy. We have a small team of like-minded inspectors, chosen by the editor and thoroughly rehearsed in recognizing what we want. While we very much appreciate readers' reports – see below – they are not our main source of information.

Last but by no means least, we're independent – there's no payment for inclusion.

So what exactly do we look for?
• An attractive, preferably peaceful setting.
• A building that is either handsome or interesting or historic, or at least with a distinct character.
• Ideally, we look for adequate space, but on a human

scale: we don't go for places that rely on grandeur, or that have pretensions that could intimidate.

• Decoration must be harmonious and in good taste, and the furnishings and facilities comfortable and well maintained. We like to see interesting antique furniture that is there because it can be used, not simply revered.

• The proprietors and staff need to be dedicated and thoughtful, offering a personal welcome, *without being intrusive*. The guest needs to feel like an individual.

Whole-page entries
We rarely see all of these qualities together in one place; but our warmest recommendations – whole page, with photograph – usually lack only one or two of these qualities.

Small entries
Lack of space means that some hotel entries have shorter descriptions and no photograph. We consider all these hotels worthy to be in the guide.

Pet hates
We are, naturally, enthusiastic about French hotels in general. But we are not blind to their faults. Here is a list of our current pet hates.

The 'confused' booking You make a booking, even send a deposit, and on arrival find that you're not expected. If you can't be accommodated and are put up in some other house in the village, there is the teeniest suspicion that what is at work is not confusion but greed.

The soggy bed As we've observed in our British edition, it's the easiest thing in the world to fail to spot the gradual decay of a bed unless you take the precaution of occasionally testing every one in the house.

The dreary breakfast We know that the French aren't very keen on breakfast, but hoteliers ought to be aware that many other people are – especially when travelling, and a good start to the day is important.

The second-class pensionnaires' meals If you're tempted to stay on pension or demi-pension terms, be sure you know what choice of dishes will be open. There may be none at all; or you may be confined to the cheapest menu.

The windowless garden room Quite a few French country hotels accommodate some or all of their guests in single-storey outbuildings with glazed doors opening on to the garden or the pool. And quite a few provide no ventilation other than those doors, which most travellers would naturally be reluctant to leave open at night.

The rough deal for vegetarians The acceptance of vegetarianism in France is still very limited, and progressing very slowly. Too many cooks, waiters and

proprietors of small hotels find it hard to conceal the fact
that they think vegetarians are mad, and a great nuisance.

No fear or favour
Unlike many guides, there is no payment for inclusion. The
selection is made *entirely* independently.

Check the price first
See page 9 for the system we adopt in giving prices; to avoid
unpleasant surprises, always double check the price at time
of booking. Sometimes they go up after we've gone to
press, sometimes there is a seasonal or other variation from
the printed version.

How to find an entry
In this guide, the entries are arranged in geographical
groups. First, the whole country is divided into three major
sections; we start with Northern France and proceed to
Central and finally Southern France. Within these sections,
the entries are dealt with in regions consisting of groups of
départements. See page 5 for a list of the regions we have
used.

Each regional section follows a set sequence:

> • First comes an Area introduction – an
> overview of that region, incorporating (if there's
> space) a summary of the tourist highlights. Under
> the heading 'Contenders', we list hotels that have
> failed to make an entry this year, but which we
> believe to be strong candidates for an entry in
> future. These listings may be useful if
> recommended hotels are full, or if there are no
> recommendations in a particular area. We
> particularly welcome reports on these hotels.

> • Then come the main, full-page entries for that
> region, arranged in alphabetical order by town.
> These are generally the hotels that we judge most
> attractive.

> • Finally come the shorter, quarter-page entries for
> that region, similarly arranged alphabetically by
> town. These are generally not as special as the
> hotels given a full-page entry; but don't disregard
> them – they are still hotels we would happily
> stay at, and many are clear candidates for
> 'promotion' in later editions.

To find a hotel in a particular area, simply browse through

Introduction

the headings at the top of the pages until you find that area – or use the maps following this introduction to locate the appropriate pages. The maps show not only the place-name under which each hotel appears, but also the page number of the entry.

To locate a specific hotel or a hotel in a specific place, use the indexes at the back, which list the entries alphabetically, first by name and then by place-name.

How to read an entry
At the top of each entry is a coloured bar highlighting the name of the town or village where the establishment is located, along with a categorization which gives some clue to its character.

Fact boxes
The fact box given for each hotel follows a standard pattern; the explanation that follows is for full entries – short, quarter-page entries have less detailed fact boxes.

Under **Tel** we give the full 10-digit telephone number.We now also give **Fax** numbers where appropriate.

Under Location we give information on the setting of the hotel and on its car parking arrangements, as well as pointers to help you find it. It is worth bearing in mind that many of our hotels are in remote spots where a large-scale road map is more-or-less essential for reliable route-finding.

Under **Meals** we list the meals available.

The basic **Prices** in this volume – unlike our volume on Britain and Ireland – are **per room**. We normally give the range of prices you can expect to pay for a room – from the cost of the cheapest single room in low season to the cost of the dearest double in high season. If the room price we give includes breakfast, we say so; otherwise, space permitting, we normally give the price of breakfast separately; where it is not given, allow 40F to 70F, according to the room price. We then give the prices of other meals, concentrating on fixed-price menus, or of prices for a room plus meals – either for dinner, bed and breakfast (DB&B), or for full board (FB) – all meals included. All these meal-inclusive prices are **per person**. Prices includes tax and service.
  Wherever possible we have given prices for 1995, but for many hotels these were not available when the guide was prepared. Bear in mind also that proprietors may change

their prices from one year to another by more than the rate of inflation, particularly if the hotel has been upgraded in some important respect. Always check when booking.

Under **Rooms** we summarize the number and style of bedrooms available. Our lists of facilities in bedrooms cover only mechanical gadgets, and not ornaments such as flowers or consumables such as toiletries or free drinks.

Under **Facilities** we list public rooms and then outdoor and sporting facilities which are either part of the hotel or immediately on hand; facilities in the vicinity of the hotel but not directly connected with it (for example, a nearby golf course) are not listed here, though they sometimes feature at the end of the main description in the **Nearby** section, which presents interesting things to see or do in the locality.

We use the following abbreviations for **Credit cards:**

AE American Express
DC Diners Club
MC MasterCard (Access/Eurocard)
V   Visa (Barclaycard/Bank Americard/Carte Bleue etc)

The final entry in a fact box is normally the name of the proprietor(s); but where the hotel is run by a manager we give his or her name instead.

Please write and tell us about your experiences of small hotels, guest-houses and inns, whether good or bad, whether listed in this edition or not. As well as hotels in France, we are interested in hotels in Britain and Ireland, Italy, Spain, Austria, Germany, Switzerland and the USA. We assume that reporters have no objections to our publishing their views unpaid, either verbatim or in edited form.

Readers who report regularly and reliably may be invited to join our Travellers' Panel. Members give us notice of their own travel plans; we suggest hotels that they might inspect, and contribute to the cost of accommodation.

The address to write to is:

Duncan Petersen Publishing Ltd
31 Ceylon Road, London W14 0YP, England.

Checklist
Please use a separate sheet of paper for each report; include your name and address on each report.

Your reports will be received with particular pleasure if they are typed, and if they are organized under the following headings:

Name of establishment
Town or village it is in, or nearest
Full address, including post code
Date and duration of visit
The building and setting
The public rooms
The bedrooms and bathrooms
Comfort (chairs, beds, heat, light, hot water)
Standards of maintenance and housekeeping
Atmosphere, welcome and service
Food
Value for money

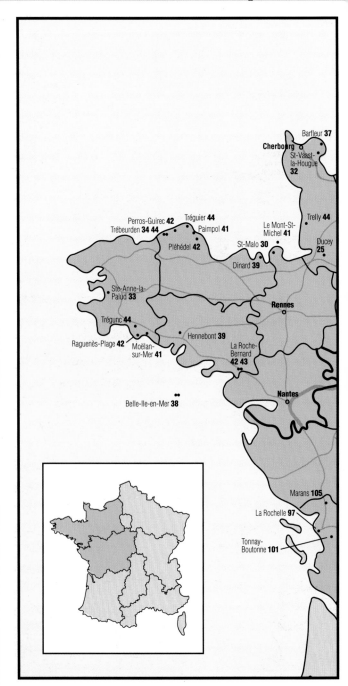

Barfleur **37**

Cherbourg
St-Vaast-
la-Hougue
32

Trelly **44**

Perros-Guirec **42**   Tréguier **44**
Trébeurden **34 44**   Paimpol **41**

Le Mont-St-
Michel **41**

Ducey
25

Pléhédel **42**

St-Malo **30**

Dinard **39**

Ste-Anne-la-
Palud **33**

Rennes

Trégunc **44**

Hennebont **39**

Raguenès-Plage **42**
Moëlan-
sur-Mer **41**

La Roche-
Bernard
42 43

Belle-Ile-en-Mer **38**

Nantes

Marans **105**

La Rochelle **97**

Tonnay-
Boutonne **101**

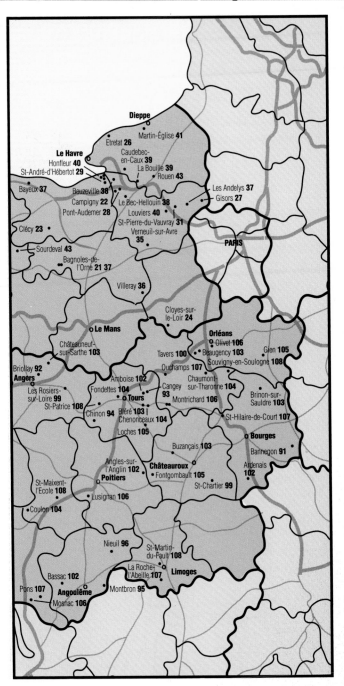

Dieppe
Martin-Église **41**
Etretat **26**
Caudebec-en-Caux **39**
Le Havre
Honfleur **40**
St-André-d'Hébertot **29**
La Bouille **39**
Rouen **43**
Bayeux **37**
Beuzeville **38**
Les Andelys **37**
Gisors **27**
Campigny **22**
Le Bec-Hellouin **38**
Pont-Audemer **28**
Louviers **40**
St-Pierre-du-Vauvray **31**
Clécy **23**
Verneuil-sur-Avre **35**
PARIS
Sourdeval **43**
Bagnoles-de-l'Orne **21 37**
Villeray **36**
Cloyes-sur-le-Loir **24**
Le Mans
Orléans
Châteauneuf-sur-Sarthe **103**
Olivet **106**
Tavers **100**
Beaugency **103**
Glen **105**
Souvigny-en-Sologne **108**
Briollay **92**
Ouchamps **107**
Angers
Amboise **102**
Chaumont-sur-Tharonne **104**
Les Rosiers-sur-Loire **99**
Fondettes **104**
Cangey **93**
Brinon-sur-Sauldre **103**
St-Patrice **108**
Tours
Montrichard **106**
Chinon **94**
Bléré **103**
Chenonceaux **104**
St-Hilaire-de-Court **107**
Loches **105**
Bourges
Buzançais **103**
Bannegon **91**
Angles-sur-l'Anglin **102**
Châteauroux
Ardenais **102**
Poitiers
Fontgombault **105**
St-Maixent-l'Ecole **108**
St-Chartier **99**
Lusignan **106**
Coulon **104**
Nieuil **96**
St-Martin-du-Fault **108**
Bassac **102**
La Roche-l'Abeille **107**
Limoges
Pons **107**
Angoulême
Montbron **95**
Mosnac **106**

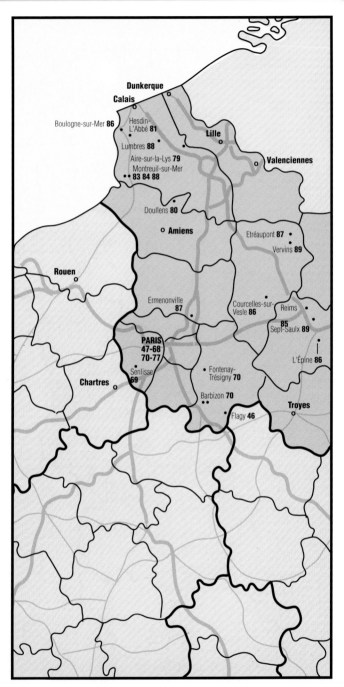

Dunkerque

Calais

Boulogne-sur-Mer **86**

Hesdin-
L'Abbé **81**

Lille

Lumbres **88**

Aire-sur-la-Lys **79**
Montreuil-sur-Mer
83 84 88

Valenciennes

Doullens **80**

Amiens

Etréaupont **87**

Vervins **89**

Rouen

Ermenonville
87

Courcelles-sur-
Vesle **86**

Reims

85
Sept-Saulx **89**

PARIS
**47-68
70-77**

L'Épine **86**

Senlisse
69

Fontenay-
Trésigny **70**

Chartres

Barbizon **70**

Troyes

Flagy **46**

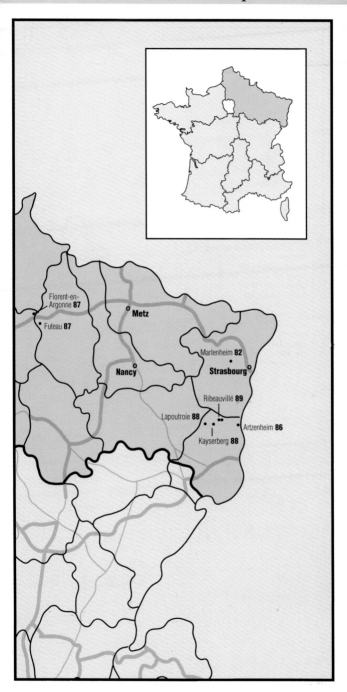

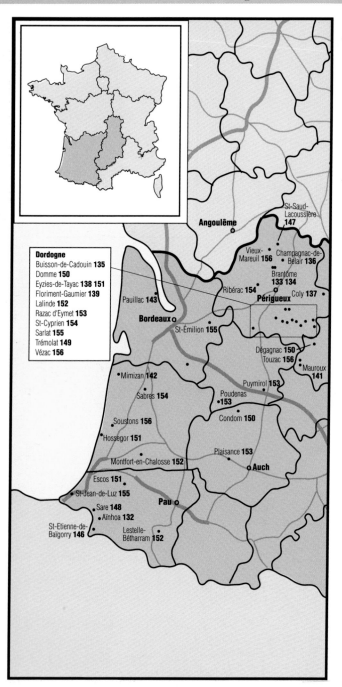

Dordogne
Buisson-de-Cadouin **135**
Domme **150**
Eyzies-de-Tayac **138 151**
Floriment-Gaumier **139**
Lalinde **152**
Razac d'Eymet **153**
St-Cyprien **154**
Sarlat **155**
Trémolat **149**
Vézac **156**

St-Saud-Lacoussière **147**

Angoulême

Vieux-Mareuil **156**

Champagnac-de-Belair **136**

Brantôme **133 134**

Ribérac **154**

Périgueux

Coly **137**

Pauillac **143**

Bordeaux

St-Émilion **155**

Dégagnac **150**
Touzac **156**

Mauroux **141**

Mimizan **142**

Puymirol **153**

Poudenas **153**

Sabres **154**

Soustons **156**

Condom **150**

Hossegor **151**

Plaisance **153**

Montfort-en-Chalosse **152**

Auch

Escos **151**

St-Jean-de-Luz **155**

Pau

Sare **148**
Aïnhoa **132**

St-Etienne-de-Baïgorry **146**

Lestelle-Bétharram **152**

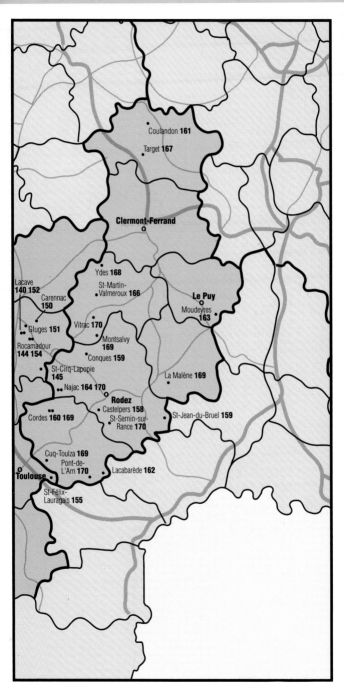

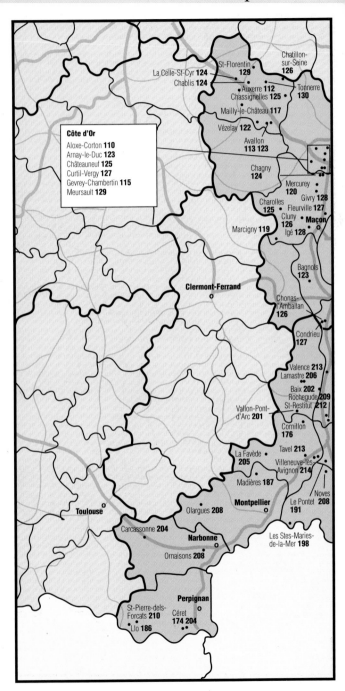

St-Florentin **129**

Chatillon-sur-Seine **126**

La Celle-St-Cyr **124**

Chablis **124**

Auxerre **112**

Chassignelles **125**

Tonnerre **130**

Mailly-le-Château **117**

Vézelay **122**

Avallon **113 123**

Côte d'Or

Aloxe-Corton **110**
Arnay-le-Duc **123**
Châteauneuf **125**
Curtil-Vergy **127**
Gevrey-Chambertin **115**
Meursault **129**

Chagny **124**

Mercurey **120**

Givry **128**

Charolles **125**

Fleurville **127**

Cluny **126**

Mâcon

Marcigny **119**

Igé **128**

Bagnols **123**

Clermont-Ferrand

Chonas-l'Amballan **126**

Condrieu **127**

Valence **213**

Lamastre **206**

Baix **202**

Rochegude **209**

St-Restitut **212**

Vallon-Pont-d'Arc **201**

Cornillon **176**

La Favède **205**

Tavel **213**

Villeneuve-lès-Avignon **214**

Madières **187**

Montpellier

Noves

Le Pontet **191**

Toulouse

Olargues **208**

Carcassonne **204**

Narbonne

Les Stes-Maries-de-la-Mer **198**

Ornaisons **208**

Perpignan

St-Pierre-dels-Forcats **210**

Céret **174 204**

Llo **186**

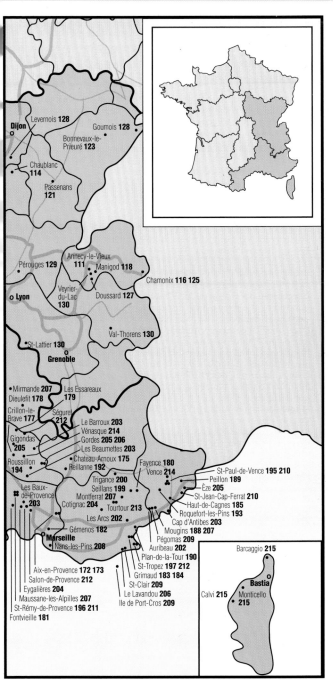

Levernois **128**

Dijon

Goumois **128**

Bornevaux-le-Prieuré **123**

Chaublanc **114**

Passenans **121**

Pérouges **129**

Annecy-le-Vieux **111**

Manigod **118**

Chamonix **116 125**

Veyrier-du-Lac **130**

Doussard **127**

o **Lyon**

Val-Thorens **130**

St-Lattier **130**

Grenoble

Mirmande **207**
Dieulefit **178**

Les Essareaux **179**

Crillon-le-Brave **177**

Séguret **212**

Le Barroux **203**
Vénasque **214**
Gordes **205 206**
Les Beaumettes **203**

Gigondas **205**

Roussillon **194**

Chateau-Arnoux **175**
Reillanne **192**

Fayence **180**
Vence **214**

St-Paul-de-Vence **195 210**

Trigance **200**
Seillans **199**
Montferrat **207**

Peillon **189**

Èze **205**

St-Jean-Cap-Ferrat **210**

Haut-de-Cagnes **185**

Les Baux-de-Provence **203**

Cotignac **204**

Tourtour **213**

Roquefort-les-Pins **193**

Les Arcs **202**

Cap d'Antibes **203**

Gémenos **182**

Mougins **188 207**

Marseille

Nans-les-Pins **208**

Pégomas **209**

Auribeau **202**

Barcaggio **215**

Aix-en-Provence **172 173**

Plan-de-la-Tour **190**

Salon-de-Provence **212**

St-Tropez **197 212**

Eygalières **204**

Grimaud **183 184**

Bastia

Maussane-les-Alpilles **207**

St-Clair **209**

Calvi **215**

Monticello **215**

St-Rémy-de-Provence **196 211**

Le Lavandou **206**

Fontvieille **181**

Ile de Port-Cros **209**

The North-West

The North-west is familiar territory to many British visitors. Lush Normandy, full of apple orchards and contented cows, is close enough to be convenient for a weekend break, and many people who live in the west of Britain prefer to use the Normandy ports when aiming further south. Further to the west, Brittany is bucket-and-spade country, and has much in common with Cornwall – a dramatic coastline, and a vigorous climate. On the border between the two regions is the most popular tourist sight in France: Mont St Michel.

Contenders in the North-west

Agneaux, Château d'Agneaux 02.33.57.65.88 Severe-looking little manor house, immaculately furnished.

Balisne, Moulin de Balisne 02.32.32.03.48 'Well-restored water mill' with good furnishings and extensive lawn.

Bazouges, Hostellerie de Mirwault 02.43.07.13.17 'Relaxing' English-run Logis with gardens overlooking the Mayenne.

Bénouville, La Pommeraie 02.31.44.62.43 Renowned restaurant with modern bedrooms in new building in grounds.

Brélidy, Château de Brélidy 02.96.95.69.38 Stern little stone manor house in peaceful setting.

Concarneau, Le Galion 02.98.97.30.16 Cosily beamed restaurant with rooms in old town, with neat modern rooms across the way.

Creully, Hostellerie Saint Martin 02.31.80.10.11 Shuttered Logis on village square with charming vaulted restaurant serving good-value menus.

Honfleur, Hostellerie Lechat 02.31.89.23.85 Smartly renovated inn, with bold colour schemes; central – parking not easy.

Lisieux, La Ferme des Poiriers Roses 02.31.64.72.14 Superbly furnished timbered house in a beautiful garden doing bed and wonderful breakfast.

Mür-de-Bretagne, Auberge Grand'Maison 02.96.28.51.10 One-star restaurant with rooms – some quite swish, though winning no prizes for taste.

Percy, La Voisinière 02.33.61.18.47 A pair of rustic cottages with prettily furnished rooms, in a beautiful flowery garden with pond.

Pleugueneuc, Château de la Motte Beaumanoir 02.99.69.46.01 Elegantly decorated 15thC château in ornamental grounds.

Plouharnel, Les Ajoncs d'Or 02.97.52.32.02 Cottagey stone-built Logis in shady, flowery garden.

Plozevet, Moulin de Brenizenec 02.98.91.30.33 Traditionally furnished old water mill in wooded grounds.

Pluherlin, Château de Talhouet 02.97.43.34.72 Slightly severe 16th/17thC château in grassy grounds, tastefully furnished and run as a B&B.

Pornichet, Hôtel Sud Bretagne 02.40.11.65.00 Smooth, luxurious seaside hotel (close to beach) with attractive garden.

Roscoff, Le Brittany 02.98.69.70.78 Neatly furnished stone manor house with particularly attractive restaurant, and indoor pool.

St-Briac-sur-Mer, Manoir de la Duchée 02.99.88.00.02 Little manor house B&B deep in countryside, handsomely furnished.

St-Pierre-de-Plesguen, Le Petit Moulin du Rouvre 02.99.73.85.84 Neatly restored 17thC water mill by a small lake.

The North-West

Manoir du Lys

The addition of an outdoor swimming-pool further enhances this delightful, typically Norman half-timbered hunting lodge, with geraniums at its foot and dripping from its balconies. It was reopened as a hotel by the Quintons in 1985 after a long period of disuse, and many improvements have been introduced. The new building is harmonious, and the bedrooms are very attractive – all spacious and well equipped, with stylish furnishings far removed from the French norm. Most have balconies overlooking the gardens.

Marie-France oversees the smart dining-rooms (also overlooking the gardens, through floor-to-ceiling windows) where you can enjoy her son Franck's delicious cuisine, which is rooted in local tradition but acknowledges modern preferences. In good weather you can dine outside. There is also a polished little bar/sitting-room with a huge open fire and a grand piano (played on Friday nights).

The Quintons organise popular educational 'mushroom' weekends, during which up to 120 varieties may be picked in the surrounding woods; English-language tuition can be laid on.

Nearby Andaines forest – walking, riding, cycling.

La Croix Gauthier, Route de Juvigny, 61140 Bagnoles-de-l'Orne
Tel 02.33.37.80.69
Fax 02.33.30.05.80
Location in middle of countryside in forest of Andaines; with car parking
Meals breakfast, lunch, dinner
Prices rooms 300F-780F; menus 135F-265F
Rooms 20 double, 19 with bath, one with shower; 3 suites; all have phone, TV, minibar

Facilities dining-room, sitting-room/bar, billiards; tennis court, swimming-pool
Credit cards AE, DC, MC, V
Children welcome; special menu 85F
Disabled 1 bedroom
Pets dogs accepted in bedrooms only 35F
Closed 6 Jan to 14 Feb; Sun evening and Mon from Nov to Easter
Proprietor Marie-France and Paul Quinton

The North-West

Hostellerie du Moulin du Vey

Just when we were beginning to wonder about this old, creeper-clad water-mill, a burst of readers' reports reassures us about its continuing appeal. 'Very pleasing,' says one. 'Bright, tastefully decorated rooms, excellent restaurant, friendly service.'

The Moulin is at the heart of some of the best scenery in the region, where the river Orne has carved a majestic valley between green, rolling hills. It is within easy driving distance of the ferry at Caen, and makes an attractive first- or last-night stop.

Both the buildings and the gardens are beautifully kept, and there is a pleasant waterside terrace for eating and drinking, with a garden beyond. Food in the half-timbered, rather barn-like restaurant, just across the courtyard from the main building, is carefully prepared and served, and the less expensive menus are sound value. Bedrooms are comfortable, furnished simply but with touches of style, and reasonably priced. Some rooms are in annexes: the Manoir de Placy, 400 metres away, and the Relais de Surosne, 3 km away on the other side of the village – a peaceful, small Gothic-style house with a lush garden.

Nearby Suisse Normande region; Thury-Harcourt (10 km) – ruined château; Falaise (30 km) – castle.

Le Vey 14570 Clécy
Tel 02.31.69.71.08
Fax 02.31.69.14.14
Location 2 km E of Clécy and 35 kms S of Caen; with river terrace and car parking
Meals breakfast, lunch, dinner
Prices rooms 390F-520F; menus 138F-360F
Rooms 17 double (7 twin) all with bath; 2 family rooms, one with bath, one with shower; all rooms have central heating, phone, colour TV

Facilities dining-room, banqueting-room, conference room
Credit cards AE, DC, MC, V
Children accepted
Disabled no special facilities
Pets accepted but not in dining-room
Closed Dec and Jan
Proprietor Denise Leduc

The North-West

Le Petit Coq aux Champs

A thatched house with its own heliport – it sounds unlikely, but convention counts for little at this smart, secluded retreat, amid rolling meadows and sweeping forests in the Risle valley. Le Petit Coq offers an intriguing mixture of the rustic, the sophisticated and the downright idiosyncratic – a cocktail that may be too heady for some, to judge by our empty postbag.

The building, mostly 19th century, has two main wings with a spacious, airy, modern extension in between. The style varies considerably – modern cane furniture in the large sitting-room, while antiques predominate in the restaurant, which has a huge open fireplace at one end. An intimate piano bar has been squeezed into the new building. The bedrooms are all furnished and arranged in different ways, some brightly coloured, others more restrained; none is particularly large.

Jean-Marie Huard, who has returned to his Norman roots after some years in highly reputed restaurants in Paris, pays serious attention to detail, presentation and local tradition in his cooking – with impressive results.

Nearby fishing, golf; Pont-Audemer – half-timbered houses, church of Saint-Ouen; Honfleur (30 km) – old port.

Campigny 27500 Pont-Audemer
Tel & Fax 02.32.41.04.19
Location in countryside, 6 km S of Pont-Audemer; in gardens with ample car parking
Meals breakfast, lunch, dinner
Prices rooms 460F-720F; breakfast 57F; menus 185F-310F
Rooms 12 double (4 twin), one family room, one suite, all with bath; all rooms have central heating, phone, TV, hairdrier
Facilities sitting-room, 4 dining-rooms, bar; swimming-pool
Credit cards AE, DC, MC, V
Children very welcome
Disabled dining-rooms and 8 bedrooms are on ground floor
Pets welcome
Closed January
Proprietors Fabienne Desmonts and Jean-Marie Huard

The North-West

Country inn, Cloyes-sur-le-Loir

Le St-Jacques

Has this old coaching inn, for some years now enjoying a new lease of life as an *étape gastronomique*, lost its way? It has certainly lost its Michelin star – as predicted by a reader who ate there before the event. He also records a poor reception, and a mediocre bedroom. But other reporters have been much happier, and we retain a soft spot for the place. For the moment, look before you book – and let us know your conclusions.

The dining-room, looking out over the garden, is pleasantly intimate. But in good weather meals are served in the shade of the trees in the garden, which is a lush expanse leading down to the banks of the little Loir. The bedrooms (at the back, looking over the garden) have been smartly done out in designer fabrics and cherry-wood reproduction antiques.

Nearby Châteaudun (10 km) – feudal château; Vendôme – la Trinité, Porte St Georges; Beaugency (45 km) – bridge, keep.

Place du Marché aux Oeufs
28220 Cloyes-sur-le-Loir
Tel 02.37.98.40.08
Fax 02.37.98.32.63
Location in village, 28 km NE of Vendôme; with garden and car parking
Meals breakfast, lunch, dinner
Prices rooms 360F-480F; suite 680F; breakfast 50F; menus 170F
Rooms 22 double, 18 with bath, 4 with shower (5 twin); one family room; all rooms have central heating, phone, TV
Facilities dining-room, sitting-room, bar
Credit cards MC, V
Children welcome
Disabled lift/elevator
Pets accepted in room and dining-room
Closed Nov to Mar
Proprietor Eric Thureau

The North-West

Auberge de la Sélune

We have nothing but positive reports on file for this splendid small hotel, which has undergone extensive improvements recently. It offers excellent value for money and tends to be pretty busy in high season. But do give it a try.

It is difficult to decide whether the housekeeping or the food earns the prize, as both are first-class. The whole place is pleasantly decorated – mainly in bright and stylish prints – and spotlessly kept; there are fluffy towels and endless hot water, crisp linen and sound beds. Jean-Pierre Girres's cooking is excellent; his fish, seafood and *pâtisserie* are particularly well regarded; crab pie is one of his noted specialities. There are two dining-rooms, though eating here is popular with locals, and dinner can take some time to serve – but there is not much else to occupy your time in the evening here. Breakfast is above average, too. Josette Girres is not a chatty hostess, but her welcome is warm. The hotel fronts directly on to the street, so parking is awkward. To compensate, there is a little garden at the back beside the Sélune.

Nearby Salmon fishing (river Sélune); Avranches (10 km) – museum; Le Mont-St-Michel (15 km) – fortified abbey on island.

2 Rue St-Germain 50220 Ducey
Tel 02.33.48.53.62
Fax 02.33.48.90.30
Location by river in village, on N176 11 km SE of Avranches; with small garden and some car parking
Meals breakfast, lunch, dinner
Prices rooms 270F-290F; breakfast 40F; menus 80F-200F
Rooms 19 double, all with bath (5 twin); one single; one family room with bath; all rooms have central heating, phone; TV on request
Facilities sitting-room, bar, conference room; salmon fishing
Credit cards DC, MC, V
Children accepted
Disabled no special facilities
Pets not accepted
Closed mid-Jan to mid-Feb
Proprietor Jean-Pierre Girres

The North-West

Le Donjon

This extraordinary little hotel set on a steep hill used to be one of our favourite places for a short break (it's only half an hour from Le Havre). Recent reports suggest, however, that standards of service and food may no longer match the high prices charged.

It is a former hilltop castle, with venerable origins and secret subterranean channel to the sea, now safely surrounded by the leafy suburbs of Etretat. Inside, all is bright and light, decorated with a Parisian sophistication by Madame Abo-Dib. The dining-room, candle-lit and mirrored, is wonderfully atmospheric; the cocktail bar overlooks Etretat's famous cliffs; and there is an impeccably kept small swimming pool surrounded by sunshades and loungers. But it is perhaps the eight bedrooms which best show off Madame Abo-Dib's creative skills: all are different, and immensely stylish. The largest, almost circular, has an Eastern theme, with black chintz drapes and gigantic mirror; another is in bright Impressionist hues, and one has a large fireplace for real log fires. Bathrooms, some in the turrets, are spacious and elegant in pure white; five have whirlpool baths.

The menu offers rather more possibilities for *pensionnaires,* with the option of choosing dishes from the *carte,* as well as the four-course *menu du Gentleman.* We welcome further reports.

Nearby Etretat – cliffs; Fécamp (17km) – Benedictine distillery.

Chemin de Saint Clair
76790 Etretat
Tel 02.35.27.08.23
Fax 02.35.29.92.24
Location on hill behind resort, 28 km N of Le Havre; with garden and car parking
Meals breakfast, lunch, dinner
Prices DB&B 600F-800F; menus 130F- 260F
Rooms 10 double, 9 with bath, one with shower (5 with whirlpool baths); all have cen-tral heating, phone, TV
Facilities dining-room, sitting-room; swimming-pool
Credit cards AE, V
Children accepted
Pets accepted
Disabled access difficult
Closed never
Proprietor Mme Abo-Dib

The North-West

Château hotel, Gisors

Château de la Râpée

'A comfortable stay, although we found the decoration, with carpets for wallcoverings, rather idiosyncratic,' commented one reporter on this 19th-century Gothic mansion. Well, yes: perhaps we should have warned about the carpet; but it is more-or-less confined (along with the antlers) to the reception area. The rest of this grandly conceived but small-scale period piece is less eccentric.

The château lies in a peaceful setting at the end of a long, rutted forest track from Bazincourt. Inside, original features have been carefully preserved and, although the public areas are rather dark in places, the house has been pleasantly furnished with antiques and reproductions. Some of the spacious, calm bedrooms are quite stately, with fine country views, plenty of antiques and creaky wooden floors; others verge on the eccentric (but are antler-free). Immediately next to the house is a small, pleasant flower-garden.

Pascal and Philippe Bergeron take their cooking seriously – classic dishes, with some regional influences and occasional original flourishes.

Nearby Gisors – castle; Jouy-sous-Thelle (25 km) – church.

Bazincourt-sur-Epte 27140
Gisors
Tel 02.32.55.11.61
Location in countryside 4 km
NW of Gisors; in small park
with ample car parking
Meals breakfast, lunch, dinner
Prices rooms 425F-525F;
apartment 750F; menus 165F-
215F
Rooms 13 double, 11 with
bath, 2 with shower (5 twin); 2
rooms form an apartment; all
rooms have central heating,
phone
Facilities sitting-room,
2 dining-rooms, bar,
banqueting-room; riding
stables next door
Credit cards AE, DC, V
Children by arrangement
Disabled no special facilities
Pets small ones accepted
Closed Feb and mid to end
Aug; restaurant Wed
Proprietors M. and Mme
Bergeron

The North-West

Town inn, Pont-Audemer

Auberge du Vieux Puits

Our latest report on this wonderful, half-timbered, 17thC building is short and to the point: 'Excellent.' It might equally well have said: 'Unchanging'.

Although war-damaged Pont-Audemer still has a charming historic centre, it is rather dwarfed by the nondescript suburbs which have grown up around it. The Vieux Puits shines out like a beacon – all crooked beams and leaded windows. The inside is a medievalist's dream, with its twisting wooden staircases and dark beams hung with shining copper and ancient pewter.

Jacques Foltz and his charming wife bring out the best in the building, by keeping the style simple and restrained. The small, intimate salon and dining-rooms are carefully furnished with antiques, and are decorated with fresh flowers. Three of the bedrooms in the old building have been converted into a family apartment; the other three are quite small but full of character. Across the peaceful, flowery courtyard a new wing provides six bedrooms – smarter and well equipped, but in keeping.

M. Foltz sees the *auberge* very much as a restaurant with rooms, and those who want to stay are encouraged to have dinner. To do so is hardly a penance, given the kitchen's high standards and the interesting dishes on the seasonal menus and *carte*.

Nearby Half-timbered houses, church of St-Ouen, the canalised Risle; Honfleur (25 km)

6 Rue Notre-Dame-du-Pré 27500 Pont-Audemer
Tel 02.32.41.01.48
Location near middle of town; with small garden and car parking
Meals breakfast, lunch, dinner
Prices rooms 270F-430F; breakfast 46F; menus, 198F-310F
Rooms 12 double (4 twin), 7 with bath, 4 with shower; 11 have phone

Facilities dining-rooms, bar/sitting-area
Credit cards MC, V
Children welome; special meals on request
Disabled 2 ground-floor rooms, specially equipped
Pets accepted in dining-room
Closed end-Dec to late Jan; Mon evening, Tue in low season
Proprietors Jacques and Hélène Foltz

The North-West

Country hotel, St-André-d'Hébertot

Auberge du Prieuré

The Millets have improved and extended their country home so vigorously over the last few years we can't help worrying that they might spoil their retreat simply by being too enterprising.

The former 13thC priory, built of pale stone beneath a steep slate roof, has made a delicious little hotel. Inside, it is all beams, stone walls, country antiques and earthy colours. There is a surprisingly big dining-room, with a black and white stone-flagged floor and heavy wood tables gleaming with polish. At one end, there are easy chairs before an open fire. On the first floor, a cosy sitting-room offers books and board games; next door is a billiard room. Bedrooms in the main house are full of character, and attic rooms are no less spacious than those on the first floor, although rather dark. A new but harmonious annexe accommodates about half the rooms.

Outside, a lush garden is surrounded by Norman orchards and meadows, and features one of the Millets' earliest improvements – a neat heated pool. Traditional food is prepared by Madame Millet and offers one mid-priced menu and a more expansive *carte*.

Nearby Pont-l'Évêque; Honfleur (15 km); Deauville (20 km).

St-André-d'Hébertot 14130 Pont-l'Évêque
Tel 02.31.64.03.03
Fax 02.31.64.16.66
Location by church in village, S of N175 7 km E of Pont-l'Évêque; in gardens with some private car parking
Meals breakfast, lunch, dinner
Prices rooms 310F-840F; breakfast 60F, meals 145F-320F
Rooms 13 double (5 twin), 11 with bath; all rooms have central heating, phone, TV, radio, hairdrier
Facilities billiard room, library; swimming-pool
Credit cards MC, V
Children welcome; special meals
Disabled ground-floor rooms
Pets 30F supplement
Closed restaurant only, Wed
Proprietors M. and Mme Millet

The North-West

Town mansion, St-Malo

La Korrigane

Jean-Maurice Marchon took over this handsome, turn-of-the-century mansion in late 1992, but its appeal remains unchanged: it is an elegantly furnished home, which you feel privileged to share. The bedrooms are individually decorated, and have comfortable armchairs, beautiful lamps and mirrors, and antique paintings dotted about. There are two harmonious sitting-rooms; you can have your breakfast in the small, pretty garden. An excellent place for a romantic short break without the children but note that there is no restaurant at present.

Nearby Emerald Coast; Château du Bosq (10 km); Dinan

39 Rue Le Pomellec 35400 St-Malo	**Facilities** 2 sitting-rooms, bar
Tel 02.99.81.65.85	**Credit cards** AE, DC, MC, V
Fax 02.99.82.23.89	**Children** accepted
Location in S part of town, near harbour; with gardens and enclosed car parking	**Disabled** no special facilities
	Pets dogs accepted (50F)
	Closed never
Meals breakfast	**Proprietor** Jean-Maurice Marchon
Prices rooms 450F-800F; breakfast 55F	
Rooms 10 double/twin, all with bath or shower; all rooms have central heating, phone, TV	

The North-West

Hostellerie St-Pierre

'Perfect for a short break,' says one report on this unusual hotel on the banks of the Seine. Could be; we've always seen it as an ideal stopover – reliably well run, and located only a short drive from the Paris-Rouen motorway. It is a bizarre concoction: a modern building, triangular in plan with a turret on one corner, half-timbered like a traditional Norman manor-house. It sounds naff, but don't dismiss it.

Not the least of the attractions is the cuisine – classical in style but inventive and light in approach, and of excellent quality, with the emphasis on fish and seafood – witness the enormous tank of langoustes and other consumables dominating the heavily decorated dining-room (which has big picture windows looking on to the river). The hotel's other public areas are limited, and solid rather than elegant – the baroque/rococo decoration does not suit all tastes – but the bedrooms are comfortable and well equipped, and many have balconies overlooking the river. (For the full flavour of this eccentric establishment, opt for the top room in the turret, with exposed beams and token four-poster.) The garden, which stretches down to the water's edge, is a relaxing place to sit. The hotel is family-run; service is friendly.

Nearby Louviers – church of Notre-Dame; Acquigny (10 km) – château; Gaillon (15 km) – château.; Giverny (30 km)

Chemin des Amoureux 27430 St-Pierre-du-Vauvray
Tel 02.32.59.93.29
Fax 02.32.59.41.93
Location on edge of village 8 km E of Louviers, beside Seine; with gardens and car parking
Meals breakfast, lunch, dinner
Prices DB&B 550F-645F; menus 195F-295F
Rooms 14 double (4 twin), all with bath; all rooms have central heating, phone, TV;
most have minibar
Facilities dining-room, sitting-room
Credit cards V
Children accepted
Disabled lift/elevator
Pets accepted at extra charge
Closed 12 Nov to 20 Dec and 2 Jan to 13 Mar; restaurant only, Tue lunch
Proprietors Potier family

The North-West

Seaside town hotel, St-Vaast-la-Hougue

Hotel de France et des Fuchsias

'The garden is still in good order, as are the fuschias, and the conservatory where we ate a memorable, beautifully presented meal is very enticing; friendly and efficient staff.' So says a reporter, confirming that the essential attractions of this perennially popular halt for Cherbourg ferry passengers (French and British alike) are unchanged.

The emphasis is on the restaurant; and the expressions of delight at the superb seafood platters, or the wonderfully presented produce from the Brix family farm, prove that the customers are happy. The wine list offers plenty of half-bottles and good-value options, the service is friendly and efficient, the atmosphere warm – whether in the cosy dining-room or in the conservatory, recently redecorated by a local *décorateur anglais.*

At the far end of the delightful English-style garden, where free chamber music concerts are held on the last ten days of August, is the hotel's annexe. Here bedrooms are more spacious and decoration more sophisticated than in the fairly simple ones in the main part of the hotel. A suite sleeping two or three people and a ground-floor bedroom have been created.

Nearby museum, fortifications; Normandy beaches.

18 rue Marechal Foch
50550 Saint-Vaast-la-Hougue
Tel 02.33.54.42.26
Fax 02.33.43.46.79
Location in quiet street near fishing port and marina; with garden
Meals breakfast, lunch, dinner
Prices rooms 150F-500F; menus 78F (weekdays only), 125F-260F (weekends)
Rooms 33 double, 28 with bath, 2 with shower; all rooms have central heating, phone,

TV
Facilities dining-room, sitting-room
Credit cards AE, DC, MC, V
Children welcome; special menu available
Disabled access only to dining-room
Pets tolerated
Closed early Jan to late Feb; Mon, mid-May to mid-Sep
Proprietor Mme Brix

The North-West

Hôtel de la Plage

A seaside hotel indeed – yards from the shore, with a vast strand of pale sand just next door. But this is far from being a bucket-and-spade holiday hotel. Although prices are not high by the elevated standards of fellow Relais & Châteaux members, they are high by summer-fortnight-with-the-kids standards. And although children are welcome, as usual in France, there are no special facilities for them.

It's as a place for relaxing, pampering breaks with an outdoors element that the Plage wins a place here. The hotel combines its splendid, peaceful seaside setting – plus attractive pool and tennis court – with one of the best kitchens in Brittany (specialising, of course, in seafood), which earns a star from Michelin and two *toques* from Gault-Millau. Within the manicured grounds is a bar in a separate thatched cottage. Mme Le Coz and her staff generate a welcoming atmosphere; service is sometimes a little slow but always friendly, and details are not overlooked. Bedrooms are comfortable, even if they do tend towards traditional French styles of decoration, and some have stunning views (worth booking ahead).

Nearby Beach; Locronan (10 km) – town square; Quimper.

Ste-Anne-la-Palud 29127 Plonévez-Porzay
Tel 02.98.92.50.12
Fax 02.98.92.56.54
Location in countryside 4 km W of Plonévez and 25 km NW of Quimper; with garden and ample car parking
Meals breakfast, lunch, dinner
Prices rooms 800F-1300F; breakfast 70F
Rooms 20 double (10 twin), 2 single, 4 family rooms, all with bath; all rooms have central heating, TV, phone, minibar
Facilities sitting-room, dining-room, bar, conference room
Credit cards AE, DC, MC, V
Children welcome
Disabled lift/elevator
Pets accepted but not in dining-room
Closed mid-Nov to Apr
Proprietor M. Le Coz

The North-West

Ti Al-Lannec

Happy reports about this handsome house on the 'pink granite' coast of Brittany suggest that the hotel manages to pamper while at the same time coping with the families who are drawn to this seaside holiday area.

The house stands high above the sea with a path down to the beach; its south-facing terrace has a splendid view over the bay of Lannion. It is a supremely comfortable hotel, with that elusive private-house feel. Bedrooms are thoughtfully decorated, light and airy but cosy, with fresh flowers and books, small tables and table lamps liberally used. Some have terraces or verandas. The dining-room has the sea view, and is crisp and fresh with rich drapes and old stone walls. Antique and modern furnishings mix well in the comfortable sitting-room, dotted with pot plants.

The house was completely renovated and opened as a hotel in 1978 by Gérard and Danielle Jouanny, and is run by them with a convincing blend of charm, taste and efficiency. Danielle's food is 'consistently delicious', the service 'five-star' and the welcome for children genuine – witness the swing and seesaw on the lawn.

Nearby Perros-Guirec (15 km) – large resort; Tréguier (30 km).

Allée de Mezo-Guen, BP 3
22560 Trébeurden
Tel 02.96.15.01.01
Fax 02.96.23.62.14
Location in wooded grounds above resort, 10 km NW of Lannion; with car parking
Meals breakfast, lunch, dinner
Prices rooms 620F-1,080F; lunch 108F, dinner menus 185F-390F, children's 92F
Rooms 20 double, 2 single, 7 family rooms, all with bath; all rooms have phone, TV

Facilities dining-room, 2 sitting-rooms, bar, billiards room, play room, beauty and fitness centre, sauna, jacuzzi
Credit cards AE, MC, V
Children welcome; early meals, baby-sitting available
Disabled lift/elevator; some bedrooms and WCs suitable
Pets accepted in bedrooms at extra charge
Closed mid-Nov to mid-Mar
Proprietors Danielle and Gérard Jouanny

The North-West

Manor house hotel, Verneuil-sur-Avre

Le Clos

Le Clos remains one of our favourite upmarket French hotels – partly because it remains just affordable by ordinary mortals, but also because it avoids the pretension and vulgarity that afflict so many château-style places.

The hotel is on the edge of the pleasant little country town of Verneuil, in a quiet back street – though with a busy bypass visible (and just audible) in the background. It is a rather comical turn-of-the-century building of highly patterned brick-work, with a mock-medieval tower, set in well-kept leafy grounds with lawns and creeping willows that are overlooked by a large terrace. Inside, everything is of the highest quality: smart, antique-style cane chairs, heavy linen tablecloths and huge bunches of flowers in the dining-room, neat reproduction armchairs in the salon, chintzy drapes in the bedrooms, deep pile carpets everywhere – even in the luxurious bathrooms. The bedrooms are light and airy, and furnished in individual style. The kitchen wins no awards, but produces a range of classical dishes with absolute professionalism and finesse.

Nearby Church of la Madeleine (flamboyant tower); Château de Pin au Haras (40 km) – stud farm; Chartres – cathedral.

98 Rue de la Ferté-Vidame
27130 Verneuil-sur-Avre
Tel 02.32.32.21.81
Fax 02.32.32.21.36
Location on edge of town, 56 km NW of Chartres and 39 km SW of Evreux; with gardens and car parking
Meals breakfast, lunch, dinner
Prices rooms 550F-800F, suites 900F; apartments 950F-1,100F; DB&B 775F-925F; breakfast 80F
Rooms 4 double, 2 suites, all with bath; 4 apartments (3 ground-floor garden rooms); all rooms have central heating, phone, satellite TV
Facilities 2 dining-rooms, sitting-room, bar; tennis court, jacuzzi **Credit cards** AE, DC, MC, V **Children** welcome
Disabled no special facilities
Pets accepted **Closed** mid-Dec to mid-Jan; restaurant Mon, except holiday periods
Proprietors Patrick and Colette Simon

The North-West

Moulin de Villeray

This grand old mill – restored from dereliction and gradually improved over a 20-year period (a heated outdoor swimming-pool is the most recent addition) – was taken over by the Eelsens in 1992. It remains one of our favourite ports of call in southern Normandy, and worth the detour from the A11 Nantes-Paris *autoroute.*

It is no longer what you would call a simple rustic retreat; but the mill-wheel is still there, and the setting is delectable – beside the rushing river Huisne, on the edge of a neat village of red-roofed stone houses, in rolling, wooded farmland on the fringe of the distinctive Perche region. Its membership of the Relais du Silence group is justified, even if prices are approaching Relais & Chateaux levels.

Much of the tall, white-painted mill has been rebuilt rather than restored, but its main focus, the restaurant, is thoroughly traditional, retaining old beams and a huge fireplace – and giving a view of the mill-wheel. The 'excellent' food is more than a match for the surroundings. Guests gather for drinks in the salon. Bedrooms are very comfortable and newly refurbished. Outside there is a pleasant terrace, a large, relaxing and informal garden bordering the river and, beyond that, countryside.

Nearby Nogent – Gothic and Renaissance buildings; Chartres (55 km) – cathedral; Alençon (55 km) – lace- making.

Villeray 61110 Condeau
Tel 02.33.73.30.22
Fax 02.33.73.38.28
Location at foot of village, 10 km N of Nogent; with garden and car parking
Meals breakfast, lunch, dinner
Prices rooms 480F-950F; suite 1,150F; breakfast 70F; menus 130F-300F; DB&B between May and Sep
Rooms 16 double, all with bath and shower (3 twin); 2 suites; all rooms have phone, minibar
Facilities sitting-room, dining-room, bar; helipad; swimming-pool
Credit cards AE, DC, V
Children accepted
Disabled access to restaurant
Pets accepted (must be kept on lead)
Closed never
Proprietors Christian and Muriel Eelsen

The North-West

Riverside hotel, Les Andelys

Hôtel de la Chaîne d'Or

This old inn, superbly set beside the Seine, has jumped upmarket since it was dropped from the guide some years ago. Bedrooms vary in size and style, but many share the restaurant's river views. Not the least of the improvements is in the food, which is now seriously good.

■ 27 Rue Grande, 27700 Les Andelys (Eure) **Tel** 02.32.54.00.31 **Fax** 02.32.54.05.68 **Meals** breakfast, lunch, dinner **Prices** rooms 395F-740F; breakfast 65F, lunch 138F, menus 230F-298F **Rooms** 11, all with bath, central heating, phone, TV **Credit cards** AE, MC, V **Closed** early Jan to early Feb; restaurant only, last week of Aug

---

Spa hotel, Bagnoles-de-l'Orne

Bois Joli

The Gattis, who took over this upright little 19thC building about eight years ago, are now well into their stride, to judge by our most recent report – 'pretty, airy bedroom; very good dinner; excellent service; excellent value.' There is a pleasant garden, leading into the forest. Sauna and solarium.

■ 12 Avenue Philippe du Rozier, 61140 Bagnoles-de-l'Orne (Orne) **Tel** 02.33.37.92.77 **Fax** 02.33 37.07.56 **Meals** breakfast, lunch, dinner **Prices** rooms 195F-495F; menus 115F-295F **Rooms** 20, all with bath, central heating, phone; TV on request **Credit cards** AE, DC, MC, V **Closed** never; restaurant only, Jan

---

Town hotel, Barfleur

Le Conquérant

A shell's throw from the port, this fine grey-stone 17thC building offers a peaceful halt for travellers, and is inviting enough for a longer stay, with its spacious garden. Recent renovations have concentrated on making the bedrooms more comfortable. Delicious crêpes in the *salon de thé*.

■ 16-18 Rue St-Thomas Becket, 50760 Barfleur (Manche) **Tel** 02.33.54.00.82 **Fax** 02.33.54.65 .25 **Meals** breakfast, tea, light suppers **Prices** rooms 200F-350F; breakfast 25F-45F, supper 75F-98F **Rooms** 16, all with bath or shower, phone; some have satellite TV **Credit cards** MC, V **Closed** mid-Nov to mid-Feb

---

Town mansion, Bayeux

Hôtel d'Argouges

'Comfortable, quiet, helpful people,' runs the latest telegraphic report on this 18thC house. There is a rather formal sitting-room and a small garden; bedrooms vary in size and are traditionally furnished; some are in an annexe across the courtyard. No restaurant.

■ 21 Rue St-Patrice, 14400 Bayeux (Calvados) **Tel** 02.31.92.88.86 **Fax** 02.31.92.69.16 **Meals** breakfast **Prices** rooms 280F-420F, suites 480F; breakfast 39F **Rooms** 25, all with bath or shower, central heating, phone, minibar **Credit cards** AE, DC, MC, V **Closed** never

The North-West

Village inn, Le Bec-Hellouin

Auberge de l'Abbaye

The archetypal atmospheric Norman inn, simple and welcoming, with tiled floors, rough stone walls and gleaming furniture. Bedrooms are cheerful and rustic, meals are typical of the region – with apples, cider and quantities of cream.

■ Le Bec-Hellouin, 27800 Brionne (Eure) **Tel** 02.32.44.86.02 **Fax** 02.32.46.32.23 **Meals** breakfast, lunch, dinner **Prices** rooms 390F-580F; half-board 400F; breakfast 40F, menus 130F-250F **Rooms** 11, all with bath, central heating, phone **Credit cards** MC, V **Closed** restaurant only, Mon evening and Tue Nov to Apr

---

Seaside hotel, Belle-Ile-en-Mer

Le Clos Fleuri

A new and stylishly simple hotel in grassy grounds 600m from the main port of Le Palais on Belle-Ile, 45 minutes by ferry from Quiberon. The catering is as fresh as the decoration, with meals tailored to guests' requirements, and the option of a substantial brunch instead of standard breakfast.

■ Bellevue, Route de Sauzon, Le Palais, 56360 Belle-Ile-en-Mer (Morbihan) **Tel** 02.97.31.45.45 **Fax** 02.97.31.45.57 **Meals** breakfast or brunch, lunch, dinner **Prices** rooms 470F-570F; suites 580F; breakfast 45F, brunch 75F; menu around 150F **Rooms** 20, all with bath, central heating, phone, cable TV **Credit cards** AE, DC, MC, V **Closed** never

---

Country hotel, Belle-Ile-en-Mer

La Désirade

La Désirade, drawn to our attention by a satisfied reader, calls itself a 'hôtel-village'; it is an unusual creation – a grouping of new, traditional-style houses around a neat heated pool (beside which you can have breakfast in good weather). Stylishly simple furnishing in the rooms.

■ 56360 Belle-Ile-en-Mer (Morbihan) **Tel** 02.97.31.70.70 **Fax** 02.97.31.89.63 **Meals** breakfast, dinner **Prices** rooms 430F-550F; breakfast 60F, menu 200F **Rooms** 26, all with bath, central heating, phone, TV, hairdrier **Credit cards** AE, DC, MC, V **Closed** Jan, Feb

---

Town hotel, Beuzeville

Cochon d'Or et Petit Castel

Two small hotels on opposite sides of the main street and under the same ownership. The Petit Castel offers simple, pleasant modern-style bedrooms; the Cochon d'Or has cheaper, rather more old-fashioned bedrooms with fewer facilities. The food is above average and excellent value.

■ Place du General-de-Gaulle, 27210 Beuzeville (Eure) **Tel** 02.32.57.70.46 (Cochon) 02.32.57.76.08 (Peti t Castel) **Fax** 02.32.42.25.70 **Meals** breakfast, lunch, dinner **Prices** rooms 205F-335F; breakfast 35F, menus 82F-240F **Rooms** 20, all with bath or shower, central heating, phone; some have TV **Credit cards** MC, V **Closed** mid-Dec to mid-Jan

The North-West

Restaurant with rooms, La Bouille

Le Saint-Pierre

Despite high prices at this smart, thriving restaurant-with-rooms by the Seine, there were no regrets from a recent visitor. 'The food was first class, and thoroughly merits its rating – it was very special.' Showy modern decoration dominates, especially in the airy riverside restaurant; cooking is professional and inventive; bedrooms mostly overlook the river.

■ La Bouille, 76530 Grand Couronne (Seine-Maritime)
Tel 02.35.18.01.01 **Fax** 02.35.18.12.7 6 **Meals** breakfast, lunch, dinner
Prices rooms 280F-350F; menus 180F-260F **Rooms** 7, all with bath or shower, central heating, phone, TV **Credit cards** AE, DC, MC, V
Closed Mon; Sun eve

Riverside hotel, Caudebec-en-Caux

Le Normandie

A friendly and well-cared-for hotel, if uninspiring in style, in a good position on the Seine. Bedrooms are simple but comfort able, many with river views. Food is carefully prepared and sound value – typical of a two-fireplace Logis.

■ 19 Quai Guilbaud, 76490 Caudebec-en-Caux (Seine-Maritime)
Tel 02.35.96.25.11 **Fax** 02.35 .96.68.15 **Meals** breakfast, lunch, dinner
Prices rooms 210F-360F; breakfast 35F; menus 59F-190F **Rooms** 16, all with bath or shower, central heating, phone, TV **Credit cards** AE, DC, MC, V **Closed** Feb

Seaside hotel, Dinard

Roche Corneille

A tall château-style building in the middle of Dinard, recently renovated in a crisp and confident style by new owners, and run with clear attention to detail – fresh flowers, fluffy towels, impeccable housekeeping. A gastronomic restaurant has just been opened, with weekly changing menus.

■ 4 Rue G Clemenceau, 35800 Dinard (Ille-et-Vilaine) **Tel** 02.99.46.14.47
Fax 02.99.46.40. 80 **Meals** breakfast **Prices** rooms 280F-600F; breakfast 50F; menus 93F-240F **Rooms** 28, all with bath, central heating, phone, TV
Credit cards AE, MC, V **Closed** mid-Nov to mid-Mar

Château hotel, Hennebont

Château de Locguénolé

A Dutch reader writes to recommend inclusion of this refined country house looking down on the estuary of Le Blavet. Splendid spacious bedrooms, plentiful sitting-rooms, very good (Michelin-starred) food. Lots of ways to mitigate the damage – walks, tennis, bikes, as well as a good-sized pool, sauna and turkish bath.

■ Route de Port-Louis en Kervignac, 56700 Hennebont (Morbihan)
Tel 02.97.76.29.04 **Fax** 02.97.76.82.35 **Meals** breakfast, lunch, dinner
Prices rooms 660F-1,480F; breakfast 82F, menus 190F-480F **Rooms** 22, all with bath, central heating, phone, TV; most have hairdriers
Credit cards AE, DC, MC, V **Closed** early Jan to early Feb

The North-West

Country hotel, Honfleur

La Chaumière

Set peacefully in an orchard garden with the sea in view (and direct access to the shore), this typically Norman timbered building offers deeply comfortable, relaxing accommodation. The bedrooms are decorated with flair and taste, and warmly furnished. Serious cooking of regionally-based dishes.

■ Route du Littoral, Vasouy, 14600 Honfleur (Calvados) **Tel** 02.31.81.63.20 **Fax** 02.31.89.5 9.23 **Meals** breakfast, lunch, dinner **Prices** rooms 990F-1,350F; breakfast 85F; menus 190F-380F **Rooms** 9, all with bath, central heating, phone, TV, minibar, hairdrier **Credit cards** AE, MC, V **Closed** never; restaurant only, Tue, and Wed lunch

---

Country hotel, Honfleur

La Ferme Saint-Siméon

This fine old farmhouse used to be a favourite haunt of the Impressionist painters, and is still a tranquil spot. Cooking blends bold innovation with the traditional. Extensive wine list. Indoor heated swimming-pool, sauna, steam room and solarium. Reports please.

Rue Adolphe-Marais, 14600 Honfleur (Calvados) **Tel** 02.33.31.89.23.61 **Fax** 02.33.31.89.48.48 **Meals** breakfast, lunch, dinner **Prices** rooms 790F-2,690F; apartments 2,300F-3,510F; menus 240F-550F **Rooms** 29, 4 apartments, all with bath or shower, central heating, phone **Credit cards** AE, MC, V **Closed** never

---

Country hotel, Honfleur

Le Manoir du Butin

The Boelen family, who already own La Chaumière and La Ferme Saint-Siméon (see above) go from strength to strength. Their latest hotel, also in the Honfleur area, is a typical Normandy house with a peaceful situation. Rustic beams, polished wood and huge open fireplaces create a welcoming atmosphere. Normandy cuisine in the attractive dining-room.

■ Phare du Butin, 14600 Honfleur (Calvados) **Tel** 02.31.81.63.00 **Fax** 02.31.89.59.23 **Meals** breakfast, dinner **Prices** rooms 640F-1,970F; menus 128F-265F **Rooms** 9, all with bath or shower, central heating, phone, TV, minibar **Credit cards** AE, MC, V **Closed** restaurant only, Mon and Tue lunch

---

Country hotel, Louviers

La Haye-le-Comte

There's an energetic air about this pleasant little country house with *pétanque*, tennis, table-tennis, mountain bikes and local walks on offer. Bedrooms are neat and airy. Food is quite wide-ranging, with as much seafood as meat in evidence. Reports welcome.

■ 4 Route de la Haye-le-Comte, 27400 Louviers (Eure) **Tel** 02.32.40.00.40 **Fax** 02.32.25.03. 85 **Meals** breakfast, lunch, dinner **Prices** rooms 250F-470F; breakfast 45F, menus 100F-190F, children's 70F ; 10% reduction for 3 nights **Rooms** 16, all with bath, central heating, phone, satellite TV **Credit cards** AE, DC, MC, V **Closed** mid-Dec to end March; restaurant only, Mon and Tues lunch

The North-West

Village inn, Martin-Église

Auberge du Clos Normand

A report just in confirms the delights of this simple old auberge built of patterned brick and timber with a flowery garden and stream behind. Bedrooms in a converted outbuilding are attractive and comfortable. Food is classically Norman, involving much cholesterol and alcohol.

■ 22 Rue Henri IV, Martin-Église, 76370 Neuville-les-Dieppe (Seine-Maritime) **Tel** 02.35.04.40.34 **Fax** 02.35.04.48.49 **Meals** breakfast, lunch, dinner **Prices** rooms 300F-470F; breakfast 38F; DB&B 350F-445F **Rooms** 8, all with bath or shower, central heating, phone, TV **Credit cards** AE, MC, V **Closed** mid-Nov to mid-Dec; Mon, Tue

---

Converted mill, Moëlan-sur-Mer

Les Moulins du Duc

The main building of this unusual hotel is a former mill but the spacious and well equipped accommodation is in two-storey cottages scattered around the secluded grounds. Breakfast can be had on the terrace by the pond. A reporter rates the food 'totally delicious'. Indoor swimming-pool.

■ 29350 Moëlan-sur-Mer (Finistère) **Tel** 02.98.39.60.73 **Fax** 02.98.39.75.56 **Meals** breakfast, lunch, dinner **Prices** rooms 440F-805F; suites 1,100F-1,300F; breakfast 55F, menus150F-350F, children's 60F **Rooms** 27, all with bath or shower, phone, TV, minibar **Credit cards** AE, DC, MC, V **Closed** mid-Jan to Mar

---

Town hotel, Le Mont-St-Michel

Auberge Saint-Pierre

The Saint-Pierre is the pick of the hostelries that line the main street at the foot of France's premier tourist attraction. Its diningrooms are satisfyingly rustic, its bedrooms (half in an annexe up many steps) tastefully decorated and comfortable. Efficient service, good plain food.

■ BP16, 50116 Le Mont-St-Michel (Manche) **Tel** 02.33.60.14.03 **Fax** 02.33.48.59.82 **Meals** breakfast, lunch, dinner **Prices** rooms 480F-890F; breakfast 50F, dinner 120F-180F **Rooms** 20, all with bath or shower, central heating, phone, TV, hairdrier **Credit cards** AE, V **Closed** Dec to Feb

---

Quayside hotel, Paimpol

Le Repaire de Kerroc'h

Set in an enviable position right on the quay, this handsome 18thC house has been beautifully restored. Bedrooms are well furnished and equipped. Excellent breakfasts. In the guide since our first edition, a new chef, Louis Le Roy, has just taken over the cooking (one Michelin star). A recent reporter was well satisfied.

■ 29 Quai Morand, Port de Plaisance, 22500 Paimpol (Côtes-d'Armor) **Tel** 02.96.20.50.13 **Fax** 02.96.22.07.46 **Meals** breakfast, lunch, dinner **Prices** rooms 290F-580F; DB&B 790F (for two); breakfast 50F, menus 115F-365F **Rooms** 13, all with bath, phone, TV, minibar **Credit cards** MC, V **Closed** Jan to mid-Feb

The North-West

Seaside villa, Perros-Guirec

Le Sphinx

There are splendid sea views from this tall house atop low cliffs on the 'pink granite coast' – both from the dining-room and the best of the spacious, tastefully decorated bedrooms. Service is friendly, food reliably good and night-time silence absolute .

■ Chemin de la Messe, 22700 Perros-Guirec (Côtes-d'Armor)
Tel 02.96.23.25.42 **Fax** 02.96.9 1.26.13 **Meals** breakfast, lunch, dinner
Prices rooms 510F-560F; breakfast 45F; menus 130-F290F
Rooms 20, all with bath or shower, central heating, phone, alarm, TV
Credit cards AE, MC, V **Closed** Jan to mid-Feb

Château hotel, Pléhédel

Château de Coatguélen

This fine 19thC château, set in a large park, has a relaxed and friendly atmosphere. Families are well catered for – playroom, good sports facilities (including its own golf course) and a network of 'bush trails'. In the guide since the beginning; more reports welcome.

■ Pléhédel, 22290 Lanvollon (Côtes-d'Armor) **Tel** 02.96.55.33.40
Fax 02.96.22.37.67 **Meals** breakfast, lunch, dinner **Prices** rooms 450F-950F; breakfast 55F, menus 100F-380F **Rooms** 17, (14 with bath, 3 with shower), central heating, TV **Credit cards** AE, DC, V **Closed** never

---

Seaside hotel, Raguenès-Plage

Chez Pierre

A family seaside Logis completely without pretension and offering reliably good, traditional, sea-based cooking. 'Superb' family rooms in the modern annexe (2 suitable for the disabled) next to the turn-of-the-century main house have single beds upstairs and doubles downstairs. Big garden, early meals for kids.

■ Raguenès-Plage, 29920 Nevez (Finistère) **Tel** 02.98.06.81.06
Fax 02.98.06.62.09 **Meals** breakfast, lunch, dinner **Prices** rooms 185F-410F; breakfast 32F, menus 100F-270F, children's 75F **Rooms** 14 with shower, 7 single, all with phone **Credit cards** MC, V **Closed** Oct to Mar

---

Country inn, La Roche-Bernard

Auberge Bretonne

Food takes pride of place at this small, welcoming auberge; people come from far afield for Jacques Thorel's cooking (two Michelin stars). There is a formidable cellar, too. Bedrooms are prettily furnished in rural Breton style; the rustic dining-room surrounds the vegetable garden.

■ 2 Place Duguesclin, 56130 La Roche-Bernard (Morbihan)
Tel 02.99.90.60.28 **Fax** 02.99.90 .85.00 **Meals** breakfast, lunch, dinner
Prices rooms 480F-1400F; breakfast 80F, menus 150F-450F **Rooms** 8, all with central heating **Credit cards** AE, MC, V **Closed** mid-Nov to early Dec; 2 weeks in Jan

The North-West

Town hotel, La Roche-Bernard

Auberge des Deux Magots

A warm welcome awaits inside this prim-looking 17thC stone house. The furniture in the elegant dining-rooms and bedrooms may be reproduction, but it is all part of a careful, fresh decorative scheme. Good-value menus concentrate on traditional regional dishes.

■ 1 Place du Bouffay, 56130 La Roche-Bernard (Morbihan) **Tel** 02.99.90.60.75 **Fax** 02.99.90. 87.87 **Meals** breakfast, lunch, dinner **Prices** rooms 280F-320F, family rooms 380F-480F; breakfast 35F, menus 80F-320F, children's 50F **Rooms** 14, all with bath or shower, phone, satellite TV **Credit cards** MC, V **Closed** Sun eve and Mon, except long weekends; restaurant only Mon, except long weekends

---

Manor house hotel, La Roche-Bernard

Manoir du Rodoir

This plain-looking house, recently taken over by a new owner, attracts golfing guests, who enjoy discounts at some of the excellent courses in southern Brittany. But with its peaceful wooded setting, relaxed ambience and tasteful decoration it also appeals to many others. Reports welcome.

■ Rte de Nantes, 56130 La Roche-Bernard (Morbihan) **Tel** 02.99.90.82.68 **Fax** 02.99.90.76.22 **Meals** breakfast, lunch, dinner **Prices** rooms 350F-490F; suites 800F-950F; breakfast 52F; DB&B 385F-485F; menus 95F-235F **Rooms** 26, all with bath or shower, central heating, phone, TV **Credit cards** AE, MC, V **Closed** 1 week Nov, 1 week Dec

---

Town hotel, Rouen

Hôtel de la Cathédrale

This ancient, rambling, half-timbered hotel is tucked away down a pedestrian street, only yards from the cathedral. Most of the chintzy bedrooms have been renovated over recent years. Delightful courtyard with a mass of flowers. No restaurant but plenty of choice nearby. 'Friendly service'.

■ 12 Rue St-Romain, 76000 Rouen (Seine-Maritime) **Tel** 02.35.71.57.95 **Fax** 02.35.70.15.54 **Meals** breakfast **Prices** rooms 270F-355F; breakfast 35F **Rooms** 24, all with bath or shower, central heating, phone, TV **Credit cards** MC, V **Closed** never

---

Bed and breakfast guest-house, Sourdeval

La Maurandière

A chambres d'hôtes establishment, where you share the sitting and dining room of Mme Dupart. Her lovely stone farmhouse, in an idyllic setting, was beautifully restored about ten years ago. The bedrooms are spacious and delightful. Breakfast can be served in the garden in summer.

■ 50150 Sourdeval (Manche) **Tel** 02.33.59.65.44 **Meals** breakfast **Prices** rooms 210F with breakfast **Rooms** 4, all with bath or shower, central heating **Credit cards** MC **Closed** never

The North-West

Manor house hotel, Trébeurden

Manoir de Lan-Kerellec

A member of the Relais & Châteaux group, but one of the least pretentious and most captivating, this handsome and unusual family house stands in trees high above the rocky shore, with splendid sea views from all rooms. Very relaxing and welcoming.

■ 22560 Trébeurden (Côtes-d'Armor) **Tel** 02.96.23.50.09 **Fax** 02.96.23.66.88 **Meals** breakfast, lunch, dinner **Prices** rooms 500F-2,000F; breakfast 70F, menus 140F-350F **Rooms** 20, all with bath, central heating, phone, TV **Credit cards** AE, DC, MC, V **Closed** mid-Nov to mid-Mar; restaurant only, Mon (and Tue lunch in low season)

Manor house hotel, Tréguier

Kastell Dinec'h

We have received enthusiastic reports in the past on this 'oasis' – a handsome old farmhouse, tucked away in lush wooded gardens. Bedrooms are small – beware the stable block – but comfortable and stylishly decorated. Food rated 'good' to 'excellent'. Neat heated pool.

■ Rte de Lannion, 22220 Tréguier (Côtes-d'Armor) **Tel** 02.96.92.49.39 **Fax** 02.96.92.34.02 **Meals** breakfast, dinner **Prices** rooms 400F-490F; breakfast 55F, menus 120F-310F **Rooms** 14, all with central heating, phone **Credit cards** MC, V **Closed** Jan to mid-Mar, 2 weeks end of Oct; Tue evening and Wed out of season

---

Country hotel, Trégunc

Les Grandes Roches

From the roadside this looks much like any other simple Logis, but in the extensive flowery grounds are charmingly restored farm buildings containing some of the bedrooms. 'Comfortable, peaceful, friendly, good value.' What more could you ask?

■ Route des Grandes Roches, 29910 Trégunc (Finistère) **Tel** 02.98.97.29.97 **Fax** 02.98.50.29.19 **Meals** breakfast, dinner; lunch weekends and holidays **Prices** rooms 250F-550F; breakfast 45F; DB&B 290-450F; menus 98F-250F **Rooms** 21, all with bath or shower, central heating, phone **Credit cards** MC **Closed** mid-Dec to mid-Jan, Feb holidays; restaurant only mid-Nov to end-Mar

---

Country inn, Trelly

La Verte Campagne

Pascal Bernou has won the Michelin star he set his sights on when he bought this 18thC farmhouse from his former employer. Reporters agree that the food is delicious, but service can be slow. Bedrooms in the main building are delightful but vary widely in size.

■ Hameau Chevalier, 50660 Trelly (Manche) **Tel** 02.33.47.65.33 **Fax** 02.33.47.38.03 **Meals** breakfast, lunch, dinner **Prices** rooms 260F-380F; menus 140F-350F **Rooms** 7, all with central heating, phone **Credit cards** MC, V **Closed** 3 weeks in Jan; restaurant Sun dinner and Mon out of season

Ile-de-France

We've lumped together Paris and the surrounding *départements* of Ile de France because for many visitors they are sensible alternatives. If you're passing through the area and need a stopover, your instinct will probably be to stay out of the city; and if you're bent on a sightseeing holiday or a romantic break you'll probably want to be in the heart of things. But it's not necessarily so: an overnight stop in Paris can work perfectly well, and a rural base for city sightseeing can be very restful.

Paris is a compact city – much more so than London, for example – and for many visitors choice of location is not very important (from the convenience point of view) unless you intend to spend a lot of time in one place (the Louvre, say).

From the point of view of atmosphere and charm, location can make a deal of difference. It pays to know something about the districts (*arrondisements*) that make up the city. The one-digit or two-digit number at the end of Paris postcodes is the number of the *arrondisement*. Thus 75006 is the 6th, for example.

The *arrondisements* are numbered in a clockwise spiral starting in the centre on the Right Bank of the Seine (the northern bank). You'll mainly be interested in the first turn of the spiral.

The 1st is an upmarket area extending from the Place de la Concorde past the Louvre to Les Halles; we have a few entries here. We have none in the 2nd and only one in the 3rd (Pavillon de la Reine) to the east. But the spiral then turns back towards the Seine, and we have a number of entries in the 4th – in the revitalised Marais, east of the Pompidou centre, and around Notre Dame.

Across the river, the 5th, 6th and 7th make up the Left Bank, with the Boulevard St-Germain its main axis. Between the Jardin des Plantes in the east and the Eiffel Tower in the west, there are more Charming Small Hotels here than anywhere else. The spiral crosses the river again to the 8th, and the Champs Elysées area, where we have a couple of entries. Outside this first central spiral, all our entries are to the north, in the 9th, 17th and 18th (Montmartre).

Ile-de-France

Converted mill, Flagy

Hostellerie du Moulin

Over the years since its inclusion in our first edition, we have received a steady flow of readers' reports approving of this imaginatively converted flour mill an hour from Paris.

The setting, with tables in the grassy garden beside the stream that still gently turns the mill wheel, is idyllic. Beyond the neat gardens you look out on to cultivated fields which until the 1950s supplied the grain that was milled here. The heavy beams, wheels and pulleys of the mill dominate the cosy sitting-room, and the bedrooms, named after cereals, are as quirkily captivating as you would hope in a building of this character; space is at a premium, and low beams lead some guests to move about with a permanent stoop.

The cooking is satisfying and mildly adventurous, though our most recent report is less enthusiastic than usual. The menu and carte have English translations, underlining the Moulin's popularity with British travellers. Claude Scheidecker is a charming and friendly host who gives his little hotel, which he has been running for twenty years, an exceptionally welcoming atmosphere. And he still manages to keep his prices admirably low.

Nearby Fontainbleau Château; Sens (40 km) – cathedral.

2 Rue du Moulin 77940 Flagy
Tel 01 60.96.67.89
Fax 01.60.96.69.51
Location in village, 23 km SE of Fontainebleau, 10 km W of Montereau; with car parking
Meals breakfast, lunch, dinner
Prices rooms 260F-500F; breakfast 50F; menus 180F-250F
Rooms 7 double, 3 family rooms, all with bath; all rooms have phone

Facilities dining-room, bar, sitting-room; fishing
Credit cards AE, DC, MC, V
Children accepted
Disabled access to dining-room, not to bedrooms
Pets accepted
Closed 14-26 Sep, 21 Dec-23 Jan; Sun evening and Mon (except public holidays at Easter and 14 Jul: closed Mon evening and Tue)
Proprietor Claude Scheidecker

Ile-de-France

Town hotel, Paris

Hôtel de l'Abbaye

If we gave awards, this gorgeous hotel would be a very strong contender on all counts. Indeed, we find it hard to fault at all, save to say that the standard bedrooms are fairly small (and feel even smaller compared to the spaciousness of the public rooms); you would do well to upgrade to a larger room if you can afford it. One on the ground floor has its own terrace, as do the four duplex apartments. Take note that you should book well in advance, as the hotel is usually full.

The moment we walked in to this skilfully converted former abbey we felt calmed and cosseted. The hotel has a reputation for attentive yet unobtrusive service which it justly deserves: the courteous staff seem genuinely eager to be of help. The public rooms are inviting yet chic, with several sitting areas, the sofas and armchairs attractively upholstered in floral or striped fabrics, warmly lit by huge table lamps and filled with fresh flowers; in cool weather there's an open fire. The breakfast room/bar must be one of the most alluring in Paris, conservatory style, with walls covered in trellis and pretty leaf print curtains surrounding French doors which overlook a large courtyard garden complete with fountain. Here you can take breakfast or a drink in warm weather. Worth every penny.

Nearby Jardin de Luxembourg; blvd Saint-Germain.

10 rue Cassette, 75006 Paris
Tel 01.45.44.38.11
Fax 01.45.48.07.86
Location close to the junction with rue de Meziers; parking at Saint-Sulpice; metro Saint-Sulpice
Meals breakfast
Prices 900F-1,950F; breakfast included
Rooms 42 double and twin, all with bath; 4 duplex apartments; all rooms have phone, satellite TV, air-conditioning, hairdryer
Facilities 2 sitting rooms, breakfast room/bar, courtyard garden **Credit cards** AE, MC, V **Children** accepted
Disabled two rooms on ground floor **Pets** not accepted **Closed** never
Proprietors M. & Mme Lafortune

Ile-de-France

Hôtel d'Angleterre

One of the most peaceful, comforting and gracious small hotels in Paris, the Angleterre has a faintly English air, befitting a building which was once the British Embassy. In 1783, Benjamin Franklin refused to enter it to sign the Treaty of Paris because he considered it to be British soil. Had he done so, he would have found well-proportioned rooms, fine mantlepieces, a beautiful staircase decorated with *trompe l'oeil* murals and a lovely courtyard garden, all of which are still in place.

The feeling of spacious calm in the public rooms is echoed in the bedrooms, all different but characteristically roomy, elegant and comfortable. One of our inspectors had a deluxe room with one of the largest hotel bathrooms he had seen, all marbled and mirrored glamour, based on a bathroom in the London Ritz. Another bathroom has a charming handpainted suite, with the basin set into a splendid wood and tiled washstand. A couple report that they stayed in the hotel's smallest room – normally let out as a single but with a double bed so that two can share if they wish. Their verdict? Despite the size, they were happy to enjoy the benefits and ambience of the Angleterre at a very modest price. Their only quibble was with the nose-in-air attitude of the receptionists, though not the manageress.

Nearby blvd Saint-Germain; Musée d'Orsay.

44 Rue Jacob 75006 Paris
Tel 01.42.60.34.72
Fax 01.42.60.16.93
Location in the stretch of rue Jacob between rues Bonaparte and Saints-Pères; parking at blvd Saint-Germain (rue du Dragon); metro Saint-Germain des-Près
Meals breakfast
Prices 600F-1,400F; breakfast 50F

Rooms 24 double and twin, all with bath; 3 apartments; all rooms have phone, cable TV, air-conditioning, hairdrier, safe **Facilities** sitting-room, breakfast room, bar, courtyard garden, lift/elevator to some rooms **Credit cards** AE, DC, MC, V **Children** accepted **Disabled** no special facilities **Pets** not accepted **Manager** Mme Michèle Blouin

Ile-de-France

Hôtel de Banville

This 1930s town house hotel offers an attractive combination of style, comfort and middle-of-the-road prices. Convenient, too, at least for motorists: finding your way from the Périphérique to boulevard Berthier is easy, and parking here does not pose an insoluble problem.

With its flower-filled window boxes, the airy art deco building – the work of a celebrated architect, we're told – looks promising, and does not disappoint. Inside, all is tastefully decorated and comfortable, bordering on the luxurious. There is an elegantly furnished sitting area/bar in reception, where a pianist often plays in the evenings. Another welcoming sitting-room (with antique pieces as well as comfy sofas), which can be closed off for meetings, puts the Banville comfortably ahead of the Parisian norm. Murals create a garden effect in the breakfast room. In the bedrooms, light furniture and wallpaper give a spacious feel; fabrics have been thoughtfully chosen, with antiques dotted throughout. Flower arrangements add a personal touch, as do such small details as having your bed turned down – a rare thing in the city nowadays. Peace is ensured by the efficient sound-proofing. Staff are extremely friendly, and we suspect that this hotel would be far more expensive if it were on the Left Bank.
Nearby Arc de Triomphe; Champs-Elysées; Palais des Congrès.

166 blvd Berthier, 75017 Paris
Tel 01.42.67.70.16
Fax 01.44.40.42.77
Location on service road off major boulevard, N of Arc de Triomphe; parking at blvd Berthier in street and garage metro Porte de Champerret;
Meals breakfast
Prices 635F-922F; breakfast 50F
Rooms 39 double, 33 with bath, 6 with shower; 2 triple, one family room, all with bath; all rooms have phone, air-conditioning, satellite TV, hairdrier, safe **Facilities** sitting area/bar, sitting-room, small dining-room, lift/elevator
Credit cards AE, MC, V
Children accepted **Disabled** no special facilities **Pets** accepted **Closed** never
Proprietor Mme Lambert

Ile-de-France

Hôtel de la Bretonnerie

A distinctive 17thC townhouse, converted with sympathy and style, which, though conveniently placed in the middle of the picturesque and (now) fashionable Marais district, is – as a recent reporter points out – 'in a rather scruffy street' too close to the Pompidou Centre, an area which has become 'very run down, with the French version of lager louts and pickpockets'. The reporter continues, 'however once inside the hotel all is calm and peaceful'.

The exposed beams in the public areas and the upper bedrooms are echoed throughout the house by the sturdy hardwood furniture (some antique, some reproduction). The small basement breakfast- and sitting-rooms attempt a medieval flavour, with pale stone vaulted ceilings, iron light fittings, richly coloured fabrics and polished tiled floors. Considering the apparent size of the hotel, the bedrooms are surprisingly roomy, also comfortable and pretty, and every one is different; some are arranged with the beds on a mezzanine gallery with the 'downstairs' used as a small sitting area. All have a glossy modern bathroom and guests will not find any lack of comfort.

Good-humoured staff extend a warm welcome, and cope admirably when all their guests arrive at the same time.

Nearby Hôtel de Ville; Pompidou Centre; Les Halles.

22 Rue Ste-Croix-de-la-Bretonnerie 75004 Paris **Tel** 01.48.87.77.63 **Fax** 01.42.77.26.78 **Location** between rue des Archives and rue Vielle du Temple; parking at Hôtel de Ville; metro St Paul/Hôtel de Ville/Rambuteau **Meals** breakfast **Prices** 630F-1,100F; breakfast 48F	**Rooms** 27 double, 3 family rooms, all with bath; all rooms have phone, TV, minibar, hairdrier, safe **Facilities** sitting area off lobby, cellar breakfast room, lift **Credit cards** MC, V **Children** accepted **Disabled** no special facilities **Pets** not accepted **Closed** 4 weeks end Jul-Aug **Proprietor** M. Sagot

Ile-de-France

Hôtel Degrés de Notre-Dame

Almost all the small hotels of Paris are without a dining room. Here, however, is an exception – the kind of family-run establishment well-known in the French countryside, but rarely found in the city: a restaurant with rooms. The restaurant has the feel of a simple *auberge*, and serves correspondingly rustic food. Guests also take breakfast here (served at any time) which, assures the *patron*, (who does not speak English) features the freshest of bread, orange juice squeezed on the spot, and good coffee.

A wooden staircase, (staff carry your bags) decorated with charming murals leads to the bedrooms, which are good value: well equipped, with beamed ceilings and smart wooden furnishings including the bathroom mirrors. Some rooms have views over Notre-Dame; the ones at the front are the largest, with triple windows onto the street (with the exception of the first floor room). No. 24 is particularly handsome, with an expansive desk in the centre. In complete contrast is the attic conversion, very popular with Japanese guests, which swops Gallic character for modern decor, a private bar and a huge contoured bath. Rooms are spotlessly kept, and are often graced with that rare thing in Paris hotels – a vase of fresh flowers.

Nearby Notre-Dame; Sainte-Chapelle; Musée de Cluny.

10 rue des Grands Degrés 75005 Paris **Tel** 01.43.25.88.38 **Fax** 01.40.46.95.34 **Location** on a tiny square at junction with rue Fréderic-Sauton, close to quai de Montebello; parking at place Maubert; metro Saint-Michel; **Meals** breakfast, lunch, dinner **Prices** 380F-500F; breakfast	30F; dinner: set menus from 67F-145F **Rooms** 10 double, all with bath; all rooms have phone, fax/modem plug, TV, mini-bar, fridge, hairdrier **Facilities** restaurant, bar **Credit cards** V **Children** accepted **Disabled** not suitable (no lift) **Pets** accepted **Closed** never **Proprietor** M. Tahir

Ile-de-France

Hôtel Duc de St-Simon

A stylish hotel on a stylish street, just off the boulevard St-Germain. First glimpsed through two pairs of French windows which lie beyond a pretty courtyard, the interior of the Duc de St-Simon looks wonderfully inviting; and so it is – there is a warm, beautifully furnished salon with the distinctly private-house feel that the Swedish proprietor seeks to maintain, and elegant yet cosy bedrooms, all individually decorated with not a jarring note. The twin bedrooms are more spacious than those with double beds. Everywhere you look – both upstairs and downstairs – there are rich fabrics, gloriously overstuffed pieces of furniture, antique mirrors and cleverly conceived paint effects. The kilim-lined lift is a particularly original idea.

The white-painted 19thC house backs on to an 18thC building behind, also part of the hotel, with a tiny secret garden wedged in between. Breakfasts can be had here, or in the intimate cellar bar; service is smiling and courteous. But as the hotel's own brochure points out, there are two famous cafés (the Deux Magots and the Flore) only a few yards away. Prices are high, but not unreasonable we felt after our recent visit, especially in comparison with other hotels in this category, and Gun Karin Lalisse, the manager, runs the hotel with great charm and efficiency.
Nearby Hôtel des Invalides; Musée d'Orsay; Rodin Museum.

14 rue de St-Simon, 75007 Paris
Tel 01.44.39.20.20/reservations 01.42.20.07.52
Fax 01.45.48.68.25
Location between blvd St-Germain and rue de Grenelle; parking at blvd Raspail; metro Rue du Bac/Solférino
Meals breakfast, light meals
Prices 1,025F-1,850F; breakfast 70F

Rooms 29 double, 28 with bath, one with shower; 5 suites; all rooms have phone, hairdrier, safe; TV on request; some rooms have air-conditioning **Facilities** 2 sitting-rooms, bar, lift **Credit cards** not accepted **Children** accepted **Disabled** no special facilities **Pets** not accepted **Closed** never **Proprietor** M. Lindqvist

Ile-de-France

Town hotel, Paris

Hôtel Eber

Jean-Marc Eber remains as committed as ever to the little hotel he took over in the late 1980s after more than a decade practising his hotelkeeping in four-star Paris hotels.

The turn-of-the-century house, easily missed in a quiet residential street not far from the Champs Elysées and near the Parc Monceau, is well cared for and prettily furnished and decorated, and M. Eber's combination of warmth and professionalism makes sure that the hotel stays well out of the rut. The public areas are tiny, but inviting – there is a small beamed sitting area off the reception and a pretty little courtyard. Breakfast may be taken in either of these places, or in your bedroom. These vary in size and feel, priced accordingly – our inspector's had a little sitting-room and a shower room as well as a bathroom. Some have lofty ceilings, others are small-scale, all are attractive, using neutral colours with elegant flower-patterned curtains. Best of all is the top-floor apartment with its own private terrace, much favoured, says Monsieur Eber, by fashion directors during Parish Fashion Week. The house rule is to 'make yourself at home' – after a hard day's sightseeing, an inviting prospect.

Nearby Parc Monceau, Arc du Triomphe, Champs Elysées.

18 Rue Léon Jost 75017 Paris
Tel 01.46.22.60.70
Fax 01.47.63.01.01
Location in residential area, close to Champs Elysées; parking rue de Courcelles; metro Courcelles
Meals breakfast
Prices rooms 610F-660F, suites 1,000F-1,300F; breakfast 50F
Rooms 18 double (3 twin), all with bath; all rooms have central heating, cable TV, phone, minibar, hairdrier
Facilities some rooms have private sitting-area
Credit cards AE, DC, MC, V
Children accepted
Disabled no special facilities
Pets accepted
Closed never
Proprietor Jean Marc Eber

Ile-de-France

Town hotel, Paris

Hôtel Ermitage

We were entranced when we found the Ermitage, a stone Baroque style building tucked away behind Sacré Coeur. Only a sober wall plaque announces that this is a hotel, the door opening onto a smart little gold and cream lobby, followed by a dark blue hall with deep red carpet strewn with rugs. From the reception you can see a charming kitchen with its faience stove from Lorraine (breakfast is prepared here and served in your room) and a little terrace beyond. Also on the ground floor: an old fashioned parlour, with green velvet hangings, filled with antiques and photographs. Par for the course so far, you may think, yet the Ermitage has a decorative surprise which starts in the hall and continues all the way up the stairs, on walls, doors, glass panels, skirtings: the charming, shadowy paint effects and murals of the artist Du Buc – those in the reception area, sketchy scenes of Montmartre, were done in 1986 when he was an old man.

Eclectic and friendly, the Ermitage is the creation of Maggie Canipel, its endearing *patronne*. Bedrooms are by and large light and spacious, with old fashioned charm: floral wallpapers, lace curtains, large *armoires*. Those on the ground floor benefit from the leafy terrace with views of eastern Paris. Bathrooms are tiny, many with mini baths, with showers above.

Nearby Sacré Coeur; Place du Tertre.

24 rue Lamarck, 75018 Paris
Tel 01.42.64.79.22
Fax 01.42.64.10.33
Location at eastern end of rue Lamarck, close to Sacré Coeur; parking in nearby private garage; metro Lamarck Caulaincourt
Meals breakfast
Prices 330F-680F; breakfast included
Rooms 12 double; 1 family room; 11 rooms have bath or mini bath and shower; all rooms have phone, hairdrier
Facilities sitting-room
Credit cards not accepted
Children accepted
Disabled 2 rooms on ground floor
Pets accepted
Closed never
Proprietor Maggie Canipel

Ile-de-France

Town hotel, Paris

Hôtel de Fleurie

A model hotel, rightly very popular, where charm, efficiency and up-to-date comforts go hand-in-hand. Renovated seven years ago by the Marolleau family, who used to own the well-known Latin Quarter brasserie, Balzar, it combines an immaculate appearance (not least the pretty façade, elegantly lit at night, complete with statues in the niches) with a cosy, intimate feel. The hands-on owners – parents and two sons – are determined to keep it so, and the place always feels fresh, clean and well cared for.

Instantly eye-catching in the terracotta-tiled reception is a delightful *faience* stove picked up by Madame Marolleau in the Saint Antoine flea market; the adjoining sitting room, with its exposed beams and section of ancient wall, has a discreet bar and little tables covered in Provençal cloths. The basement *cave*, where a generous breakfast is served, is equally cosy, cleverly lit by uplighters.

The spotless bedrooms do not disappoint. You will find pretty billowing curtains, walls of panelled wood and grasspaper, period style furniture, inviting beds and - a rare touch - fresh flowers. Bathrooms, all in pink-hued marble, are well equipped with thick towels on heated rails and towelling bath robes.

Nearby Saint-Sulpice; Jardin de Luxembourg.

32 rue Grégoire-de-Tours
75006 Paris
Tel 01.43.29.59.81
Fax 01.43.29.68.44
Location between blvd Saint-Germain and rue des Quatres-Vents; parking at rue de l'Ecole de Médecine; metro Mabillon, Odéon
Meals breakfast
Prices 650F-1200F; breakfast 50F

Rooms 29 all with bath or shower; all rooms have phone, satellite TV, fax/modem plug, air-conditioning, minibar, hairdryer, safe
Facilities sitting room, bar, breakfast room, lift
Credit cards AE, DC, MC, V
Disabled no special facilities
Pets not accepted
Closed never
Proprietors Marolleau family

Ile-de-France

Town hotel, Paris

Hôtel du Jeu de Paume

We feature no less than four hotels in the delightful rue Saint-Louis-en-l'Ile; but whereas the others are homely, this one is highly original with considerable panache,

As its name implies, the building was the site of a 17thC *jeu de paume* court, built in the days when the 'palm game', forerunner to tennis, was all the rage; when the proprietors acquired it ten years ago, however, it was a run-down warehouse. Monsieur Prache is an architect and he wrought something of a miracle on the building, opening out the heart of it right up to the roof, exposing all the old timber construction and slinging mezzanine floors around a central well. The impression of light and transparency is reinforced by a glass-walled lift and glass balustrades around the upper floors. Stone walls and all those beams add a reasuringly rustic feel. The sitting area close to the entrance has the appearance of a sophisticated private apartment with leather sofas, subtle lighting and handsome stone fireplace. Nearby, at the reception desk, the chic, laid-back staff adjust their designer shawls and coolly deal with the guests while a stylish sheepdog pads around. Madame Prache is charming. Bedrooms are small-ish, perfectly pleasant, but nothing like as exciting as the rest of the hotel.

Nearby Marais; Nôtre-Dame; Latin Quarter.

54 rue Saint-Louis-en-l'Ile
75004 Paris
Tel 01.43.26.14.18
Fax 01.40.46.02.76
Location halfway along the island's main street, near the junction with rue des Deux Ponts; car parking at Pont-Marie; metro Pont Marie, Cité
Meals breakfast
Prices 820F-2490F; breakfast 80F

Rooms 32, all with bath; all rooms have phone, satellite TV, minibar, hairdrier
Facilities breakfast room, sitting-room, bar, courtyard garden, sauna, 2 conference rooms, lift **Credit cards** AE, DC, MC, V **Children** accepted
Disabled access difficult
Pets accepted – 50F per day
Closed never **Proprietors** M. and Mme Prache

Ile-de-France

Hôtel Mansart

A stone's throw from the Ritz, spacious bedrooms which recall an earlier, more gracious era, attentive service, fair prices – these are the principle attributes of the excellent Mansart. Recently restored, the aged hotel's former proportions were left mercifully intact. The large modern lobby, with its expanse of marble floor and walls boldly painted in geometric patterns based on Mansart's drawings for the gardens of Versaille (he was also architect of place Vendôme) is impressive, but it doesn't prepare you for the bedrooms, which you might expect to be similarly contemporary. In fact, though newly decorated, they have a dignified, old-fashioned flavour quite different from downstairs. We loved no. 205, which feels like a private flat with its own entrance hall opening onto a large room with antique mirrored *armoir* and regal prints on the white walls, the panelling picked out in gold. The separate bathroom has a pretty tiled floor, as do all the bathrooms. A cheaper option, but equally stately, is no. 212, a huge room with space for table and chairs, with large gilt-framed mirrors, attractive curtains, panelled walls and a green and white bathroom – at 830F excellent value, we felt. Be warned, though – one or two singles are pokey. The breakfast room, with stained-glass windows and marble fireplace, is very elegant.

Nearby place Vendôme; Opéra Garnier; place de la Concorde.

Rue des Capucines 75001 Paris
Tel 01.42.61.50.28
Fax 01.49.27.97.44
Location on the corner of place Vendôme; parking at place Vendôme; metro Opéra, Madeleine
Meals breakfast
Prices 530F-1,500F; standard double 830F
Rooms 57, 50 double with bath, 3 with shower; 4 single all with bath; all rooms have phone, minibar, satellite TV, hairdrier, safe
Facilities sitting-room, bar, lift
Credit cards AE, DC, MC, V
Children accepted
Disabled no special facilities
Pets not accepted
Closed never
Proprietor M. Dupaen

Ile-de-France

Hôtel de Nice

Here is a wonderfully wacky two star hotel, every bit as comfortable and twice as enjoyable as many a more expensive three star. We thought it a terrific find, instantly intrigued and not disappointed by what lay behind the vivid turquoise front door and up the tightly winding stairs.

The Nice is the enchanting creation of a previously high-flying professional couple who love both collecting and entertaining. The fruits of their hobby are everywhere – masses of period engravings and prints – particularly of Paris – mirrors, old doors, postcards, even a splendid portrait of Lady Diana Cooper. The effect is charming and highly individual – the panelled *salon*, for example, where you can also take breakfast, is a harmony of uncoordinated colours, fabrics (the ceiling is tented in Indian cotton) and furniture: antique, painted, modern, garden. The use of wallpaper copied from French 18thC designs makes the smallish bedrooms feel fresh and pretty, with the off-beat addition of Indian cotton bedspreads, and doors and skirtings boldly painted in turquoise, orange or pillar-box red. Two attic rooms on the top floor are particularly charming, with their own little balconies. Others look out on to a pretty square. You'll find only basic amenities here (no television) but plenty of character.
Nearby Marais; Les Halles; Ile Saint-Louis; Nôtre Dame.

42 bis rue de Rivoli 75004 Paris **Tel** 01.42.78.55.29 **Fax** 01.42.78.36.07 **Location** on corner of rue de Rivoli and little square of rue du Bourg Tibourg; parking at Hôtel de Ville (rue de Lobau); metro Hôtel de Ville **Meals** breakfast **Prices** 350F-400F; breakfast 30F	**Rooms** 23; 5 with bath, 12 with shower; 5 single, 3 with bath, 2 with shower; one family room; all rooms have phone, hairdrier **Facilities** sitting-room/breakfast room, lift **Credit cards** MC, V **Children** accepted **Disabled** no special facilities **Pets** accepted **Closed** never **Proprietors** M. and Mme Vaudoux

Ile-de-France

Hôtel Parc Saint-Séverin

Of the many bedrooms described in this book, no. 70 at the Parc Saint-Séverin remains this writer's favourite. And although it's an expensive choice, its assets are far greater than, say, a standard double room at the Pavilion de la Reine (page 60) or the Relais Christine (page 61) which cost some 200F per night more. Overall, of course, those are far superior hotels, but this room is special: a light, sophisticated and beautifully decorated pent-house suite which is entirely encircled by a broad private terrace affording breathtaking views across the rooftops of all the land-mark buildings as far as the Eiffel Tower in one direction, Sacré-Coeur in another. Taking breakfast on a warm summer morning is sheer bliss. Less expensive, but nonetheless very impressive, are two more rooms, each with a broad terrace on three sides. On lower floors, room nos 50 and 12 both have style and space. The rest are pleasant, if unexceptional, pastel coloured, with predom-inantly grey modern furniture; bathrooms are generally quite spacious with generous basins. The large ground floor lobby, which divides into three areas for reception, breakfast and sitting, is a disappointment, another example of contemporary colours - grey, pink, mauve – abstract paintings and minimalist furniture failing to inspire.

Nearby Notre-Dame; Sainte-Chapelle; Musée de Cluny.

22 rue de la Parcheminerie
75005 Paris
Tel 01.43.54.32.17
Fax 01.43.54.70.71
Location in a pedestrian area close to Saint-Séverin and the junction with rue des Prêtres Saint-Séverin; parking at rue Lagrange; metro Saint-Michel
Meals breakfast
Prices 500F-1,500F; suite 1,500F

Rooms 22 double and twin, 1 family room, 4 single, all with bath; all rooms have phone, satellite TV, minibar, hairdrier, safe; half are air-conditioned **Facilities** break-fast room, sitting area, lift
Credit cards AE, DC, MC, V
Children accepted
Disabled no special facilities
Pets not accepted **Closed** never **Manager** M. Lebouc

Ile-de-France

Town hotel, Paris

Pavillon de la Reine

Set back from the gloriously harmonious Place des Vosges, approached through a calming courtyard garden, the Pavillon de la Reine has our vote for the most perfect location in Paris. Like its sister hotel, the Relais Christine (see page 61) it is run with calm professionalism by a dedicated and friendly team, although, it lacks the intimacy of a truly Charming Small Hotel (at 55 bedrooms it is one of our largest, but feels delightfully contained).

The fine 17thC mansion was once the residence of Ann of Austria, wife of Louis XIII. Rescued from near ruin a dozen years ago, it now feels more like a baronial country house, with an impressive entrance hall, a handsome panelled sitting-room with comfy leather sofas and a huge stone fireplace complete with roaring log fire, stone-vaulted breakfast room and two flowery courtyards. For us, the only jarring note was the use of reproduction old masters throughout. We were told about the guest of another hotel who had replaced an expensive original canvas with a copy, but still, we felt it was a misconceived idea. Upstairs, via a lift cleverly disguised by *trompe l'oeil*, bedrooms and suites contrive to be both smart and pretty, immaculately maintained and suitably luxurious, with ornaments here and there adding a personal touch. New to the guide this year.

Nearby Musée Carnavalet; Musée Picasso; Notre-Dame.

28 place des Vosges 75003 Paris
Tel 01.42.77.96.40
Fax 01.42.77.63. 06
Location northern side of place des Vosges; free private garage; metro Saint-Paul
Meals breakfast; light meals served in room at any time
Prices 1,300F-2,700F; continental breakfast 95F; cooked 140F

Rooms 55, all with bath and shower; all rooms have phone, satellite TV, air conditioning, minibar, hairdrier
Facilities sitting-room, breakfast room, 2 courtyard gardens, lift, garage **Credit cards** AE, DC, MC, V **Children** accepted **Disabled** ground floor bedrooms **Pets** accepted **Closed** never
Manager M. Sudre

Ile-de-France

Hôtel Relais Christine

The Relais Christine used to be the *sixième*'s most prestigious hotel. Back in the 1980s, companies took whole floors and never asked the price; now in the money-conscious '90s the hotel finds itself competing with less expensive establishments for the same clients, and we are including it in the guide for the first time this year. If you can afford it, though, you are unlikely to be disappointed: it has the calm, luxurious feel of a grand hotel but on a far more intimate scale; in this it is matched only by its sister hotel, the Pavillon de la Reine (see page 60).

Approached through a handsome courtyard, the Relais Christine is an oasis of dignified calm. The reception hall is coolly tiled and strewn with Persian rugs, and the ceiling retains its original painted beams. In the handsome panelled sitting room, a help-yourself drinks table enhances the feel of a private room. Traces of the building's medieval roots are visible in the elegant stone-vaulted breakfast room which has a huge hearth and a massive central pillar. Bedrooms are decorated with the same sense of restrained luxury as at the Pavillion de la Reine, with plenty of cupboard space, pretty paintings, and bathrooms (all with separate W.C.'s) in which it is a pleasure to idle away time. All the bedrooms are a fair size, especially the duplex rooms.

Nearby blvd Saint-Germain; Ile de la Cité; Latin Quarter.

3 Rue Christine 75006 Paris
Tel 01.43.26.71.80
Fax 01.43.26.89.38
Location in a quiet street between rue Dauphine and rue des Grands Augustins; free private garage; metro Odéon
Meals breakfast
Prices 1,630F-3,100F; breakfast 95F
Rooms 38 double and twin, 13 suites, all with bath (separate W.C.); all rooms have phone, satellite TV, air-conditioning, minibar, hairdrier
Facilities sitting-room, breakfast room, bar, meeting room, lift, garage
Credit cards AE, DC, MC,V
Children accepted **Disabled** access difficult **Pets** accepted
Closed never
Manager M. Monnin

Ile-de-France

Town hotel, Paris

Le Relais du Louvre

In a quiet side street hard by the Louvre and the river, this sophisticated little hotel, new to the guide this year, proves that, in the right hands, even the most featureless of bedrooms can be made to feel charming and welcoming. Most are standard box-shape, no more than adequate in size, although some have the benefit of beamed ceilings and floor length windows. Ours had a terrific view on to the gables and gargoyles of Saint-Germain-l'Auxerrois opposite and, though small, felt extremely welcoming and comforting, with its pink hydrangea curtains and matching bedspread, elegant desk and bedside tables, each with a decent-sized lamp. On the walls were pretty 19thC fashion plates, and the television could be popped away in the upholstered box on which it sat. The marble-clad bathroom was equipped with generous towels. Breakfast is served in your bedroom. Downstairs, an elegant beamed reception room, with a polished antique table serving as the reception desk, sets the hotel's tone.

Rooms are cleverly arranged so that a pair can be taken together, closed off behind a communal front door; two ground floor rooms have access onto a little patio. The manageress, Sophie Aulnette, and her close-knit staff pride themselves on trying to accommodate clients in the best, most budget-conscious way.

Nearby Louvre; Ile de la Cité; Samaritaine store (rooftop view).

19 rue des Prêtres-Saint-Germain-l'Auxerrois 75001 Paris
Tel 01.40.41.96.42
Fax 01.40.41.96.44
Location in a quiet side street parallel to Quai du Louvre; public car park opposite; metro Pont Neuf, Louvre Rivoli
Meals breakfast
Prices 600F-1,450F; breakfast 50F
Rooms 18 double, all with bath; 5 single all with shower; 2 junior suites; all rooms have phone, cable TV, minibar, hairdryer, safe **Facilities** sitting area, lift **Credit cards** AE, DC, MC, V **Children** accepted **Disabled** two ground floor bedrooms **Pets** accepted **Closed** never **Manager** Sophie Aulnette

Ile-de-France

Town hotel, Paris

Le Relais Saint-Germain

New to the guide this year, and irresistible, if you can afford it: a sumptuous 17thC house whose mini-lift and cramped public rooms – albeit artfully mirrored and glossily decorated – give no hint of the wonderfully spacious bedrooms upstairs. Expensive though the Relais Saint Germain undoubtedly is, bear in mind that what is termed a 'standard double' here would be called a 'junior suite' elsewhere – that is, a bedroom large enough for a sitting area as well. Most 'standard' rooms in Paris give you just enough room to swing a cat. The de-luxe rooms are enormous, with two sets of French windows overlooking the street; they are embellished with stunning antiques – mostly French country – plump sofas, lovely fabrics and well-chosen prints and pictures. One is notable for its pair of stone angels culled from a medieval chapel, another for two beautiful matching bookcases. The top floor suite is a dashing yellow, with black and white prints on the walls, ancient sprouting beams and a tiny sun-trap terrace.

In the morning, it's hard to choose whether to take breakfast in bed or in the adjoining café, now part of the hotel and closed to the public until noon. Here you can enjoy the ambience of an authentic 1930s café once frequented by Hemingway, Picasso *et al*, married to slick hotel service.

Nearby blvd Saint-Germain; Saint-Sulpice; Latin Quarter.

9 carrefour de l'Odéon 75006 Paris
Tel 01.43.29.12.05
Fax 01.46.33.45.30
Location off blvd Saint-Germain, at the corner of rue Monsieur Le Prince; parking at rue l'Ecole de Médecine; metro Odéon
Meals breakfast
Prices 1,280F-1,950F; breakfast included

Rooms 21, 1 suite, all with bath; all rooms have phone, cable TV, video, fax/modem plug, air-conditioning, mini-bar, hairdrier, safe
Facilities 2 small sitting-rooms, breakfast room/ bar, lift **Credit cards** AE, DC, MC, V **Children** accepted
Disabled not suitable
Pets accepted **Closed** never
Proprietor Alexis Laipsker

Ile-de-France

Town hotel, Paris

Hotel Le Saint-Gregoire

A chic, if pricey, little hotel in a tall 18thC town house, run with affable charm by manager Francois de Bené. Le Saint-Gregoire was designed by Christian Badin of David Hicks – dusty pink walls, maroon carpets, floral peachy curtains, and crisp white linen bedspreads and chair covers – and a warm intimate atmosphere prevails. An open fire blazes in the salon on wintry afternoons, a room dotted with antiques and knickknacks, picked up by Madame Bouvier, the owner's wife, in flea markets and antique shops. These range from a basket of fir cones on the mantlepiece to a pretty tin table decorated with an Italian scene, but are liable to change weekly as new acquisitions are made. Trellis on the walls and large French windows leading on to a tiny enclosed garden, full of flowers and ferns, make the back part of the sitting room feel more like a conservatory.

The colour scheme leads from the ground floor upstairs to equally attractive bedrooms, with beautiful antique chests of drawers, tables and mirrors; two bedrooms have private terraces. Bathrooms are typically white tiled and small but well designed. The ubiquitous cellar breakfast room is a particularly pretty one, with woven floor, rush chairs and baskets decorating one wall.

Nearby Musée Bourdelle; Jardin du Luxembourg; blvd St-Germain.

43 rue de l'Abbé-Gregoire
75006 Paris
Tel 01.45.48.23.23
Fax 01.45.48.33.95
Location between blvd Raspail and blvd du Montparnasse; parking rue de l'Abbé-Gregoire in garage by arrangement
metro St Placide/Rennes;
Meals breakfast
Prices rooms 790F-1,390F; breakfast 60F
Rooms 20, all with bath; all rooms have phone, satellite TV, air-conditioning, hairdrier **Facilities** sitting room, breakfast room, lift
Credit cards AE, DC, MC, V
Children welcome
Disabled no special facilities
Pets small pets accepted
Closed never
Proprietor M. Bouvier

Ile-de-France

Town hotel, Paris

Hôtel Saint-Merry

One of the most distinctive small hotels in Paris, the Saint-Merry has a church-like, medieval atmosphere all its own, with heavily beamed ceilings, pale stone walls, wrought iron fittings and splendid carved wood neo-Gothic furnishings. Everything is kept simple: bedrooms and bathrooms are spotless though mostly small; there are no public rooms to speak of, and breakfast, which is brought to your room, is prepared in a tiny galley behind the reception; a spiralling staircase is the only means by which you can reach your room; only three bathrooms have baths; and TVs and minibars are nowhere to be seen.

This former presbytery of the adjacent church of Saint-Merri became a private residence after the 1789 revolution, and served for a time as a brothel before it was rescued from decay by its committed proprietor, Christian Crabbe, in the 1960s. He decided on its memorable – if sombre – style after acquiring some neo-Gothic furnishings which were languishing in the basement of the church. The hotel is famous for room 9, where flying buttresses form a low canopy over the bed, whilst rooms 12 and 17 have remarkable bedheads. Even after 35 years, work on the hotel, says M. Crabbe "never ends". Recently he created a charming suite, complete with huge stone chimney breast, tucked under the eves.
Nearby Pompidou Centre; Les Halles; Marais; Notre-Dame.

78 rue de la Verrerie 75004 Paris
Tel 01.42.78.14.15
Fax 01.40.29.06.82
Location in a pedestrianized zone, on the corner of rue de la Verrerie and rue Saint-Martin; parking at Hôtel de Ville (rue de Lobau); metro Hôtel de Ville
Meals breakfast
Prices 400F-1,500F; breakfast 50F
Rooms 11 with bath, 8 with shower, 2 without WC; 2 family rooms, both with shower only; 1 suite; all rooms have phone, hairdrier
Facilities small sitting area
Credit cards not accepted
Children accepted
Disabled not suitable (no lift)
Pets accepted **Closed** never
Proprietor Christian Crabbe

Ile-de-France

Hôtel Saint-Paul

We like this hotel very much, as have friends to whom we have recommended it. The owner's family have been talented hoteliers in France for generations; she married an Englishman, and now their friendly and capable daughter, Marianne Hawkins, is in charge, along with her father's cat, Perkins. It is new to the guide this year.

The Saint-Paul, a 17thC building, was renovated in 1987. The public rooms are stylish in an unfussy way with beamed ceilings, a mixture of stone and colour-washed walls, Indian rugs, *haute epoque* and good country antiques, dark pink drapes and attractive pink and green checked armchairs. Facing the entrance, a courtyard garden is set behind a glass wall, carefully tended and full of colour year round. The cellar breakfast room is a particularly elegant variation on the theme, with high-backed tapestry chairs and round wooden tables. If the reception rooms have a rural feel, so do the bedrooms, all of which are differently decorated, with walls covered in grass cloth or enlivened with a dash of bright colour, and smart, carefully lit bathrooms clad in ginger or reddish marble. Our room under the eaves felt cosy, with views over the rooftops; others have four-posters or antique brass bedsteads. All in all easy going and well run: a pleasure to stay in.
Nearby Latin Quarter; Musée de Cluny; Jardin de Luxembourg.

43 Rue Monsieur Le Prince
75006 Paris
Tel 01.43.26.98.64
Fax 01.46.34.58.60
Location halfway along street, in section between rue Racine and rue de Vaugirard; parking at rue l'Ecole de Médicine, rue Soufflot; metro Odéon. **Meals** breakfast
Prices 565F-1,065F; continental breakfast 48F, cooked 68F **Rooms** 31, all with bath or shower; all rooms have phone, satellite TV, air-conditioning, minibar, haridrier, safe **Facilities** sitting-room, breakfast room, lift/elevator**Credit cards** AE, DC, MC, V **Children** accepted **Disabled** 1 room on ground floor **Pets** accepted **Closed** never **Proprietors** Hawkins family

Ile-de-France

Hôtel Le Sainte-Beuve

All is discretion and understatement at this essentially simple little hotel with luxurious touches: plain cream walls, restrained patterns in the rich fabrics; beds draped in white, simple furniture mixing modern designs with country antiques, attractive pictures, fresh flowers strategically placed. A log fire burns in the classically-styled *salon*, and there is also a bar, complete with barman in the evening.

Thanks to its owner, Bobette Compagnon, the Sainte-Beuve, though no more than a bed-and-breakfast hotel, has an inate sense of style which rescues it from the rut and sets it apart, along with some pampering extra services. "We just want people to be happy," says the hotel's manager, Yves Meteigner, and so the excellent breakfast — which arrives on a tray beautifully laid with porcelain – can be ordered at any time of day or night, as well as a selection of cold dishes. During our stay we met someone who had benefited from the hotel's policy of upgrading guests, whenever possible, to a more expensive room than was booked, and another who was accompanied by her three cats – every bit as stylish as their owner – one of which had inadvertently escaped and which we found wandering down the winding staircase – a dizzying sight from the top floor – as we passed.

Nearby Montparnasse; blvd Saint-Germain.

9 rue Sainte-Beuve 75006 Paris
Tel 01.45.48.20.07
Fax 01.45.48.67.52
Location off blvd Raspail, between place Lafou and place Picasso; street parking or car park in blvd Montparnasse; metro Notre Dame des Champs, Vavin
Meals breakfast; cold dishes also available

Prices 700F-1700F; standard double 950F; breakfast 80F
Rooms 23; all rooms have phone, satellite TV, minibar, hairdryer and safe
Facilities sitting room/breakfast room, bar, lift **Credit cards** AE, MC, V **Children** accepted **Disabled** access difficult **Pets** accepted **Closed** never **Proprietor** Bobette Compagnon

Ile-de-France

Town hotel, Paris

Hôtel Solférino

Particularly handy for the Musée d'Orsay, this is a simple hotel with an appealing old-fashioned flavour. We have added it to the guide this year despite the fact that our stay was almost blighted by the family member on duty, whose utter disdain eventually won him second prize in our Rudest Receptionist in Paris competition. He proved, however, to be an exception; subsequent receptionists were perfectly friendly and helpful. As we heaved our luggage towards the original, coffin-shaped lift (while he sat back and read a book), we took in the plain white façade of the hotel, the elegant, high ceilinged *salon*, with its fringed, paisley-print armchairs, potted palms and huge Baroque canvas, and the charming, spring-like breakfast room with its glass ceiling, pastel-coloured panelled walls decorated with pretty plates, and marble-topped tables and wicker chairs. Our room on the second floor was entered by slightly scruffy double doors painted blue. Inside, it was fairly spacious, decorated with floral-print wallpaper, with dowdy curtains and a shower room in *passé* plain blue ceramic tiles (at least made a change from modern white). An alcove for the bedside light added a focal point. All in all, the hotel had that characteristic French feel of a faded *pension*, now occupied by transient tourists rather than the habitués of a novel by Balzac.
Nearby Musée d'Orsay; Tuileries; Louvre; blvd Saint-Germain.

91 rue de Lille 75007 Paris
Tel 01.47.05.85.54
Fax 01.45.55.51.16
Location between blvd Saint-Germain and rue de Solférino; parking at rue du Bac; metro Assemblée Nationale
Meals breakfast
Prices 300F-700F; breakfast included
Rooms 33; 24 double and twin, 19 with bath, 5 with shower; 9 single with shower; all rooms have phone; 4 rooms have TV
Facilities sitting room, breakfast room, lift
Credit cards MC, V
Children accepted
Disabled access difficult
Pets accepted
Closed 21st Dec - 3rd Jan
Proprietor M. Cornic

Ile-de-France

Village hotel, Senlisse

Auberge du Gros Marronnier

Mme Trochon advises us of further improvements to this rustic little inn, which have been going on steadily since we first encountered the place in 1990. Much of the older parts of the interior have been renovated, the sitting-room has been smartened up, and a new glass veranda with lovely views over the valley has become the restaurant.

The Gros Marronier is tucked away next door to the church (it used to be the presbytery) in an affluent residential village. It's a captivating place for a night or two when passing through the Paris area – close enough to the metropolis for sightseeing expeditions, and handily placed for the Normandy ferry ports. The bedrooms are spacious and prettily decorated, and the food, served on a flowery terrace overlooking the informal grassy garden, is interesting, excellent and well presented. The staff are smiling and helpful, but not over-numerous; the pace of service at dinner is elegantly described by one reporter as 'a good tempo for digestion and civilized discourse'. More reports please.

Nearby Versailles (15 km); Paris (35 km).

3 Place de l'Église, 75720 Senlisse
Tel 01.30.52.51.69
Fax 01.30.52.55.91
Location in heart of village, next to church, 12 km NE of Rambouillet on D91; with garden and limited car parking
Meals breakfast, lunch, dinner
Prices rooms 280F–375F; breakfast 40F–45F, menus 135F–295F
Rooms 15 double, one single, 4 family rooms, 12 with bath, 8 with shower; all rooms have central heating, phone
Facilities dining-room, TV room, bar, terrace
Credit cards AE, V
Children welcome
Disabled no special facilities
Pets accepted
Closed one week at Christmas
Proprietor Mme Trochon

Ile-de-France

Inn, Barbizon

Hôtellerie du Bas-Breau

Half of Europe's political grandees have been guests at this handsome and luxurious (Relais & Châteaux) inn. The best rooms are in the inn itself; but the majority are in a modern chalet set amid the beautifully tended flower gardens. Excellent food. Swimming-pool.

■ 22 Rue Grande, 77630 Barbizon (Seine-et-Marne) **Tel** 01.60.66.40.05 **Fax** 01.60.69.22.89 **Meals** breakfast, lunch, dinner **Prices** rooms 950F-2,800F; breakfast 90F, dinner from 500F **Rooms** 20, all with bath, central heating, phone, TV, hairdrier **Credit cards** AE, MC, V **Closed** never

---

Restaurant with rooms, Barbizon

Hostellerie de la Clé d'Or

The key attraction is the shady courtyard where meals (well cooked, ample portions) are served in summer. Bedrooms are in a handsome single-storey extension. Smart dining-room with an open fireplace and walls covered in daubs by local artists. Delightful garden.

■ 73 Grande Rue, 77630 Barbizon (Seine-et-Marne) **Tel** 01.60.66.40.96 **Fax** 01.60.66.42.71 **Meals** breakfast, lunch, dinner **Prices** rooms 290F-850F; menus 160F-230F, children's 75F **Rooms** 16, all with bath or shower, central heating, phone, TV, minibar **Credit cards** AE, DC, MC, V **Closed** never

---

Manor house hotel, Fontenay-Trésigny

Le Manoir

From the outside, this half-timbered turn-of-the-century mansion in gloriously spacious gardens (with pool) looks English. But its interior is distinctively French – rich and ornate and occasionally gloomy. Bedrooms differ widely in style. Good classic cooking.

■ 77610 Fontenay-Trésigny (Seine-et-Marne) **Tel** 01.64.25.91.17 **Fax** 01.64.25.95. 49 **Meals** breakfast, lunch, dinner **Prices** rooms 830F-1,190F, breakfast 70F; menus 240F-350F **Rooms** 20, all with bath, phone, TV, minibar **Credit cards** AE, DC, MC, V **Closed** never

---

Town hotel, Paris

Hôtel Beaubourg

Although this six-storey town house dates back to the 1600s, the hotel is not lacking in modern comforts; bedrooms and public rooms are pleasantly furnished and effectively lit. Some bedrooms overlook the courtyard garden, full of trailing plants.

■ 11 Rue Simon Lefranc, 75004 Paris **Tel** 01.42.74.34.24 **Fax** 01.42.78.68.11 **Meals** breakfast **Prices** rooms 490F-580F (extra bed 150F); breakfast 40F **Rooms** 28, all with bath or shower, central heating, phone, TV, radio, minibar **Credit cards** AE, DC, MC, V **Closed** never

Ile-de-France

Town hotel, Paris

Hôtel Bersoly's Saint-Germain

On a quiet street in the administrative heart of Paris, this 17thC former convent makes an excellent sightseeing base. Each of the bedrooms – generally on the small side – has been thoughtfully done out in a favourite colour of the impressionist painter it is named after. Car parking. Reports welcome.

■ 28 Rue de Lille, 75007 Paris **Tel** 01.42.60.73.79 **Fax** 01.49.27.05.55 **Meals** breakfast, snacks **Prices** rooms 600F-750F; breakfast 50F **Rooms** 16, all with bath or shower, central heating, air-conditioning phone, TV, radio, hairdrier, safe **Credit cards** AE, MC, V **Closed** 2 weeks in Aug

---

Town hotel, Paris

Hôtel Caron de Beaumarchais

If the *décor* is a mite chi-chi for our taste, most other guests find it enchanting, and everyone agrees that it is an extremely congenial place in which to stay. Monsieurs Bigeard *père et fils* genuinely want their guests to be contented. Beneath the surface gloss is a real heart. New to the guide this year.

■ 12 rue Vieille-du-Temple, 75004 Paris **Tel** 01.42.72.34.12 **Fax** 01.42.72.34.63. **Meals** breakfast; brunch **Prices** 560-730F; breakfast 48F; brunch 78F **Rooms** 19, 17 with bath, 2 with shower; all rooms have phone, fax/modem plug; satellite TV, air-conditioning, minibar, hairdrier **Credit cards** AE, DC, MC, V **Closed** never

---

Town hotel, Paris

Hôtel Chopin

With a charming façade, the Chopin stands at the end of passage Jouffroy, a 19thC glass-and-steel roofed arcade.This is no tourist trap: the welcome is warm and friendly, and a caring hand (that of owner Philippe Bidal) was immediately in evidence in the decoration. All the rooms are quiet. New to the guide this year.

■ 10 blvd Montmartre (46 passage Jouffroy) 75009 Paris **Tel** 01.47.70. 58.10 **Fax** 01.42.47.00.70 **Meals** breakfast **Prices** rooms 355-565F; breakfast 38F **Rooms** 36, all with bath or shower; all rooms have phone, TV **Credit cards** AE, DC, MC, V **Closed** never

---

Town hotel, Paris

Hôtel Le Clos Médicis

The charming Pascal Beherec owns the Clos Médicis, the equally charming Olivier Méallet manages it, but it is architect, Jean-Philippe Nuel, whose presence is most strongly felt. The entire interior, down to the light fittings and the wave-shaped headboards in the bedrooms, is his creation, circa 1994 – and a great success.

■ 56 rue Monsieur le Prince, 75006 Paris **Tel** 01.43 29 10 80 **Fax** 01.43.54.26.90 **Meals** breakfast **Prices** rooms 786-986F; breakfast 60F **Rooms** 38, all with bath, two with private terrace; all rooms have phone with private line, fax facility and baby listening, cable TV, air-conditioning, minibar, hairdrier **Credit cards** AE, DC, MC, V **Closed** never

Ile-de-France

Town hotel, Paris

Hôtel des Deux Iles

As Roland Buffat's well-known converted townhouse moves into its third decade as an archetypical charming small hotel, a couple of recent guest reported a rather 'uncaring' atmosphere during their stay, and felt that complacency had crept in; another was entirely satisfied. We would welcome more comments.

■ 59 rue Saint-Louis-en-l'Ile, 75004 Paris **Tel** 01.43.26.13.35 **Fax** 01.43.29.60.25 **Meals** breakfast **Prices** 720-830F; breakfast 45F **Rooms** 17, all with bath or shower; all rooms have phone, cable TV, air-conditioning, hairdrier **Credit cards** AE, V **Closed** never

---

Town hotel, Paris

Hôtel du Globe

A gem of a hotel – tiny and quaint. In the entrance – the building is 17thC, once part of the Abbey of Saint-Germain-des-Prés – a door set in a wrought iron grill leads to perhaps the smallest *salon* in Paris. No breakfast room – it is brought to you. Bedooms have an old fashioned charm. For its appeal, location and price, the Globe is hard to beat. New to the guide this year.

■ 15 rue des Quatre-Vents, 75006 Paris **Tel** 01.43.26.35.50 **Fax** 01.46.33.17.29 **Meals** breakfast; light meals served in room **Prices** 255-450F; breakfast 45F **Rooms** 15, 5 with shower, 1 with W.C. and basin only; all rooms have phone, TV **Credit cards** not accepted **Closed** never

---

Bed and breakfast guest-house, Paris

Hôtel des Grandes Écoles

The name refers to the Sorbonne, next door; the far-from-grand hotel retains the ambience of a country house, aided by its court-yard-garden. Bedrooms are modestly furnished and some have thin walls; but a recent visitor was very pleased, especially by Mme LeFoch's 'cheerful disposition'.

■ 75 Rue de Cardinal Lemoine, 75005 Paris **Tel** 01.43.26.79.23 **Fax** 01.43.25.28.15 **Meals** breakfast **Prices** rooms 490F-650F; breakfast 45F **Rooms** 50, all with central heating , phone **Credit cards** MC, V **Closed** never

---

Town hotel, Paris

Hôtel des Grands Hommes

Conflicting views on this handsome and well placed hotel, named after the artists and writers who used it in the past, the critics taking the view that prices are rather high for what you get. More reports would be welcome. If you opt for a view of the Panthéon, be prepared for a little street noise.

■ 17 Place du Panthéon, 75005 Paris **Tel** 01.46.34.19.60 **Fax** 01.43.26.67.32 **Meals** breakfast **Prices** rooms 606F-792F **Rooms** 32, all with bath or shower, central heating, air-conditioning, cable TV, radio, minibar, hairdrier **Credit cards** AE, DC, MC, V **Closed** never

Ile-de-France

Town hotel, Paris

Le Jardin des Plantes

Situated directly opposite the botanical gardens, this bright little hotel has floral decorative themes for each of its five floors. Rooms on the top floor have the best views and some open on to the roof terrace. Breakfast can be served here, or in a café-style room. Sauna,

■ 5 Rue Linné, 75005 Paris **Tel** 01.47.07.06.20 **Fax** 01.47.07.62.74 **Meals** breakfast, lunch **Prices** rooms 450F-550F; breakfast 49F, lunch 55F-90F **Rooms** 33, all with bath or shower, central heating, phone, TV, minibar, hairdrier **Credit cards** AE, DC, MC, V **Closed** restaurant only, Aug

---

Town hotel, Paris

Hôtel Lenox

The more central of a pair of polished sister hotels, both marked out by smoothly traditional furnishings. The Lenox started life at the turn of the century as a pension, but is now quite a suave hotel, with a clubby bar. Notably tasteful decoration in the bedrooms.

■ 9 Rue de l'Université, 75007 Paris **Tel** 01.42.96.10.95 **Fax** 01.42.61.52.83 **Meals** breakfast **Prices** rooms 640F-1,500F; breakfast 45F **Rooms** 34, all with bath or shower, cent ral heating, phone, TV, hairdrier **Credit cards** AE, DC, MC, V **Closed** never

---

Town hotel, Paris

Résidence Lord Byron

In an area of grand hotels, the Lord Byron stands out for its personal service and (by local standards) reasonable prices. Bedrooms tend to be smallish, but are modern and comfortable, with a mix of old and new furnishings. There is a little courtyard garden.

■ 5 Rue de Chateaubriand, 75008 Paris **Tel** 01.43.59.89.98 **Fax** 01.42.89.46.04 **Meals** breakfast **Prices** rooms 700F-1,300F; breakfast 55F **Rooms** 31, all with bath or shower, central heating, phone, TV, minibar, hairdrier, safe **Credit cards** AE, MC, V **Closed** never

---

Town hotel, Paris

Hôtel du Lys

Ideally situated in a quiet street parallel to blvd Saint Germain, the Hôtel du Lys has been a family-run hotel run along *pension* lines for more than 50 years. Nowadays it is in the hands of Marie-Helène Decharne, daughter of the original owners, and her husband who see it as more a house than a hotel. Some clients have been returning regularly for 40 years.New to the guide this year.

■ 23 rue Serpente, 75006 Paris **Tel** 01.43.26.97.57 **Fax** 01.44.07. 34.90 **Meals** breakfast **Prices** 450-580F with breakfast **Rooms** 22, 6 with bath, 16 with shower; all rooms have phone, TV, hairdrier **Credit cards** not accepted **Closed** never

Ile-de-France

Town hotel, Paris

Hôtel Mayflower

In the same ownership as the Lord Byron and right next door to it, the Mayflower shares the same refined but relaxed atmosphere and is similarly well run. Bedrooms are pretty and calm, and mainly spacious. Elegant and comfortable sitting-room.

■ 3 Rue de Chateaubriand, 75008 Paris **Tel** 01.45.62.57.46 **Fax** 01.42.56.32.38 **Meals** breakfast **Prices** rooms 650F-950F; breakfast 50F **Rooms** 24, all with bath, central heating, phone, satellite TV, minibar **Credit cards** MC, V **Closed** never

---

Town hotel, Paris

Hôtel de la Place des Vosges

Set in a quiet street only 25 metres from one of the loveliest squares in Paris, this 17thC house is entirely in harmony with the surrounding area. The salon is suitably traditional and rustic in style; bedrooms have less character but are well kept – and reasonably priced.

■ 12 Rue de Birague, 75004 Paris **Tel** 01.42.72.60.46 **Fax** 01.42.72.02.64 **Meals** breakfast **Prices** rooms 315F-460F; breakfast 30F; children under 2 free **Rooms** 16, all with bath or shower, central heating, phone **Credit cards** DC, MC, V **Closed** never

---

Town hotel, Paris

Hôtel Prima-Lepic

Set in bustling Montmartre, this is a cheerful bed and breakfast place. The ground floor is done out as an indoor courtyard giving an airy and peaceful effect; bedrooms are individually and well decorated, though not over-spacious. Breakfast is buffet-style.

■ 29 Rue Lepic, 75018 Paris **Tel** 01.46.06.44.64 **Fax** 01.46.06.66.11 **Meals** breakfast **Prices** rooms 350F-700F; breakfast 40F **Rooms** 38, all with bath or shower, central heating, phone, TV, hairdrier **Credit cards** MC, V **Closed** never

---

Town hotel, Paris

Hôtel Prince Albert

Reasonably priced hotels of any comfort are hard to come by in the 1er arondissement; the Prince Albert – well placed for culture, entertainment and shopping alike – is an exception. New owner, M. Jiua, writes to tell us that following the recent renovation of the breakfast-room, the reception and main sitting area are now undergoing a transformation. The corridors upstairs are rather dim, but lead to bedrooms that are well cared for and comfortable.

■ 5 Rue St-Hyacinthe, 75001 Paris **Tel** 01.42.61.58.36 **Fax** 01.42.60.04.06 **Meals** breakfast **Prices** rooms 430F-580F, extra bed 160F; breakfast 35F **Rooms** 30, all with bath or shower, central heating, phone, satellite TV, minibar, safe **Credit cards** AE, MC, V **Closed** never

Ile-de-France

Town hotel, Paris

Hôtel Riboutté Lafayette

Not one of the most conspicuous of the city's charming small hotels, but a reasonably priced and cheerful base. Bedrooms are small, friendly and individual; all rooms are quiet, whether overlooking the courtyard or the street.

■ 5 Rue Riboutté, 75009 Paris **Tel** 01.47.70.62.36 **Fax** 01.48.00.91.50 **Meals** breakfast **Prices** rooms 370F-460F; breakfast 30F **Rooms** 24, all with bath or shower, phone, satellite TV **Credit cards** AE, MC, V **Closed** never

---

Town hotel, Paris

Hôtel Les Rives de Notre Dame

Its outlook is the Ile de la Cité across the traffic-heavy quai Saint-Michel and the Seine, but the Degravi's hearts are firmly in Provence and Tuscany, and the decoration is designed to transport you to the south. The well proportioned bedrooms are stylish – less precious than downstairs – Provençal fabrics, wood framed windows and charming fabric bedheads. A new entry this year.

■ 15 quai Saint-Michel, 75005 Paris **Tel** 01.43.54.81.16 **Fax** 01.43. 26.27.09 **Meals** breakfast; 24hour rooms service for hot and cold dishes and drinks **Prices** 995-2600F; breakfast 85F **Rooms** 10, all with bath; all rooms have phone fax/modem plug; satellite TV, air-conditioning, minibar, hairdrier, safe **Credit cards** AE, DC, MC, V **Closed** never

---

Town hotel, Paris

Hôtel St-Dominique

Recent refurbishments in a confident, colourful style, have helped to restore the St-Dominique's reputation. The reception-cum-sitting-room is very much part of the appeal – a pleasant, comfortable spot. Bedrooms are small but well-equipped, breakfast delicious and beautifully presented. Drinks can be had outside in the small, flowery courtyard.

■ 62 Rue St-Dominique, 75007 Paris **Tel** 01.47.05.51.44 **Fax** 01.47. 05.81.28 **Meals** breakfast **Prices** 450F-600F; breakfast 40F **Rooms** 34 all with bath or shower; all rooms have central heating, phone, TV, minibar **Credit cards** AE, DC, MC, V **Closed** never

Town hote, Paris

Town hotel, Paris

Hôtel Saint-Germain-des-Prés

This small Left Bank hotel stands out for charm and individuality, if not for notably good taste or coherence of interior design – its bedrooms are all furnished in different styles and colours. Large salon-cum-breakfast-room.

■ 36 Rue Bonaparte, 75006 Paris **Tel** 01.43.26.00.19 **Fax** 01.40.46.83.63 **Meals** breakfast **Prices** rooms 760F-1,600F **Rooms** 30, all with bath or shower, central heating, phone , TV, radio, minibar; some have air-conditioning **Credit cards** AE, MC, V **Closed** never

Ile-de-France

Bed and breakfast guest-house, Paris

Hôtel Saint-Louis

Sister hotel to the Saint-Louis Marais, the welcoming atmosphere and its ideal location on the Ile-St-Louis for sightseeing make up for any lack of facilities (only one public room) and the small size of the bedrooms.

■ 75 Rue St-Louis-en-l'Ile, 75004 Paris **Tel** 01.46.34.04.80 **Fax** 01.46.34.02.13 **Meals** breakfast **Prices** rooms 695F-795F; breakfast 45F **Rooms** 21, all with bath or shower, phone, safe **Credit cards** MC,V **Closed** never

---

Town guest-house, Paris

Hôtel Saint-Louis Marais

A sound, friendly choice if you are looking for a peaceful, reasonably priced base close to the Bastille. The beamed bedrooms are far from spacious, but are prettily decorated with antiques, wall hangings and fresh flowers.

■ 1 Rue Charles V, 75004 Paris **Tel** 01. 48.87.87.04 **Fax** 01. 48.87.33.26 **Meals** breakfast **Prices** rooms 495F-700F; breakfast 40F **Rooms** 15, all with bath or shower, central heating, phone **Credit cards** MC, V **Closed** never

---

Town hotel, Paris

Hôtel des Saints-Pères

Nearly all the bedrooms in this calmly sophisticated hotel look on to a leafy, glass-sided internal courtyard where you can breakfast or take a drink in the summer sunshine. Bedrooms are restful and fairly spacious, and there are good paintings on the walls. New to the guide this year.

■ 65 rue des Saints-Pères, 75006 Paris **Tel** 01.45.44.50.00 **Fax** 01.45. 44.90.83 **Prices** 550F-1620F; breakfast 55F; bar **Rooms** 36, all with bath or shower; all rooms have phone, satellite TV, minibar, hairdrier **Credit cards** AE, MC, V **Closed** never

---

Restaurant with rooms, Paris

Thoumieux

Set in the shadow of the Eiffel Tower, this efficient, friendly place revolves around its popular brasserie-style restaurant, which offers good country-style cooking and drinkable house-wine. Bedrooms are modern and comfortable, with tasteful fabrics and stylish furniture.

■ 79 Rue St-Dominique, 75007 Paris **Tel** 01. 47.05.49.75 **Fax** 01. 47.05.36.96 **Meals** breakfast, lunch, dinner **Prices** rooms 550F-600F; breakfast 35F; meals about 150F **Rooms** 10 , all with bath, central heating, phone, TV, radio **Credit cards** MC **Closed** never

Ile-de-France

Town hote, Paris

Hôtel des Tuileries

The Poulle-Vidal family offer a pleasant combination of a quiet but convenient setting, comfortable accommodation and a warm welcome. The two small *salons* have velvet seats and paintings and tapestries on plains wells. Bedrooms are pretty and individually decorated, bathrooms small but very smart. Breakfast is a better-than-average buffet.

■ 10 Rue St-Hyacinthe 75001, Paris **Tel** 01.42.61.04.17 **Fax** 01.49. 27.91.56 **Meals** breakfast **Prices** 690F-1,200F; breakfast 60F **Rooms** 26, all with bath; all rooms have central heating, air-conditioning, phone, satellite TV, minibar, hairdrier, safe **Credit cards** AE, DC, V **Closed** never

Town hotel, Paris

Hôtel de l'Université

This dignified town house in an area of quiet, elegant streets is not cheap, but does offer reasonable value – antiques in the beamed public areas and in the comfortable bedrooms, efficient and friendly service and breakfasts well above the Parisian norm in quality but not price.

■ 22 Rue de l'Université, 75007 Paris **Tel** 01.42.61.09.39 **Fax** 01.42.60.40.84 **Meals** breakfast, light snacks **Prices** rooms 650F-1,500F; breakfast 45F **Rooms** 28, all with bath or shower, phone, TV **Credit cards** MC, V **Closed** never

Town hotel, Paris

Hotel Verneuil-St-Germain

Be prepared for one of the zaniest reception areas in Paris – a truly original and eclectic mixture. Bedrooms are similarly eclectic but more restrained, the marble-clad bathrooms well-equipped. In the attractive basement breakfast-room, things sober up considerably. At our latest visit we found proprietor M. Le Boudec's staff distinctly cool: more reports please.

■ 8 rue de Verneuil, 75007 Paris **Tel** 01.42.60.82.14 **Fax** 01.42.61.40.38 **Meals** breakfast **Prices** 650F-950F including breakfast **Rooms** 22, all with bath; all rooms have central heating, phone, cable TV, hairdrier, minibar **Credit cards** AE, DC, MC, V **Closed** never

The North-East

Area introduction

Our North-east region contains some large areas with not much to offer the holidaymaker, and which contain few Charming Small Hotels; there are several *départements* with no entries at all. But this region embraces four areas worth singling out for their touristic interest and their hotels.

The hinterland of the main Channel ferry ports includes some pleasant rolling countryside, and of course proximity to those ports makes this area – particularly the *département* of Pas-de-Calais, containing Calais and Boulogne – prime territory for a quick weekend away.

The *départements* of Oise and Seine-et-Marne, respectively to the north and east of the Ile de France, contain some tourist highlights (Compiègne, Chantilly, Vaux-le-Vicomte), and some desirable hotels – though they may owe their existence more to proximity to Paris than to the demands of the local tourist trade.

More or less due east of Paris, where the motorway from Paris to Strasbourg meets that coming down from Calais, is Champagne country. Wherever there is wine there is a satisfyingly cultivated landscape, and here there is also the architectural spectacle of Reims, at the heart of the Champagne business as well as the region, of which the cathedral is only one part.

And then there is Alsace, at the far eastern end of this region, against the German border. This is another wine region – a hilly one, with some wonderful scenery. The wines and the food alike are German-influenced, as you might expect.

Contenders in the North-east
Audinghen-par-Wissant, La Maison de la Houve 03.21.32.97.06 Well modernised old farmhouse B&B, comfortably furnished and well run, in flowery garden.
Illhaeusern, Hôtel des Berges 03.89.71.87.87 Luxurious barn-style lodgings at foot of garden of one of the most celebrated restaurants in Alsace.
Langres, Le Cheval Blanc 03.25.87.07.00 Neat Logis in ancient town-centre building; small terrace.
Sars-Poteries, Hôtel Fleuri 03.27.61.62.72 Old farm building, now a prettily furnished B&B hotel, with independently run Michelin-starred restaurant (Auberge Fleurie) next door.

Reporting to the guide
We're very keen to hear from readers about their hotel-going experiences. We can't visit every hotel in the guide every year; even if we could, we wouldn't be staying in them all. And it's only when you stay in a place that you find out how the plumbing deals with the demand for hot water, what that much-vaunted 70F breakfast is really like, and what happens when you request something extraordinary like an extra pillow. So please do let us know how you get on next time you're travelling in France.

In particular, please do write when you like a small hotel, whether or not you've chosen it with our help. People are pretty good at letting us know when we've got a place wrong (usually, we hope, because the place has gone downhill). Places that come up to expectations don't always trigger a reaction.

The North-East

Hostellerie des 3 Mousquetaires

Most visitors are thoroughly well pleased by this jolly 19thC château, equidistant from the ferry ports of Boulogne, Calais and Dunkerque, although one report indicates that the service in the restaurant at the weekend is sometime overstretched. Is the place becoming too popular for its own good?

The hotel is a family-run *logis*, a world away from the classical château pattern. The charming and vigilant Mme Venet is in charge front of house, aided by her daughter-in-law, while husband Marcel and son Philippe prepare regionally based meals offering 'enormous portions' and 'astonishing value' in the spotless open-to-view kitchen. (The cheeseboard is 'magnificent'.)

The building is an eccentric mixture of stone-and-brick stripes and pseudo-timbering beneath a steep slate roof, set in a large wooded garden with ponds and streams (ducks and swans). A reader reports delightedly that children can follow the example of the owners' own children and run around without raising eyebrows. The interior is traditionally grand in style, the best of the old bedrooms (eg 'Milady') huge and elegant (though some are much smaller); those in the annexe are sumptuously decorated in various styles – one has a Japanese theme, for example. But several guests have been worried over by street noise in these rooms.

Nearby Aire – Renaissance bailiff's court, collegiate church of St-Pierre; St Omer (20 km) – basilica, fine arts museum.

Château du Fort de la Redoute
62120 Aire-sur-la-Lys
Tel 03.21.39.01.11
Fax 03.21.39.50.10
Location in countryside off N43, 2km S of Aire; in parkland, with ample car parking
Meals breakfast, lunch, dinner
Prices rooms 250F-570F, suites 850F; breakfast 55F, menus 115F- (except weekends) 240F
Rooms 31 double (9 twin), 24 with bath, 2 with shower; one suite with bath; one family room with bath; all rooms have central heating, phone, TV
Facilities 2 sitting- rooms, 2 dining-rooms, bar; golf
Credit cards AE, MC, V
Children welcome; cots and special menu available
Disabled no special facilities
Pets accepted
Closed mid-Dec to mid-Jan
Proprietors M. and Mme Philippe Venet

The North-East

Château de Remaisnil

A visit in 1996 has encouraged us to promote this pretty 18thC mansion to a long entry. Previously the home of Bernard and Laura Ashley, founders of the fabrics and wallpaper retail chain, it is set in 35 acres, deep in the Picardy countryside. At the back of the house sheep graze placidly in the meadow, and horses in a neighbouring field are available for guests to ride. Near a grove of chestnut trees *javelot picard* can be tried – a medieval game which involves throwing giant darts underarm with as much force as you can muster at a sturdy target.

Susan and Adrian Doull left their small Manhattan apartment some ten years ago to take up residence here with their family. They are charming hosts, and although the house is extremely grand inside, with lavish rococo embellishments, tapestries and antique furniture, it is very much a family home. Bedrooms are opulent, with Laura Ashley designs still much in evidence; bathrooms are large, with fluffy, white robes. Dinner is a set four courses, and guests mingle in the library for pre-dinner drinks and for coffee and liqueurs afterwards. A remarkable white-tiled underground passageway, reminiscent of the Paris metro, links the château to the conference centre and coach house, where bedrooms are smaller, more rustic.

Nearby Doullens (8 km); Amiens; Picardy battlefields.

80600 Doullens
Tel 03 22 77 07 47
Fax 03 22 77 41 23
Location on D938 direction Auxi-le-Château, on right before Mézerolles
Meals breakfast, lunch, dinner, by arrangement
Prices 1400F-1600F château; 750F coach house; breakfast 75F; dinner 355F
Rooms 20 (9 in coach house), all with bath and shower; all have central heating, phone, TV, minibar **Facilities** 3 sitting rooms, library, breakfast/dining-room; swimming-pool, riding, javelot picard, snooker
Credit cards AE, DC, MC, V
Children accepted **Disabled** not suitable **Pets** by arrangement **Closed** late Feb to early Mar **Proprietors** Susan and Adrian Doull

The North-East

Country mansion, Hesdin-l'Abbé

Hôtel Cléry

Catherine and Didier Legros took over this elegant 18thC mansion in 1996, and judging from the delighted report we received recently, are even improving on the high standards already reached by the previous owners. Properly called the Château d'Hesdin-l'Abbé, a dignified façade dominates the fine tree-lined approach to the house, surrounded by parkland. But there is no need to be intimidated: this is not a stuffy place. Inside, there is not an antler in sight; nor are the public rooms stiff with Louis XV chairs (although there is a very fine Louis XV wrought-iron staircase), or even laden with chintz. Here, all is bright and light in harmonious pastel tones, in understated modern style.

The hotel already has an established British trade; the excellent golf at nearby Hardelot is an attraction in addition to proximity to the Channel and the merits of the place itself. Bedrooms are newly decorated, including those in the cottage annexe. There is an attractive bar, and a log fire in the sitting-room when the weather calls for it. Dinner can be taken here on weekday evenings, and there is also a large choice of restaurants in nearby Boulogne.

Nearby Hardelot, golf and beach (9km); Le Touquet (15km)

62360 Hesdin-L'Abbé
Tel 03.21.83.19.83
Fax 03.21.87.52.59
Location in tiny rural village, 9 km SE of Boulogne; with gardens and ample car parking
Meals breakfast, dinner
Prices rooms 3250F-630F; menu 125F-165F
Rooms 21 double, 12 with bath, 9 with shower (12 twin); all have central heating, phone, satellite TV

Facilities bar, sitting-room; tennis court, table tennis, mountain bikes for hire
Credit cards AE, DC, MC, V
Children accepted
Pets not accepted
Disabled no special facilities
Closed mid-Dec to end Jan
Proprietors Catherine and Didier Legros

The North-East

Village inn, Marlenheim

Le Cerf

All the signs are that the Cerf is as compelling as ever for visitors who like the cooking of Alsace as much as its wines. Michel Husser carries on the gastronomic tradition of father Robert, who has now taken a back seat; Michelin awards two stars. Bedrooms are not particularly luxurious, but are well furnished and thoroughly comfortable. There is a cobbled courtyard for drinks and breakfast – so, when the weather is fine, the shortage of sitting space should not be a problem.

Nearby Strasbourg (20 km); wine villages.

30 Rue du Général-de-Gaulle
67520 Marlenheim
Tel 03.88.87.73.73
Fax 03.88.87.68.08
Location on main road through village, 18 km W of Strasbourg; with courtyard and car parking
Meals breakfast, lunch, dinner
Prices rooms 300F-600F; menus 250F-500F
Rooms 17 double, 8 with bath, 7 with shower (6 twin); one single with shower; 2 family rooms, both with bath; all rooms have central heating, phone
Facilities dining-room, 2 function rooms
Credit cards AE,V
Children accepted
Disabled access to dining-room; 2 ground-floor bedrooms
Pets accepted
Closed restaurant, Tue, Wed
Proprietor Robert Husser

The North-East

Restaurant with rooms, Montreuil-sur-Mer

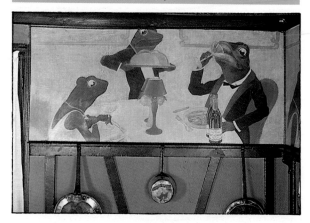

Auberge de la Grenouillère

We receive conflicting messages about this low Picardy-style farm-house (known to many as the Froggery), a popular gastronomic halt with the British. Two visitors particularly commend lunch on the terrace ('most agreeable', 'delightful') while the third relates an unhappy incident concerning undrinkable wine. An isolated blip, we trust.

The spacious gravel terrace is certainly an excellent spot for leisurely lunches, rather overshadowing the gleaming brass and polished wood of the restaurant – complete with frog-motif mural (done by an Englishman, of course). And the food is excellent, too – Michelin-starred, and not wildly expensive. Bedrooms are captivating (one is very large, and eminently suitable for families), complete with well equipped and very attractive bathrooms.

If you are normally resolute about going native once on French soil, and feel you might be put off by all those other English voices, relax. You can safely resist the temptation to carry on driving: this is a serious French enterprise and M. Gauthier has not allowed the popularity of his establishment to make him complacent.

Nearby Ramparts, citadel; Le Touquet (15 km).

La Madelaine-sous-Montreuil,
62170 Montreuil-sur-Mer
Tel 03.21.06.07.22
Fax 03.21.86.36.36
Location by river at end of lane off D139, NW of Montreuil-sur-Mer; with ample car parking
Meals breakfast, lunch, dinner
Prices rooms 400F-500F; breakfast 50F; menus 150F-380F
Rooms 2 double, 1 twin, one flat; all with bath; all rooms have central heating, phone,
Facilities dining-room, small bar
Credit cards AE, DC, MC, V
Children welcome
Disabled two ground-floor room
Pets welcome
Closed mid-Dec to end Jan; Tue and Wed from Sep to Jun
Proprietor M. Gauthier

The North-East

Château de Montreuil

'Montreuil, Château de: Charming host, exceptional food, great advice on local shopping for food and wine. Comfortable, well equipped rooms. Not cheap. Wife of patron: English.' Military man, our most recent reporter; as usual, verdict spot-on; other readers concur. No doubt about it: full entry merited, as of now.

This substantial, luxurious country house, dating from the 1930s, is a well established favourite with British travellers, who make up most of the resident guests. The house is immaculately done out, with great taste throughout. Bedrooms are splendid – decorated with real flair and furnished with character; those on the top floor are very spacious, but the first floor rooms give better views of the beautiful English-style gardens. There is a snug brick-and-beams bar for an aperitif, an airy glass-fronted sitting-room and a lovely, elegant dining-room. Although you're quite close to the town centre, the setting is quiet, the gardens secluded.

Christian Germain's cooking aims high and hits the target (the restaurant does not rely on British custom but has a loyal French following); even breakfast ('home-made everything') is delicious. **Nearby** Ramparts (still intact), citadel; Le Touquet (15 km).

4 Chaussée des Capucins
62170 Montreuil-sur-Mer
Tel 03.21.81.53.04
Fax 03.21.81.36.43
Location in quiet part of town, 38 km S of Boulogne, off N1; with large garden and ample car parking
Meals breakfast, lunch, dinner
Prices rooms 750F-950F, DB&B 1600F-1700F; menus 240F-390F
Rooms 12 double, all with bath (6 twin); 3 single; 2 family rooms all with bath or shower; all rooms have central heating, phone
Facilities sitting-room, dining-room, bar
Credit cards AE, DC, MC, V
Children welcome
Disabled 3 ground-floor bedrooms
Pets not accepted
Closed mid-Dec to end Jan
Proprietors Christian and Lindsay Germain

The North-East

Château hotel, Reims

Château des Crayères

At last! We were beginning to have doubts about our continued inclusion of this wonderful but prohibitively expensive mansion when a reporter who 'stayed in the best room and drank one of the best wines' wrote to approve of the place – singling out for praise (of all things) baby croissants that 'melt in the mouth'.

Gérard Boyer (by common consent one of the finest chefs in the land) and his wife Elyane had a good starting point: a graceful turn-of-the-century mansion (built in Louis XVI style), situated in a spacious park almost at the heart of Reims, and surrounded by the *caves* of the famous Champagne names. With Elyane's exquisite taste and skill in interior decoration, they could hardly go far wrong. There are a wonderful grand staircase, enormous windows, marble columns and tapestries; the dining-room is wood panelled and candle-lit. Bedrooms are sumptuous, individually decorated to a theme, and have views over the park; two have a large balcony.

The cooking is not merely for the benefit of Champagne grandees; it's good enough to attract businessmen from Paris. Not surprisingly, it is necessary to book well ahead.

Nearby Basilica, cathedral; Champagne Route.

64 Blvd Henry Vasnier 51100 Reims
Tel 03.26.82.80.80
Fax 03.26.82.65.52
Location on edge of city centre, near St-Remi basilica; in own grounds with ample car parking
Meals breakfast, lunch, dinner
Prices rooms 990F-2,300F; menus -650F
Rooms 19 double, all with bath (15 twin); all rooms have air-conditioning, phone, TV, radio, minibar
Facilities dining-room, bar, function room; tennis, helistation
Credit cards AE, DC, MC, V
Children welcome
Disabled access possible, lift/elevator
Pets dogs welcome
Closed 3 weeks at Christmas/New Year; restaurant only, Mon and Tue lunch
Proprietor M. Boyer

The North-East

Country hotel, Artzenheim

Auberge d'Artzenheim

'A beflowered oasis in the middle of nowhere,' says a recent report on this cosy auberge. Its focal point is the restaurant, all beams and polished wood, but there is a terrace for outdoor eating. Bedrooms (some small) are prettily decorated with rustic furniture and jolly fabrics.

■ 30 Rue du Sponeck, 68320 Artzenheim (Haut-Rhin) **Tel** 03.89. 71.60.51 **Fax** 03.89.71.68.21 **Meals** breakfast, lunch, dinner **Prices** rooms 255F-310F; menus 165F-235F **Rooms** 10, all with bath or shower, central heating, phone, TV **Credit cards** MC, V **Closed** Feb; restaurant only, Mon dinner and Tue

---

Town hotel, Boulogne-sur-Mer

Hôtel Métropole

A very pleasant hotel, centrally situated in one of the main shopping streets of Boulogne but with the bonus of a pretty and colourful garden. Bedrooms were rated 'surprisingly attractive for a modest town hotel' by a recent visitor. No restaurant but 'excellent' breakfasts. Private garage.

■ 51-53 Rue Thiers, 62200 Boulogne-sur-Mer (Pas-de-Calais) **Tel** 03.21.31.54.30 **Fax** 03.21.30.45.72 **Meals** breakfast **Prices** rooms 330F-430F; breakfast 40F **Rooms** 25, all with bath or shower, central heating, phone, TV **Credit cards** AE, DC, MC, V **Closed** mid-Dec to early Jan

---

Château hotel, Courcelles-sur-Vesle

Château de Courcelles

Set in a small formal park, this impressive – and expensive – 17thC château can name Napoléon and Jean-Jacques Rousseau among former visitors. Bedrooms are spacious and individually decorated, food rated 'very impressive' by a visitor. Pool, tennis.

■ 02220 Courcelles-sur-Vesle (Aisne) **Tel** 03.23.74.13.53 **Fax** 03.23.74.06.41 **Meals** breakfast, lunch, dinner **Prices** rooms 900F-1200F; suites 1,300F-1500F; breakfast 85F, menus 230F-360F **Rooms** 14, all with bath or shower, central heating, phone, TV, minibar **Credit cards** AE, MC, V **Closed** never

---

Village hotel, L'Épine

Aux Armes de Champagne

The main attractions here are the renowned cuisine and cellar, and the hotel's refreshing lack of pretension. The modern bedrooms are comfortable and impeccable; sixteen of the rooms are in an annexe 200 metres down the road, away from the traffic noise that afflicts the main building.

■ Avenue du Luxembourg, 51460 L'Épine (Marne) **Tel** 03.26.69.30.30 **Fax** 03.26.66.92.31 **Meals** breakfast, lunch, dinner **Prices** rooms 320F-690F; breakfast 55F, menus 110F (weekday lunch only), 280F-495F **Rooms** 37, all with bath or shower, central heating, phone, TV, minibar **Credit cards** AE, DC, MC, V **Closed** early Jan to mid-Feb; Sun eve and Mon, Nov to Mar

The North-East

Hôtel le Prieuré

Nothing has changed at this polished little B&B place, introduced to the guide a couple of years ago. The former vicarage is beautifully furnished with antiques and decorated with unusual style, with exposed beams in the attic rooms. There is a neat breakfast room and an immaculate 'English' garden.

■ Chevet de l'Eglise, 60950 Ermenonville (Oise) **Tel** 03.44.54.00.44 **Fax** 03.44.54.02.21 **Meals** breakfast **Prices** rooms 450F-600F; breakfast 50F **Rooms** 11, all with bath or shower, cen tral heating, phone, TV, minibar **Credit cards** AE, DC, MC, V **Closed** Feb

Le Clos du Montvinage

This imposing, spacious red-brick building is effectively the annexe of the cheerful Auberge du Val de l'Oise. Bedrooms are well equipped; those at the back have views of the walled garden and suffer no disturbance from the busy main road.

■ RN 2, 02580 Etréaupont (Aisne) **Tel** 03.23.97.91.10 **Fax** 03.23. 97.48.92 **Meals** breakfast, lunch, dinner **Prices** rooms 285F-430F; dinner 90F-225F **Rooms** 20, all with bath, central heating, air-conditioning, phone, TV, minibar, hairdrier **Credit cards** AE, DC, MC, V **Closed** Sun night; last week Feb; 2 weeks mid-Aug; restaurant only, Mon lunch, Sun eve

Le Jabloire

Recently refurbished and promoted to three-star status, this elegant little house fronting directly on to the street impressed a reader as 'an excellent staging post just off the A4 motorway'. The proprietor (formerly the local mayor) offers a warm welcome.

■ 51800 Florent-en-Argonne (Marne) **Tel** 03.26.60.82.03 **Fax** 03.26. 60.85.45 **Meals** breakfast **Prices** rooms 250F-380F; breakfast 35F **Rooms** 12, all with bath or shower, heating, TV **Credit cards** AE, MC V **Closed** Feb

A L'Orée du Bois

Surrounded by woods, this modest hotel enjoys perfect peace, although the mood is often jolly in the elegantly rustic restaurant at its heart. The cooking is excellent, with seafood very much the high-point. Madame serves, with great charm. Rooms are adequate: motel-style, in a ground-floor extension.

■ Futeau, 55120 Clermont-en-Argonne (Meuse) **Tel** 03.29.88.28.41 **Fax** 03.29.88.24.52 **Meals** breakfast, lunch, dinner **Prices** rooms 310F-375F; breakfast 50F, lunch 110F, menus 185-350F **Rooms** 7, all with bath, central heating, phone, TV, hairdrier **Credit cards** MC, V **Closed** one week Nov, Jan; restaurant only, Tue and Sun dinner out of season

The North-East

Village inn, Kaysersberg

Hôtel Résidence Chambard

Pierre Irrmann's sober, highly traditional-looking inn is almost better thought of as a restaurant with rooms; there is sitting space, but you'll spend most of your time (when you're not out tasting Alsatian wines) in the restaurant 50 metres away and in your elegantly furnished, spacious bedroom.

■ 13 Rue de Général de Gaulle, 68240 Kaysersberg (Haut-Rhin) **Tel** 03.89.47.10.17 **Fax** 03.89.47.35.03 **Meals** breakfast, lunch, dinner **Prices** rooms 550F-650F; suites 750F; breakfast 60F; menus 300F -450F **Rooms** 20, all with bath or shower, phone, TV, radio **Credit cards** AE, MC, V **Closed** 3 weeks Mar; restaurant only, Mon, and Tue lunch

---

Country hotel, Lapoutroie

Les Alisiers

This simple, farmhouse-style place enjoys a splendid setting, high in the Vosges, with floor-to-ceiling windows in the dining-room to exploit the view. The rustic interior has an intimate, private-house feel, the bedrooms are small but comfortable. Alsatian specialities dominate the menus. Good value.

■ 5 Faudé, 68650 Lapoutroie (Haut-Rhin) **Tel** 03.89.47.52.82 **Fax** 03.89.47.22.38 **Meals** breakfast, lunch, dinner **Prices** rooms 250F-365F; menus 80F-160F;reductions for children sharing parents' room **Rooms** 13, all with phone **Credit cards** MC, V **Closed** Tue; Jan

---

Converted mill, Lumbres

Moulin de Mombreux

An eighteenth century mill, much improved over the past few years, to judge by recent reports. Pleasant, compact bedrooms in a modern block built to match the mill; public rooms that are charmingly traditional or light and airy; 'deserved' Michelin star for food; friendly atmosphere.

■ Rte de Bayenghem, 62380 Lumbres (Pas-de-Calais) **Tel** 03.21.39.62.44 **Fax** 03.21.93.61.34 **Meals** breakfast, lunch, dinner **Prices** rooms 500F-700F; breakfast F60; menus 220F-570F (including wine) **Rooms** 24, all with bath or shower, central heating, TV, phone **Credit cards** AE, DC, V **Closed** around Christmas

---

Town hotel, Montreuil-sur-Mer

Les Hauts de Montreuil

A reader who resorted to this timbered hotel near the centre of Montreuil when our recommendations in the area were closed recommends it for a combination of well-furnished rooms (some in a modern annexe), a warm welcome from the patron and his wife, 'fantastic' traditional food and 'excellent' value.

■ 21-23, Rue Pierre Ledent, 62170 Montreuil-sur-Mer (Pas-de-Calais) **Tel** 03.21.81.95.92 **Fax** 03.21.86.28.83 **Meals** breakfast, lunch, dinner **Prices** rooms 365F-460F; breakfast 55F, menus 145F-235F **Rooms** 27, all with bath or shower, central heating, phone, TV **Credit cards** AE, DC, MC, V **Closed** never

The North-East

Country hotel, Ribeauvillé

Le Clos Saint-Vincent

The service at this elegant hotel is almost impossible to fault. The bedrooms are beautifully furnished, the staff friendly and the food delicious, reports a recent visitor. Although the restaurant is closed on Tuesday and Wednesday evenings, there are excellent alternatives in the town. Indoor swimming-pool.

■ Rte de Bergheim, 68150 Ribeauvillé (Haut-Rhin) **Tel** 03.89.73.67.65 **Fax** 03.89.73.32.20 **Meals** breakfast, lunch, dinner **Prices** rooms 700F-1,170F; menus 180F-280F **Rooms** 15, all with bath, central heating, phone, minibar; TV on request **Credit cards** MC, V **Closed** mid-Nov to mid-Mar; restaurant only, Tue and Wed

---

Restaurant with rooms, Ribeauvillé

Les Vosges

We should welcome more reports on this neat little place in the middle of one of the most attractive wine towns of Alsace. The restaurant is no longer open, but breakfast is available and rooms are pleasantly comfortable.

■ 2 Grande Rue, 68150 Ribeauvillé (Haut-Rhin) **Tel** 03.89.73.61.39 **Fax** 03.89.73.34.21 **Meals** breakfast **Prices** rooms 230F-490F; breakfast 50F **Rooms** 18, all with bath or shower, phone, TV **Credit cards** AE, DC, MC, V **Closed** Sun evening; restaurant only, mid-Nov to Apr

---

Country hotel, Sept-Saulx

Le Cheval Blanc

'Excellent food and accommodation in a lovely setting,' said the reader's report that first drew our attention to this old inn, extended over the years but still blessed with a charming garden. Food is ambitious, although no longer endorsed by Michelin with a star.

■ 51400 Sept-Saulx (Marne) **Tel** 03.26.03.90.27 **Fax** 03.26.03.97.09 **Meals** breakfast, lunch, dinner **Prices** rooms 390F-810F; suites 980F; breakfast 50F, **Rooms** 25, all with bath or shower, phone, TV, minibar **Credit cards** AE, DC, MC, V **Closed** 3 weeks Feb

---

Town mansion, Vervins

La Tour du Roy

This turreted building perched on the ramparts of Vervins is full of character, with pretty, individually decorated rooms. Recent reports include (for the first time) niggles about service and housekeeping. But no complaints about the food, except that the menus do not offer a very wide choice. More reports, please.

■ 45 Rue du Général Leclerc, 02140 Vervins (Aisne) **Tel** 03.23.98.00.11 **Fax** 03.23.98.00.72 **Meals** breakfast, lunch, dinner **Prices** rooms 350F-500F; breakfast 70F, menus 180F-450F **Rooms** 18 (2 suites, suitable for the disabled), all with bath, central heating, phone, TV, radio, minibar; some have air-conditioning **Credit cards** AE, DC, MC, V **Closed** mid-Jan to mid-Feb

Western France

Area introduction

Our Western France region has three major components of interest to tourists. First there is the Loire valley and its immediate surroundings, including the atmospheric Sologne, south of Orleans. There are almost as many Charming Small Hotels here as there are Renaissance châteaux. Secondly, the hilly Limousin, fading into the northern fringes of Périgord, around Angoulême and Limoges. And finally the hinterland of the Atlantic coast, including the canals of Poitou-Charente. We have entries in all these areas, but also dotted around the *départements* in between, and on the western side of the region on the fringes of the Massif Central.

Contenders in Western France

Aubigny-sur-Nère, Château de la Verrerie 02.48.58.06.91 Splendid turreted château in gracious parkland, run by aristocratic owners.

Blois, Le Vieux Cognet 02.54.56.05.34 Simple but well furnished B&B in quiet spot on banks of the Loire.

Challans, Château de la Vérie 02.51.35.33.44 Richly furnished manor-house in extensive grounds; pool, tennis.

Cheverny, Château du Breuil 02.54.44.20.20 18thC château in large grounds, with an elegant salon and comfortable bedrooms with antiques.

Chouzé-sur-Loire, Château des Réaux 02.47.95.14.40 Fairytale château, stylishly decorated and handsomely furnished.

Dompierre-les-Eglises, Le Moulin des Combes 05.55.68.62.09 Ancient watermill turned luxury B&B, with British owner.

Grez-Neuville, La Croix d'Etain 02.41.95.68.49 Handsome little manor-house B&B in pleasant village on the Mayenne.

Le Gua, Le Moulin de Châlons 05.46.22.82.72 Pale stone mill beside the Seudre with grassy grounds and charming rooms.

Loches, Hôtel George Sand 02.47.59.39.74 Riverside Logis with abundant beams and traditional decor.

Mondoubleau, Le Grand Monarque 02.54.80.92.10 Friendly Logis with neat (some cramped) rooms, in mature grassy garden.

Mont-près-Chambord, Manoir de Clénord 02.54.70.41.62 Secluded country house, tastefully furnished and family-run.

Montbazon-en-Touraine, Domaine de la Tortinière 02.47.26.00.19 Dinky fairytale château, smartly furnished, in wooded grounds with views and pool.

Onzain-en-Touraine, Domaine des Hauts de Loire 02.54.20.72.57 Elegantly furnished but characterful converted hunting lodge (Relais & Châteaux).

La-Roche-sur-Yon, Logis de la Couperie 02.51.37.21.19 Country house, just outside the town, run as an elegant but home-like guest-house.

St-Lambert-des-Levées, La Croix de la Voulte 02.41.38.46.66 Ancient country house B&B in lush gardens.

Tours, Jean Bardet 02.47.41.41.11 Smooth, elegant setting for some of the best food in France.

Velluire, Auberge de la Rivière 02.51.52.32.15 Unpretentious waterside Logis with some pleasant rooms.

Western France

Converted mill, Bannegon

Auberge du Moulin de Chaméron

The Moulin de Chameron is a curious animal, and difficult to categorise. At the heart of it is the original 18thC water-mill – now a combination of country museum and charmingly traditional restaurant. But the bedrooms are housed across the garden in a pair of unremarkable modern buildings of rather towny appearance – comfortable, but thin on charm. So should it be thought of as a restaurant with rooms? We think to do so would be to underestimate its appeal as a place to stay for more than a one-night stopover (though one reporter found the peace marred by the noise of early morning departures) – at least in summer, when the wooded garden and neat pool come into play, along with the restaurant's tented dining terrace beside the mill stream. Jean Merilleau's cooking is excellent.

Nearby Meillant castle (25 km); Noirlac abbey (30 km).

Bannegon 18210 Charenton-du-Cher
Tel 02.48.61.83.80
Fax 02.48.61.84.92
Location in countryside between Bannegon and Neuilly, 40 km SE of Bourges; with garden and ample car parking
Meals breakfast, lunch, dinner
Prices rooms 350F-650F; menus 150F-240F, children's 60F **Rooms** 13 double, 8 with bath, 5 with shower (5 twin); one family room with bath; all rooms have central heating, phone, TV
Facilities 2 dining-rooms, bar, 2 sitting-rooms; swimming-pool, table-tennis, fishing
Credit cards AE, MC, V
Children welcome
Disabled no special facilities
Pets accepted in bedrooms; charge **Closed** mid-Nov to early Mar; Tue in low season
Proprietors M. Candoré and

Western France

Château and manor house hotel, Briollay

Château de Noirieux

'A gem of a hotel, situated at the western end of the Loire château-belt; whereas most hotels on the Loire tourist trail are over-priced and under-enthusiastic, this one gets most things right and is thoroughly professional in the nicest way.' So says one of our most conscientious reporters. Since he's started so well, we'll let him finish.

'Dating from the seventeenth century, with Art Deco additions in 1927, it opened as a hotel in 1991. It is set in magnificent grounds, with views down to the Loir. It is outstandingly comfortable; a good test was that during three days of almost continuous rain we always felt cossetted. The salons are beautifully furnished and comfortable, the dining-room light and airy, with a terrace for fine weather. Bedrooms are split between the main building and two others – all well furnished, some quite opulently.

'The cuisine is inventive and of a high standard. The wine list is exemplary, with prices that don't take your breath away. We received a warm welcome, and all the staff were unfailingly helpful and courteous. The chateau is not cheap, but is excellent value in every respect.'

Nearby golf; Angers (12 km) – cathedral, château

26 Route du Moulin, 49125 Briollay
Tel 02.41.42.50.05
Fax 02.41.37.91.00
Location in countryside off D 52, (junction 14 off A11); with gardens and ample car parking
Meals breakfast, lunch, dinner
Prices rooms 600F-1,300F; breakfast 85F, menus 195F (lunch – weekdays only) 460F
Rooms 19 double with bath; some rooms with central heating, phone, TV, minibar, hairdrier
Facilities dining-room, sitting-room/bar; jacuzzi, swimming-pool, tennis **Credit cards** AE, DC, MC, V **Children** accepted **Disabled** 2 ground-floor bedrooms **Pets** accepted
Closed early Feb to mid-Mar; end Nov to early Dec; restaurant Sun eve, Mon mid-Oct to mid-Apr **Managers** Gérard and Anja Come

Western France

Manor house hotel, Cangey

Le Fleuray

Each year we receive glowing reports on Le Fleuray. 'I have no hesitation in recommending this small, well appointed hotel in the Loire valley,' says one reporter, 'where the loudest noise was the croaking of the little green bullfrogs in the pond.' Another enthuses about the friendly and efficient service, 'the staff obviously considering themselves lucky to be spending the summer working in such a lovely place'.

The Newingtons continue to make improvements to this formerly dilapidated house, which they opened, 'exhausted and poor', in November 1992. The hotel and restaurant are very much family-run, Hazel doing most of the cooking. In summer, they offer dining on the terrace; in winter, in front of a log fire. Bedrooms are named after local flowers. Breakfast includes hot home-made rolls, brioches, orange juice and fresh fruit.

The old house has been modernized and decorated sympathetically, and has made a very agreeable place to stay while exploring chateau country. Our reporter confirms that Hazel's cooking is 'very good indeed', and found the Newingtons 'most welcoming hosts, without being intrusive'.

Nearby Châteaux – Amboise, Chaumont, Chenonceaux, Tours.

Cangey 37530 Amboise
Tel 02.47.56.09.25
Fax 02.47.56.93.97
Location on D74, 7 km NE of Amboise; in gardens with ample car parking
Meals breakfast, dinner
Prices rooms 295F-375F; breakfast 55F, menus 115F-225F, children's 60F
Rooms 11 double, 4 with bath, 7 with shower; 9 rooms have central heating, 2 with electric heating, phone

Facilities dining-room
Credit cards MC, V
Children very welcome (special menus, games)
Disabled some ground floor rooms
Pets accepted
Closed late Oct to early Nov; Christmas and New Year
Proprietors Peter and Hazel Newington

Western France

Town mansion, Chinon

Hôtel Diderot

Surprisingly few hotels have been in these pages since the first edition while generating a steady stream of entirely complimentary reports, but here is one. And we hear that nothing has changed at the Diderot, not even the moderate prices. 'Excellent' and 'superb' are the latest verdicts.

Creeper-covered and white-shuttered, it is a handsome townhouse set in a courtyard, which conveys the benefit of convenient private parking. The French- Cypriot proprietors are charming and unstintingly helpful, and breakfast (served on the shady terrace or in a rustic room with tiled floor and massive beams) is exceptionally tasty – thanks to Madame's home-made preserves. Bedrooms are simply furnished, but are spotlessly clean and some have fine views. Some now have smart new bathrooms.

Nearby Grand Carroi, ruined château, church of St- Maurice; châteaux – Azay-le-Rideau (20 km), Langeais (30 km).

4 Rue Buffon 37500 Chinon
Tel 02.47.93.18.87
Fax 02.47.93.37.10
Location in middle of town; with courtyard and private car parking
Meals breakfast
Prices rooms 250F-400F; breakfast 40F
Rooms 28 double, 17 with bath, 11 with shower (8 twin); 3 family rooms, all with bath; all rooms have central heating, phone

Facilities bar, breakfast room
Credit cards AE, DC, MC, V
Children welcome
Disabled some ground-floor bedrooms
Pets not accepted
Closed mid-Dec to mid-Jan
Proprietor Theo Kazamias

Western France

Château hotel, Montbron

Hostellerie Ste-Catherine

The Tardoire valley is a pretty one, but the area around Montbron, east of Angoulême, is off the beaten tourist track and we presume this is why we hear so little from readers about this fine old house, once the residence of the Empress Joséphine.

The approach, along a winding drive through splendid wooded grounds, is appropriately imposing and the house – built in a pale, irregular stone – looks handsome but austere. But inside it is a different story: despite fine furnishings and immaculate housekeeping, there is none of the expected pretension, and a relaxed, informal atmosphere prevails.

Rooms are decorated and furnished with proper regard for both style and comfort: the dining-rooms (one leads in to the other) have tapestries on the walls, and a carved wooden mantlepiece stands over an old fireplace; the two sitting-rooms are inviting and relaxing. Most of the individually furnished and thoroughly comfortable bedrooms have views of the surrounding parkland; they do vary in size, and the prices reflect this. One menu and an 'interesting' *carte* are offered.

Nearby Angoulême (30 km) – cathedral, walk along ramparts; châteaux – de Brie (40 km); Rochechouart (40 km).

Route de Marthon 16220 Montbron
Tel 05.45.23.60.03
Fax 05.45.70.72.00
Location in park off D16, 4 km SW of Montbron, 28 km E of Angoulême; with ample car parking
Meals breakfast, lunch, dinner
Prices rooms 450F-800F; breakfast 49F, menu 170F
Rooms 14 double and 4 family rooms, most with bath or shower; all rooms have central heating, phone, TV
Facilities 2 dining-rooms, 2 sitting-rooms, bar; swimming-pool
Credit cards AE, DC, MC, V
Children accepted
Disabled no special facilities
Pets accepted
Closed never
Proprietor Marie-Michelle Rey

Western France

Château hotel, Nieuil

Château de Nieuil

'Our room was extremely comfortable, even though it was one of their smaller ones, and one of the best-value rooms of our holiday,' says a reporter on this fairy-tale Renaissance château, making the point that high prices can be worth paying if you get something special in return. Steep-roofed, turreted, and surrounded by parkland stretching away beyond its formal garden and ornamental 'moat', it is the picture of elegance. Inside, it is appropriately furnished throughout, with exquisite antiques, porcelain and tapestries. Some of the bedrooms are exceedingly grand.

It could be embarrassingly pretentious. But the delight of the place is that it is not at all pretentious or intimidating. The château has been in the Bodinaud family for over a hundred years, and the hotel is very much a family concern. Mme Bodinaud (an ex-design-lecturer) does all the interior decoration and oversees the cooking, earning a Michelin star for her imaginative food, while her husband administers a collection of 300 cognacs.

Recently, the Bodinauds have opened a 'winter' restaurant, La Grange aux Oies, in converted stables. Their shared interest in art has also led to a gallery.

Nearby Angoulême (40km), Limoges (65 km).

Rte de Fontafie, 16270 Nieuil
Tel 05.45.71.36.38
Fax 05.05.45.71.46.45
Location in wooded park, 2 km E of Nieuil; with extensive grounds, car parking and garage for 8 cars
Meals breakfast, lunch, dinner
Prices rooms 630F-1,350F; suites 1,400F-2,100F; breakfast 75F; menus 240F-320F
Rooms 11 double, 3 suites, all with bath; all rooms have central heating, phone, TV,

minibar; 5 have air conditioning
Facilities dining-room, sitting-room, bar; swimming-pool, tennis court
Credit cards AE, DC, MC, V
Children accepted
Disabled access possible to one bedroom and apartment
Pets welcome **Closed** Nov to Apr; restaurant 'La Grange aux Oies' mid-Apr to mid Dec
Proprietor Jean-Michel and Luce Bodinaud

Western France

33 Rue Thiers

This distinctive little guest-house continues to delight a steady stream of guests.'The lovely Maybelle's welcome makes 33 Rue Thiers a particular favourite,' says one reporter. 'It proved to be the most memorable hotel I stayed in, and one I will certainly visit again,' says another.

33 Rue Thiers is a renovated 18thC townhouse in the heart of La Rochelle. Its owner and renovator is a half-American/half-French cook-book author, Maybelle Iribe. She opened for business in 1987, the word spread like wildfire and she now has a faithful band of enthusiastic guests who return year after year.

The public rooms are filled with antiques and (mainly) stylish modern furniture. The huge bedrooms are decorated in soothing pastel shades; to say they have been furnished individually is an understatement − they are a showcase for Madame Iribe's eclectic collection of art and ornaments.

Sumptuous breakfasts and dinner can be eaten on the patio in the secluded little walled garden.

Nearby old quarter, port, and lantern tower of La Rochelle; Ile de Rey.

33 Rue Thiers, 17000 La Rochelle
Tel 05.46.41.62.23
Fax 05.46.41 10.76
Location in street next to central market; with small walled garden and car parking
Meals breakfast, dinner
Prices rooms 380F-450F; breakfast 30F, dinner 120F
Rooms 5 double, one family room, all with bath; all rooms have central heating

Facilities dining-room, sitting-room, TV room
Credit cards not accepted
Children welcome; special meals, baby-sitting available
Disabled no special facilities
Pets well-behaved dogs accepted
Closed Feb
Proprietor Maybelle Iribe

Western France

Restaurant with rooms, Les Rosiers-sur-Loire

Auberge Jeanne de Laval

This is a quintessential restaurant with rooms − you go for Michel Augereau's Michelin-starred cooking, with the option of staying the night. You're unlikely to want to spend a holiday here, but the auberge makes an excellent stopover, whether you are touring the Loire château country or on your way south. The restaurant is a warmly welcoming room with light modern furniture beneath mellow exposed beams, and with an uncompromisingly modern glazed extension. In the same main building are four of the bedrooms − two overlooking the road, two the pretty garden. Most of the rooms are a fair walk away in the château-style Ducs d'Anjou annexe shown in our photo. They are quiet, spacious and tastefully decorated. Service in the annexe is limited to breakfast, which is served in the rooms or in the pretty garden.

Nearby Saumur (15 km); Angers (30 km) − cathedral, château.

54 Rue Nationale, Les Rosiers-sur-Loire 49350 Gennes
Tel 02.41.51.80.17
Fax 02.41.38.04.18
Location in middle of village, 15 km NW of Saumur; with flower gardens and car parking
Meals breakfast, lunch, dinner
Prices rooms 350F-600F; breakfast 50F, menus 170F-420F
Rooms 10 double, all but one with bath; all rooms have central heating, phone, TV, minibar
Facilities TV room, dining-room
Credit cards MC, V
Children welcome
Disabled no special facilities
Pets dogs accepted in bedrooms
Closed mid-Nov to mid-Dec; mid to end Jan; Mon (except public holidays and high season)
Proprietors Augereau family

Western France

Château de la Vallée Bleue

The young Gasquets took over this handsome château in 1985, just in time to make an appearance in the first edition of this guide, and have been assiduously improving it ever since – a barn and stables have been renovated to provide extra space. A report from a British resident in France with three young children sums up the Vallée Bleue precisely: 'Here is complete commitment. Service was friendly and discreet – the children treated like young adults. The restaurant was one of the best we've eaten in.'

Inside, the atmosphere of the house is, as always, warm and easy. Fresh flowers and a cosy log fire in the spacious entrance hall set the tone, and personal touches are in evidence in every room. The château overlooks gardens front and back, giving all the bedrooms – big, and comfortably furnished with antiques – a pleasant outlook; just visible, beyond cows grazing in the fields, are the terracotta roof-tops of the village. Public rooms are gracious and charming, furnished with solid antiques and looking on to the garden. Cooking is regionally based but *nouvelle*-oriented and way above average in execution.

Nearby Tour de la Prison (Museum of George Sand and Vallée Noire); Sarzay (10 km) – château; Nohant (5 km) – château.

Rte de Verneuil, St-Chartier
36400 La Châtre
Tel 02.54.31.01.91
Fax 02.54.31.04.48
Location just outside hamlet, on D69 9 km N of La Châtre; in 4 acre grounds with ample car parking
Meals breakfast, lunch, dinner
Prices rooms 390F-590F; breakfast 50F, menus 140F-295F, children 70F
Rooms 11 double (3 twin), 5 with bath 6 with shower; one single with shower; 2 family rooms with bath; all rooms have central heating, phone, TV, minibar, hairdrier
Facilities 2 dining-rooms, sitting-room, fitness room; swimming-pool, bowling area
Credit cards MC, V
Children welcome; special menus available
Disabled 3 ground-floor rooms
Pets accepted at extra charge
Closed Feb
Proprietor Gérard Gasquet

Western France

La Tonnellerie

The flow of readers' reports on this fine 19th-century wine merchant's house has dried to a trickle (perhaps because the cheapest rooms are no longer cheap) but its attractions seem to us to remain undiminished.

The hotel, in the small village of Tavers, close to the Loire and not far from Beaugency, is set around a central courtyard-garden which is at the heart of its appeal. There is a pretty little swimming-pool, shady chestnut trees; tables for summer meals stand on the lawn and further away from the house on terrace areas. The country atmosphere extends indoors to the dining-rooms, both looking on to the garden, one in 'winter garden' style, the other handsomely rustic, with tiled floor and mellow woodwork. Cooking is *nouvelle* in style but recognizes the traditions of the region, and is above average in execution.

In recent years Mme Pouey has steadily improved the hotel, adding four 'apartments/suites' (pastel walls, flowery drapes, polished antiques, smart tiled bathrooms) and refurbishing other bedrooms.

Nearby Beaugency – Hôtel de Ville, Tour St-Firmin, church of Notre-Dame; châteaux – Chambord (25 km), Blois (30 km).

12 Rue des Eaux-Bleues,
Tavers 45190 Beaugency
Tel 02.38.44.68.15
Fax 02.38.44.10.01
Location in middle of village,
3 km W of Beaugency; with
garden, and private and
public car parking
Meals breakfast, lunch, dinner
Prices rooms 350F-840F,
apartments 660F-1,240F;
breakfast 65F, menus 135F-
245F
Rooms 12 double (7 twin),

3 suites, 5 apartments, all with
bath; all rooms have central
heating, phone, TV, hairdrier
Facilities 2 dining-rooms,
sitting-room; swimming-pool,
tennis, bicycle hire
Credit cards AE, MC, V
Children welcome; cots and
special meals **Disabled**
ground-floor rooms;
lift/elevator **Pets** accepted
Closed 2 Jan to end Feb
Proprietor Marie-Christine
Pouey

Western France

Village hotel, Tonnay-Boutonne

Le Prieuré

A few years ago we came close to dropping this hotel from the guide through lack of support from readers, but our perseverance has been rewarded by a renewed burst of enthusiastic reports. 'I certainly endorse the inclusion of Le Prieuré,' says one. 'At just over 800F for two it must rank as our most expensive stopover, but well worth it.' Another reporter (who describes the prices as 'reasonable') sums up Le Prieuré as 'excellent in every respect,' with 'first-rate food'.

Tonnay-Boutonne is a small, quiet village lying between the old military town of Rochefort and St-Jean-d'Angély, a former wine port. Set slightly back from the (not very busy) main road in a large grassy garden, Le Prieuré is a typical Charentaise building: plain but handsomely symmetrical, with white-shuttered windows. It was the family home of the proprietors before they opened it as a hotel, and retains a friendly atmosphere. The bedrooms and bathrooms have been revamped, leading a reporter to call them 'lovely' and justifying a move from two-star to three-star status a couple of years ago.

Nearby Rochefort – 17thC Corderie Royale, Navy Museum; La Roche Courbon (25 km) – château; Saintes (30 km).

17380 Tonnay-Boutonne
Tel 05.46.33.20.18
Fax 05.46.33.25.55
Location in village 21 km E of Rochefort; with large garden and ample car parking
Meals breakfast, lunch, dinner
Prices rooms 250F-450F; breakfast 45F, menu 140F
Rooms 16 double (6 twin), 2 family rooms; 15 with bath, 3 with shower; all rooms have phone, TV

Facilities reception/sitting-area, TV/sitting-room, 2 dining-rooms
Credit cards MC, V
Children welcome
Disabled no special facilities
Pets accepted
Closed Christmas/New Year
Proprietors M. and Mme Paul Vernoux

The West

Château hotel, Amboise

Château de Pray

A 13thC château steeped in history and in a magnificent position high up above the Loire, with superb views from the windows and terraces. All the rooms have been smartly redecorated recently, and four swish suites have been added across the garden.

■ 37400 Amboise (Indre-et-Loire) **Tel** 02.47.57.23.67 **Fax** 02.47.57. 32.50 **Meals** breakfast, lunch, dinner **Prices** rooms 470F-750F; breakfast 50F, menus 145F-295F **Rooms** 19, all with bath, phone, TV **Credit cards** AE, DC, MC, V **Closed** Jan

---

Village inn, Angles sur l'Anglin

Le Relais du Lyon D'or

A couple who visit France frequently wrote to us praising the warm welcome and high quality service they received here. The Lyon D'or is situated at the heart of a tranquil village that has been designated one of the most beautiful in France. The building, which was once a royal tythe depot and dates back to the 14thC, now provides comfortable accommodation with eight individually designed bedrooms (with more planned) open log fires, rustic beams and terracotta tiled floors. Food is based on seasonal local produce.

■ 4 Rue d'Enfer, 86260 Angles sur l'Anglin (Vienne) **Tel** 05.49.48.32.53 **Fax** 05.49.84.02.28 **Meals** breakfast, lunch, dinner **Prices** rooms 350F; breakfast 35F; menus from 98F **Rooms** 8, all with bath or shower, central heating, phone **Credit cards** MC, V **Closed** 5 Jan to 21 Feb

---

Country house, Ardenais

Domaine de Vilotte

The home of the welcoming Champenier family, this elegant rose-covered mansion offers five individually decorated bedrooms, a farmhouse-style kitchen with copper pans lining the walls and a lovely terrace. An interesting collection of antique radios, telephones and sewing machines fills the entrance. New to the guide this year, we welcome further reports.

■ Ardenais, 18170 Le Châtelet-en-Berry (Cher) **Tel & Fax** 02.48.96. 04.96 **Meals** breakfast, dinner by arrangement **Prices** rooms 330F-390F, with breakfast **Rooms** 5, all with bath, central heating **Credit cards** none **Closed** never

---

Village hotel, Bassac

L'Essille

It's years since we first heard of this modest hotel in a peaceful small village on the banks of the Charente, and a new report earns an entry: 'Comfortable hotel in delightful garden; very quiet; simple food; good parking.' 'Warm welcome, friendly but efficient service,' says an earlier report.

■ 16120 Bassac (Charente) **Tel** 05.45.81.94.13 **Fax** 05.45.81.97.26 **Meals** breakfast, lunch, dinner **Prices** rooms 270F-360F; breakfast 38F, menus 100F-220F **Rooms** 10, all with bath, central heating, phone, TV **Credit cards** MC, V **Closed** One week in Jan; restaurant only, Sun eve

The West

Village hotel, Bléré

Le Cheval Blanc

This smart-looking three-fireplace Logis on the main square of Bléré comes highly recommended, particularly for the 'outstanding' warmth of welcome and friendly service from the young staff. Food is 'imaginative and delicious,' value for money 'difficult to beat in the area.' Garden and heated swimming-pool.

■ Place de l'Église, 37150 Bléré (Indre-et-Loire) **Tel** 02.47.30.30.14 **Fax** 02.47.23.52.80 **Meals** breakfast, lunch, dinner **Prices** rooms 290F-390F; breakfast 36F, menus 99F-265F **Rooms** 12, all with bath or shower, central heating, phone, TV, minibar, hairdrier **Credit cards** AE, DC, MC, V **Closed** Jan and Feb; restaurant only, Sun and Mon dinner except Jul and Aug

---

Village hotel, Brinon-sur-Sauldre

Auberge de la Solognote

The attractions of this rather dull-looking house are within – elegantly rustic furnishing and restrained, tasteful decoration, and excellent (Michelin-starred) food. The light, attractive bedrooms earn top marks for comfort – especially those in the converted outhouse.

■ 18410 Brinon-sur-Sauldre (Cher) **Tel** 02.48.58.50.29 **Fax** 02.48.58.56.00 **Meals** breakfast, lunch, dinner **Prices** rooms 310F-420F; menus 160F-330F **Rooms** 13, all with bath or shower, central heating, phone, TV **Credit cards** MC, V **Closed** mid-Feb to mid-Mar

---

Country hotel, Buzançais

L'Hermitage

Monsieur and Madame Sureau have added a second dining-room and a veranda to this excellent Logis de France, occupying a mini manor house in leafy grounds beside the Indre. Breakfast can be had in the garden, which also provides flowers and vegetables. An open fire on winter evenings. Reporters are enthusiastic – warm welcome, good housekeeping, excellent good-value food in an otherwise pricey area.

■ 36500 Buzançais (Indre) **Tel** 02.54.84.03.90 **Fax** 02.54.02.13.19 **Meals** brea kfast, lunch, dinner **Prices** rooms 285F-335F; breakfast 29F, menus 88F-235F **Rooms** 14, all with central he ating, phone, TV **Credit cards** MC, V **Closed** Sun evening and Mon, except July/Aug

---

Riverside hotel, Châteauneuf-sur-Sarthe

Hôtel de la Sarthe

Our most recent reporter was happy with this modest Logis on a beautiful stretch of the Sarthe, but light sleepers can be disturbed by noise from the nearby through-road. Bedrooms have recently been redecorated; food is well prepared and excellent value, and served on the terrace in summer. Very welcoming proprietors.

■ 1 Rue du Port, 49330 Châteauneuf-sur-Sarthe (Maine-et-Loire) **Tel** 02.41.69.85.29 **Meals** breakfast, lunch, dinner **Prices** rooms 195F-270F; breakfast 30F, menus 86F-205F **Rooms** 7, all with bath or shower, central heating **Credit cards** MC, V **Closed** 3 weeks Oct; restaurant only, Sun dinner, Mon lunch and dinner out of season

The West

Village hotel, Chaumont-sur-Tharonne

La Croix Blanche

The 200-year-old tradition of women chefs continues at this cosy hotel, furnished with gleaming country antiques and floral-patterned fabrics. The 'superb' food is the attraction; the style of cooking is largely Périgordian (foie gras and so on). A recent visitor thought the hotel itself 'in need of a facelift'.

■ 41600 Chaumont-sur-Tharonne (Loir-et-Cher) **Tel** 02.54.88.55.12 **Fax** 02.54.88.60.40 **Meals** breakfast, lunch, dinner **Prices** rooms 290F-580F; DB&B 445F-520F; breakfast 45F, menus 145F-250F **Rooms** 16, all with bath, central heating, phone, TV, radio, minibar **Credit cards** AE, DC, MC, V **Closed** never

---

Village hotel, Chenonceaux

La Roseraie

A reader alerted us to this recently opened hotel, formerly the Ottoni, run by a 'delightful' Parisienne, Mme Fiorito. The bedrooms are tastefully decorated, the beamed dining-room is charming, but the highlight is the sunny dining terrace. There is now a heated swimming-pool, too. The splendid château is only a couple of minutes away.

■ 7 Rue du Dr Bretonneau, 37150 Chenonceaux (Indre-et-Loire) **Tel** 02.47.23.90.09 **Fax** 02.47.23.91.59 **Meals** breakfast, lunch, dinner **Prices** rooms 265F-480F; breakfast 38F, menus 98F-155F **Rooms** 18, all with central heating, phone, satellite TV **Credit cards** AE, DC, MC, V **Closed** mid-Nov to mid-Feb

---

Riverside hotel, Coulon

Au Marais

The Marais in question is a huge area of marshes west of Niort. This friendly little inn on the banks of the Sèvre-Niortaise river makes a pleasant and peaceful stop-over. The rooms are decorated in bright pastel tones and immaculately kept.

■ 46-48 Quai Louis-Tardy, 79510 Coulon (Deux-Sèvres) **Tel** 05.49. 35.90.43 **Fax** 05.49.35.81. 98 **Meals** breakfast **Prices** rooms 250F-600F; breakfast 38F **Rooms** 18, all with bath, central heating, phone, TV **Credit cards** AE, MC, V **Closed** Jan

---

Country guest-house, Fondettes

Manoir du Grand Martigny

Henri and Monique Desmarais are fluent in English, and actively seek to attract English-speaking guests to their 16thC manor house, in wooded grounds not far from the Loire. They renovated the house in the mid-1980s, and it makes a captivating place to stay, with splendid bedrooms and elegant public rooms. Excellent breakfasts.

■ Vallières, 37230 Fondettes (Indre-et-Loire) **Tel** 02.47.42.29.87 **Fax** 02.47.42.24.44 **Meals** breakfast **Prices** rooms 460F-700F with breakfast **Rooms** 7, all with bath, central heating **Credit cards** not accepted **Closed** mid-Nov to Mar

The West

Village inn, Fontgombault

Auberge de l'Abbaye

'An interesting overnight stop' sums up this unpretentious, tiny 16thC auberge – described as 'barely more than a cottage' by a recent reporter. Bedrooms are small and basic but the food is excellent and the service 'delightful' – as is the village setting, close to Fontgombault Abbey, which is famous for Gregorian chant. Reservation in advance is recommended.

■ 36220 Fontgombault (Indre) **Tel** 02.54.37.10.82 **Meals** breakfast, lunch, dinner **Prices** rooms 130F-200F; breakfast 30F, menu 115F **Rooms** 5 **Credit cards** V **Closed** never

---

Riverside hotel, Gien

Hôtel du Rivage

Christian Gaillard's modern-classic (Michelin-starred) cooking is the main attraction of this unpretentious but quite chic modern hotel. Rooms are generally comfortable, with new mattresses promised for the beds, and good value. Lovely views of the Loire are shared by some bedrooms and the pretty dining-room.

■ 1 Quai de Nice, 45500 Gien (Loiret) **Tel** 02.38.37.79.00 **Fax** 02.38.38.10.21 **Meals** breakfast, lunch, dinner **Prices** rooms 300F-520F, suites 690F; menus 140F-390F **Rooms** 19, all with bath or shower, central heating, phone, TV **Credit cards** AE, DC, MC, V **Closed** early Feb to Mar

---

Converted mill, Loches

Le Moulin

Andrew and Sue wrote to suggest that their 19thC watermill might make an entry here, and they were right. The house is on a small island in the Indre, with lawns down to the water. All the bedrooms are recently renovated, and furnished with stripped pine or antiques. French-trained Andrew Page cooks, and you can eat separately or communally, with meals beside the river in summer.

■ St-Jean, St-Germain, 37600 Loches (Indre-et-Loire) **Tel** 02.47. 94.70.12 **Fax** 02.47.94.77. 98 **Meals** breakfast, dinner **Prices** rooms 260F-300F with breakfast; menus 110F **Rooms** 5, all with bath, central heating **Credit cards** not accepted **Closed** Jan, Nov, Dec

---

Restaurant with rooms, Marans

La Porte Verte

This neat, shuttered house sits quietly on the quayside with its own invitingly shady courtyard. A good, predominantly fishy menu (and wonderful puds) from Didier Montéran's kitchen. Bedrooms are tasteful, although there are idiosyncratic touches. Two are in the Montérans' own house along the quay. Reports on the new quayside *terrasse* please.

■ 20 Quai Foch, 17230 Marans (Charente-Maritime) **Tel** 05.46.01.09.45 **Meals** breakfast, lunch, dinner **Prices** rooms 235F-265F with breakfast; menus 110F-165F **Rooms** 4, all with shower, central heating **Credit cards** MC,V **Closed** 17 Feb to 4 Mar; Wed; Sun dinner low season

The West

Château hotel, Montrichard

Château de Chissay

A small-scale fairytale château in the heart of château country, renovated in the late 1980s, with rooms ranging from the affordable to the rather less so. Cooking is above average, including fish from the Loire. Swimming-pool.

■ Chissay-en-Touraine, 41400 Montrichard (Loir-et-Cher)
Tel 02.54.32.32.01 **Fax** 02.54.32.43.80 **Meals** breakfast, lunch, dinner
Prices rooms 450F-1,500F; breakfast 65F; menus 185F-295F
Rooms 31, all with bath, central heating, phone **Credit cards** AE, DC, MC, V **Closed** mid-Nov to mid-Mar

---

Château hotel, Montrichard

Château de la Menaudière

Despite its elegant furnishings, the atmosphere of this lovely little château is not intimidating. There are two intimate and rather hushed dining-rooms, and the food is good; breakfast can be had in the courtyard in summer, and there is a pubby bar in the stables. Bedrooms are well furnished, with smart bathrooms.

■ 41401 Montrichard (Loir-et-Cher) **Tel** 02.54.32.02.44 **Fax** 02.54.71.34.58 **Meals** breakfast, lunch, dinner **Prices** rooms 500F-650F; breakfast 55F; menus 150F-290F **Rooms** 25, all with bath, central heating, phone, TV, minibar **Credit cards** AE, DC, MC, V **Closed** Nov to Mar; restaurant only, Sun dinner, Mon lunch and dinner out of season

---

Restaurant with rooms, Mosnac

Moulin de Marcouze

The food (two Michelin stars) is the main draw of this smartly converted mill – Dominique Bouchet is a graduate of the Tour d'Argent in Paris. The modern bedrooms, like the dining-room, employ a light, simple style, with antique and reproduction furniture on plain quarry-tiled floors. Swimming-pool.

■ Mosnac, 17240 Saint-Genis-de-Saintonge (Charente-Maritime)
Tel 05.46.70.46.16 **Fax** 05.46.70.48.14 **Meals** breakfast, lunch, dinner
Prices rooms 525F-700F; breakfast 70F, menus 140F-420F **Rooms** 9,
all with bath, central heating, air-conditioning, phone, TV, minibar
Credit cards AE, MC, V **Closed** Feb

Riverside hotel, Olivet

Le Rivage

Position and food are the keys to this ordinary-looking hotel. It's in a peaceful spot on the banks of the Loiret, with a riverside terrace; the food is regionally-based and rated 'excellent' and 'beautifully presented'. Chatty, friendly owner. Tennis court.

■ 635 Rue de la Reine Blanche, 45160 Olivet (Loiret)
Tel 02.38.66.02.93 **Fax** 02.38.56.31.11 **Meals** breakfast, lunch, dinner
Prices rooms 370F-490F; breakfast 50F-55F, menus 155F-290F
Rooms 17, all with bath or shower, central heating, phone, TV, minibar
Credit cards AE, DC, MC, V **Closed** 3 weeks in Jan; restaurant only, Sun dinner Nov to Easter

The West

Manor house hotel, Ouchamps

Relais des Landes

This 17thC mansion has a splendidly peaceful setting, in neat gardens leading off to the ponds and woods of the Sologne. Restful, spacious, well equipped bedrooms (most in low outbuildings); traditional food is served in a tiled, beamed dining-room. Reports welcome.

■ 41120 Ouchamps (Loir-et-Cher) **Tel** 02.54.44.03.33 **Fax** 02.54.44.03.89 **Meals** breakfast, dinner **Prices** rooms 495F-745F; DB&B 565F-855F **Rooms** 28, all with bath, central heating, pho ne, TV, minibar **Credit cards** AE, DC, MC, V **Closed** mid-Nov to end Mar

---

Town hotel, Pons

Auberge Pontoise

Ambitious and competent cooking (Michelin-starred) is the chief attraction of this simple, unpretentious hotel. The rooms (some facing the garden) are of a fair size, and there is a pleasant courtyard where meals are served in summer. Reports welcome.

■ 23 Ave Gambetta, 17800 Pons (Charente-Maritime) **Tel** 05.46.94.00.99 **Fax** 05.46.91.33.40 **Meals** breakfast, lunch, dinner **Prices** rooms 270F-450F; menus 160F-350F **Rooms** 22, all with bath or shower, central heating, phone, TV **Credit cards** MC, V **Closed** 5 weeks Dec to Jan; Sun dinner and Mon out of season

---

Converted mill, La Roche-l'Abeille

Moulin de la Gorce

A tranquil setting and renowned cooking (two stars from Michelin) are the main attractions of this neat, low-lying 16thC mill building, beside a lake amid wooded grounds. Bedrooms – some richly furnished, some more bland – are split between the main building and an ancient nearby mill. Relais & Châteaux.

■87800 La Roche-l'Abeille (Haute-Vienne) **Tel** 05.55.00.70.66 **Fax** 05.55.00.76.57 **Meals** breakfast, lunch, dinner **Prices** rooms 350F-900F; apartment 1,300F; breakfast 75F; menus 180F-480F **Rooms** 10, all with bath, phone, TV **Credit cards** AE, DC, MC, V **Closed** Oct to Apr

---

Château hotel, St-Hilaire-de-Court

Château de la Beuvrière

A beautifully restored medieval château with 11thC origins – complete with conical slate roofs atop its round towers. Inside, the scale is more domestic than in many châteaux, the atmosphere welcoming. Outside, extensive grounds. New to the guide a few years ago; reports, please.

■ St-Hilaire-de-Court, 18100 Vierzon (Cher) **Tel** 02.48.75.14.63 **Fax** 02.48.75.47.62 **Meals** breakfast, lunch, dinner **Prices** rooms 350F-460F; suite 600F; menus 150F-198F **Rooms** 15, all with bath or shower, central heating, phone **Credit card** AE, DC, V **Closed** Sun night and Mon

The West

Country hotel, St-Maixent-l'Ecole

Le Logis Saint-Martin

This neat old house, completely secluded in wooded grounds but conveniently close to the RN11 and the A10, has added new terrace for outdoor eating, and refurbished the dining-room since our last edition. Bedrooms have also been redecorated and are individually and tastefully furnished. Food is taken increasingly seriously.

■ Chemin de Pissot, 79400 St-Maixent-l'Ecole (Deux-Sèvres) **Tel** 05.49. 05.58.68 **Fax** 05.49.76.19.93 **Meals** breakfast, lunch, dinner **Prices** rooms 360F-460F; breakfast 58F; menus 140F-160F **Rooms** 11, all with bath or shower, central heating, phone, hairdrier, TV **Credit cards** AE, DC, MC, V **Closed** Jan

---

Country house hotel, St-Martin-du-Fault

La Chapelle-Saint-Martin

A neat, shuttered country house in lovely manicured grounds. The suave interior is designer-decorated and luxuriously furnished, mixing antiques, modern conveniences and rich fabrics in the best of taste; bedrooms are equally impressive. Relais & Châteaux.

■ St-Martin-du-Fault, 87510 Nieul (Haute-Vienne) **Tel** 05.55.75.80.17 **Fax** 05.55.75.89.50 **Meals** breakfast, lunch, dinner **Prices** rooms 690F-980F; suites 1,300F-1,500F; DB&B 750F-850F **Rooms** 14, all with bath, central heating, phone, TV **Credit cards** AE, MC, V **Closed** Jan

---

Château hotel, St-Patrice

Château de Rochecotte

'Travellers who stay here for only one night do themselves an injustice,' advises a recent reporter, impressed by an 'unusual degree of consideration for individual guests.' An opportunity to sample life in a château of the grandest style, looked after by the charming Mme Pasquier and her equally charming daughters and staff. Bright fabrics and elegant modern furniture complement the classical proportions of the rooms. Gastronomique cuisine.

■ St-Patrice, 37130 Langeais (Indre-et-Loire) **Tel** 02.47.96.16.16 **Fax** 02.47.96.90.59 **Meals** breakfast, lunch, dinner **Prices** rooms 580F-930F; suites 1,250F; menus 195F-285F **Rooms** 30, all with bath, central heating, phone, TV **Credit cards** AE, DC, MC, V **Closed** Feb

---

Village inn, Souvigny-en-Sologne

Auberge de la Croix Blanche

This family-run brick-and-timber auberge occupies a prime spot in the middle of a deliciously pretty village in the Sologne (the annexe is some 150 metres from the hotel itself). Bedrooms are small and simple with smartly tiled bathrooms. The *cuisine traditionelle et copieuse* is highly regarded.

■ Rue Eugenie Labiche, Souvigny-en-Sologne, 41600 Lamotte-Beuvron (Loir-et-Cher) **Tel** 02.54.88.40.08 **Fax** 02 54 88 91 06 **Meals** breakfast, lunch, dinner **Prices** rooms 120F-280F; breakfast 30F-35F, menus 76F-235F **Rooms** 9, all with central heating, phone **Credit cards** V **Closed** mid-Jan to Feb; Tue dinner, Wed lunch and dinner

Eastern France

Our Eastern France region takes in Burgundy, the Jura and most of the Alps – an exceptionally rewarding area for lovers of food, wine and the great outdoors. We have a great many potential entries for this area, listed below.

Contenders in Eastern France

Beaune, Le Cep 03.80.22.35.48 Fairly pricey B&B in centre, now much enlarged.

Bourg-St-Maurice, Hôtel l'Autantic 04.79.07.01.70 Modern stone-faced chalet on edge of town, with comfy rooms.

Le-Bourget-du-Lac, Ombremont 04.79.25.00.23 Tastefully decorated R&C villa overlooking lake; pool.

Bresson, Chavant 04.76.25.25.38 Upmarket, elegantly furnished auberge; flower-filled dining terrace; excellent food.

Buxy, Château de Sassangy 03.85.96.12.40 Tall 18thC château in lovely grounds, with freshly decorated rooms.

Chamonix-Mont-Blanc, Hôtel Albert 1er 04.50.53.05.09 Solid old town hotel with the best food in town.

Chorey-les-Beaune, Château de Chorey-les-Beaune 03.80.22.06.05 Tastefully decorated, family-run B&B in solid 17thC château.

Cordon, Le Cordonant 04.50.58.34.56 Good-value modern chalet hotel in a country setting with excellent views.

Courchevel 1850, La Sivolière 04.79.08.08.33 Warmly welcoming hotel, run with dedication; quiet, but close to centre.

Lods, La Truite d'Or 03.81.60.95.48 Old riverside mill in a narrow Jura valley, now a modest, rustic Logis.

Loué, Laurent 02.43.88.40.03 Smart Relais & Châteaux place with extravagant decor, attractive gardens with pool.

Lyon, La Tour Rose 04.78.37.25.90 Ambitious restaurant with spectacularly individual rooms decorated by Lyon silk makers.

Megève, Le Fer à Cheval 04.50.21.30.39 Tastefully rustic furnishings in a wood-built chalet on edge of town.

Mionnay, Alain Chapel 04.78.91.82.02 Luxury restaurant (one of best in France) with very expensive rooms.

Monêtier-les-Bains, l'Auberge du Choucas 04.92.24.42.73 Former farmhouse, still charming, with simple quiet rooms.

Le-Moulin-du-Milieu, Le Moulin 03.81.44.35.18 Eccentric house with large garden in a remote setting, recently opened.

Onlay, Château de Lesvault 03.86.84.32.91 Home-like 19thC manor in grounds, with special appeal for writers and artists.

Replonges, La Huchette 03.85.31.03.55 Boldly decorated, shuttered house in grassy grounds with large pool; good food.

St-Martin-en-Bresse, Au Puits Enchanté 03.85.47.71.96 Neat little Logis; exceptionally stylish decor and good-value food.

St-Sauveur-en-Rue, L'Auberge du Château de Bobigneux 04.77.39.24.33 Dinky rustic 16thC château offering simple rooms and country cooking at very low prices.

Saulieu, Bernard Loiseau 03.80.64.07.66 A temple of gastronomy, in an old inn, beautifully renovated, plus rustic-style extensions.

Veyrier-du-Lac, Auberge de l'Eridan 04.50.60.24.00 Swanky villa on lake shore; super-chef Marc Veyrat cooks.

Vienne, La Pyramide 04.74.53.01.96 Famous restaurant, revived under a new chef; tasteful, comfortable rooms.

Eastern France

Hôtel Clarion

'Highly recommended,' enthuses a recent German visitor, 'especially for its modern style in a traditional building, the superb garden views and the excellent breakfasts.'

The tiny village of Aloxe-Corton is a place of pilgrimage for lovers of great white wine. Its symbol is the château of Corton-André, a picturesque building of gleaming coloured tiles and tidy tunnels full of *premiers crus*. Next to it lies the Hôtel Clarion, a 17th-century mansion which has been cleverly converted into a small and unconventional hotel. The style is a mix of modern and old, art deco furnishings set against old timberwork and beamed ceilings. Bedrooms are well co-ordinated, mainly in matching fabrics of pastel shades. Although varied in size and price, all are thoroughly comfortable and well-equipped. Bathrooms, in marble, are large and luxurious.

Other merits of the hotel are the comfortable salon (beams, open fireplace) opening out on to the park and vineyards, and the large garden. Those breakfasts include eggs, cheese and fresh fruit in addition to the usual coffee and croissants.

Nearby Vineyards; Beaune – infirmary, wine museum; Le Rochepot (25 km) – château; Dijon (35 km).

21420 Aloxe-Corton
Tel 03.80.26.46.70
Fax 03.80.26.47.16
Location on edge of village, 3.5 km N of Beaune on N74; in large garden with ample car parking
Meals breakfast
Prices rooms 500F-800F
Rooms 10 double (7 twin), all with bath; one family room with bath ; all rooms have central heating, phone, TV, minibar
Facilities sitting-room; bicycles
Credit cards MC, V
Children welcome; cots, special meals, baby-sitting available
Disabled one ground-floor bedroom specially equipped
Pets accepted
Closed never
Proprietor Christian Voarick

Eastern France

Converted abbey, Annecy-le-Vieux

L'Abbaye

Annecy-le-Vieux is not the lovely medieval heart of Annecy, but a sprawling residential area north of the lake, and to be honest both the inspectors we've recently sent here have fretted about this weak spot in an otherwise captivating (although idiosyncratic) hotel. In promoting it to a full entry, we're influenced by a reader who summarises it as 'a very attractive hotel with delightful bedrooms,' with no niggles about the location. A room overlooking the garden is recommended.

L'Abbaye was indeed an ancient abbey. A stone archway leads into a quaint cobbled courtyard surrounded by a wooden balcony. The dining-room is a splendid, vaulted room sporting a motley array of decoration: gold mythological masks, chandeliers, Renaissance fresco, Indian print napkins. In summer, tables are set up in the shade of huge trees. The bedrooms have been beautifully furnished – again in a variety of styles – and with every modern convenience. (We're not surprised to hear that the hotel has recently stepped up to four-star status.)

It's rather surprising to find a disco in a hotel like this, but it is separate and does not disturb the peace. The food is good, and well priced; service is casual in terms of dress, but effective.

15, Chemin de l'Abbaye, 74940 Annecy-le-Vieux
Tel 04.50.23.61.08
Fax 04.50.27.77.65
Location in rural setting, 2 km NE of Annecy; with garden and car parking
Meals breakfast, dinner
Prices rooms 400F–700F; breakfast 55F, menu 125F
Rooms 15 double, 2 suites, one apartment, all with bath; all have central heating, phone, TV, minibar

Facilities dining-room, bar, terrace
Credit cards AE, DC, MC, V
Children welcome
Disabled no special facilities
Pets accepted
Closed restaurant only, Mon
Proprietors M. Menges and M. Burnet

Eastern France

Parc des Maréchaux

This substantial 1850s house, restored from near-dereliction by Espérance Hervé and her doctor husband, enjoys clear support from readers, not least because it offers excellent value.

The Hervés have cut no corners: the welcoming ambience, confident style and solid comfort of the house would do credit to any professional hotelier. For a bed-and-breakfast establishment, the public rooms are exceptionally comfortable; as well as the sitting-room, the smart little bar looking over the garden is appreciated.

The large bedrooms are beautifully done out in restrained colours, and handsomely furnished using warm wooden beds and chests in traditional styles. One reader warned against those on the noisy road side and advises booking one that overlooks the garden – the secluded, leafy 'park' from which the hotel takes its name. But Madame advises that the road-side rooms have now been soundproofed. Breakfast, which can be had outside in summer, as an alternative to the pretty breakfast room, is 'outstanding,' says one reporter, 'adequate, with more copious options,' says another.

Nearby cathedral, abbey church of St-Germain; Chablis (20 km)

6 Ave Foch 89000 Auxerre
Tel 03.86.51.43.77
Fax 03.86.51.31.72
Location close to middle of town; with gardens and car parking
Meals breakfast
Prices rooms 310F-470F (under 7s free); breakfast 47F
Rooms 19 double (7 twin), 2 single, 3 family rooms; all with bath; all rooms have central heating, phone, TV
Facilities sitting-room, bar, breakfast room
Credit cards AE, V
Children welcome
Disabled 3 ground-floor bedrooms; lift/elevator
Pets accepted
Closed never
Proprietor Espérance Hervé

Eastern France

Château hotel, Avallon

Château de Vault-de-Lugny

Recent visitors report enthusiastically on this impressive and expensive château, new to the guide a few years ago − only a couple of miles from the dear little Moulin des Templiers (page 114), but as sharp a contrast in style as you will find. 'Superb and welcoming hotel,' runs one report. 'We enjoyed both the food and the ambience, and will go again.'

The house, of plain medieval rather than fancy Renaissance origin, was restored and opened as a hotel in the mid-1980s. Some of the very grand bedrooms retain their aristocratic style, with period decoration and sparse antique furnishings that contribute more to atmosphere than comfort; others have something of a modern designer feel, with subtly coloured fabrics, and comfortable furniture that looks suspiciously like reproduction rather than the real thing. Bathrooms are ritzy, as they should be at these prices.

The extensive, well-wooded grounds include a well-used kitchen garden, contributing to the proprietors' *cuisine traditionelle*, and a fair stretch of trout fishing, as well as a tennis court. Hot-air balloon flights can be arranged.

Nearby Avallon − ramparts; Vézelay (10 km)

89200 Avallon
Tel 03.86.34.07.86
Fax 03.86.34.16.36
Location 4 km W of Avallon, 1 km N of Pontaubert, on D427 outside village of Vault-de-Lugny, in large grounds with ample car parking
Meals breakfast, lunch, dinner, snacks
Prices rooms 700F-2,200F with breakfast; dinner 280F; reductions for 5 nights plus
Rooms 12 double (4 twin), all with bath; all rooms have central heating, phone, TV, minibar; most have hairdrier, safe
Facilities sitting-room/bar, sitting-room, restaurant; tennis, fishing **Credit cards** AE, MC, V **Children** welcome; babysitting available
Disabled easy access, room on ground floor **Pets** welcome (50F charge)**Closed** mid-Nov to early Apr
Proprietor Elisabeth Audan

Eastern France

Converted mill, Chaublanc

Moulin d'Hauterive

We've no reason to doubt that this ancient watermill is as attractive as ever, but reports are few and far between; if you pay a visit, do drop us a line about it.

The wheels of the mill were still turning less than 30 years ago; only for the last decade or so has it been enjoying a new lease of life as a country hotel – offering an unusual blend of rural seclusion, good living and sporting activities. It is a handsome creeper-clad building, three storeys high, surrounded by a collection of lower outbuildings. Beyond them are the little pool (with a lift-up cover/roof which is doubtless a great aid to child safety and energy conservation when the pool is not in use, but diminishes the pleasure of swimming) and tennis court.

The interior is the epitome of rustic chic. The building contributes a network of beams, smooth stone-flagged floors, white-washed or rough pale stone walls. Against this are placed bright fabrics, delicate mellow antiques, gleaming ornaments, and vivid bowls of flowers. Bedrooms are romantically done out in pastel shades – beds are often draped or canopied with lacy fabrics. The young Moilles were new to hotel keeping when they set up the Moulin. Madame has gained a formidable reputation for her inventive dishes (two red *toques* from Gault-Millau).

Nearby Archéodrome (10 km) – archeological centre; Beaune (15 km) – medieval infirmary, wine museum.

Chaublanc 71350 St-Gervais-en-Vallière
Tel 03.85.91.55.56
Fax 03.85.91.89.65
Location 16 km SE of Beaune, off D970; in grounds with ample car parking
Meals breakfast, lunch, dinner
Prices rooms 530F-650F, suites 850F; DB&B 580F-730F; menus 160F-400F
Rooms 11 double, 11 family rooms, all with bath or shower; all rooms have central heating, phone, TV, minibar
Facilities 2 dining-rooms, bar, 3 seminar rooms; swimming-pool, tennis, spa, billiards, heliport, sauna, solarium, fitness room
Credit cards AE, DC, V
Children accepted
Disabled one room
Pets dogs accepted in bedrooms at extra charge
Closed Christmas, Jan
Proprietors Christiane and Michel Moille

Eastern France

Country hotel, Gevrey-Chambertin

Les Grands Crus

The walls are vertical and plastered, the exposed beams are straight and smooth, the windows are easily opened casements: this is a modern hotel, built as recently as 1977, and so not as immediately charming as many older places in these pages. But the Grands Crus has been done out in traditional Burgundian style, with quarry-tiled floors, lime-washed walls, tapestry fabrics and a carved-stone fireplace, and it drips with geraniums in summer – so to a degree it combines the charm of the old with the comfort of the new. More importantly, perhaps, it offers a warm welcome and friendly service – factors which repeatedly impress themselves on our reporters.

The bedrooms are not the last word in stylish decoration, but they are peaceful, spacious and thoughtfully furnished, and look out over the famous Gevrey-Chambertin vineyards. A better-than-average breakfast is served in the small flowery garden in fine weather; if you're confined indoors, there may be delays because of a shortage of space in the breakfast room, off reception. There are plenty of restaurants nearby for other meals, including some notably good ones.

Nearby Dijon – Grand Duke's palace, Place de la Libération.

Rte des Grands Crus 21220 Gevrey-Chambertin
Tel 03.80.34.34.15
Fax 03.80.51.89.07
Location in middle of village, 10 km SW of Dijon; with garden and ample car parking
Meals breakfast
Prices rooms 350F-440F; breakfast 47F; children under 4 free
Rooms 24 double (8 twin) all with bath; all rooms have phone
Facilities sitting-room
Credit cards MC, V
Children welcome
Disabled no special facilities
Pets accepted but not to be left in rooms
Closed Dec to Feb
Proprietor Mme Marie-Paule Farnier

Eastern France

Chalet hotel, Chamonix

Auberge du Bois Prin

Despite increasing competition (notably from the newish Jeu de Paume, see page 116) the Bois Prin remains our favourite spot in (or at least near) Chamonix. This is partly because of its stunning views across the valley to the spires and glaciers of Mont Blanc, Europe's highest peak. But an inspection visit also confirms its merits as a cossetting place to stay.

The Bois Prin is a traditional-style dark-wood chalet, in a pretty, flowery garden close to the foot of the Brévent cable-car, on the north side of the deep, steep-sided Chamonix valley. The Carriers have run the hotel since it was built (by Monsieur's parents) in 1976. The first impression may be of a surprising degree of formality, with crisply dressed staff. But in fact the informal and friendly approach of the young Carriers sets the tone. Bedrooms face Mont Blanc, and are luxuriously furnished, with rich fabrics and carved woodwork (much of it Denis's own work) and a sprinkling of antiques; the best have a private terrace. Food is excellent, with a good choice of menus and a 'wonderful' cheeseboard.

Nearby Mt Blanc and Le Brévent – cable-car rides, walking, rock climbing, skiing; Mont Blanc tunnel for easy access to Italy.

69 Chemin de l'Hermine, Les Moussoux 74400 Chamonix
Tel 04.50.53.33.51
Fax 04.50.53.48.75
Location on hillside, NW of town; with garden and ample car parking and garages
Meals breakfast, lunch, dinner
Prices rooms 870F-1,240F with breakfast; menus 160F-400F
Rooms 9 double (5 twin), all with bath; 2 family rooms, with bath; all rooms have phone, TV, minibar
Facilities dining-room, seminar room
Credit cards AE, DC, MC, V
Children welcome; special meals, high-chair available
Disabled no special facilities
Pets accepted
Closed mid-Apr to early May, late Oct, Nov
Proprietors Monique and Denis Carrier

Eastern France

Village mansion, Mailly-le-Château

Le Castel

We have had mixed reports, over the years, on this pleasant old *maison bourgeoise*. We're coming to the view that it's a matter of expectations. It is a modest hotel – a two-fireplace Logis, with rooms and meals at very attractive prices. But because the house and its name are rather grand, some visitors perhaps expect too much. Our latest reporter, who stayed two nights, takes a balanced view: 'Pleasant welcome (in English), good rooms, good food; restricted menus understandable in view of reasonable prices.'

Built at the end of the last century, Le Castel is a large shuttered house lying in the shadow of the village church, with a well-kept garden and a flowery terrace shaded by lime trees, where you can have breakfast. There are two dining-rooms, separated by a small salon with Empire-style furnishings and a handsome fireplace. Bedrooms vary widely – from spacious ones with touches of grandeur, such as chandeliers and drapes over bedheads, to much smaller and simpler rooms. Some much-needed refurbishment has been undertaken recently, and continues. Madame is 'the perfect hostess'.

Nearby Vézelay (30 km) – Romanesque buildings; Avallon (30 km) – ramparts; Chablis (45 km) – vineyards.

Place de l'Église 89660 Mailly-le-Château
Tel 03.86.81.43.06
Fax 03.86.81.49.26
Location in church square of village, 30 km S of Auxerre; with garden, terrace and car parking
Meals breakfast, lunch, dinner
Prices rooms 155F-400F, suite 420F; menus 75F-170F
Rooms 10 double (5 twin), 7 with bath, 2 with shower;
2 family rooms with bath ; all rooms have central heating, phone
Facilities 2 dining-rooms, sitting-room
Credit cards MC, V
Children accepted
Disabled one ground-floor bedroom
Pets accepted
Closed Wed
Proprietors M. and Mme Breerette

Eastern France

Chalet hotel, Manigod

Chalet Hôtel de la Croix-Fry

The inspector who was lucky enough to find herself spending a night in this cosy wooden chalet could scarcely contain her enthusiasm, summing it up in the end as her favourite in a week-long tour which included several delectable places.

Mountain chalets come in many styles, but the pretty-as-a-cuckoo-clock variety, two a penny in Switzerland, is all too rare in France. But this is one – built in dark wood, its terrace overflowing with bright flowers. Inside, the immediate impression is of rustic simplicity, with wood the warm, dominant material; an open fire burns on cool evenings, with benches and sofas covered by animal skins in front of it. The bedrooms, too, are charmingly rustic in style – even in the modern annexe-chalets, which offer flexible and comfortable accommodation (with kitchenettes) for all sizes of family.

Style apart, the peaceful setting is the attraction, with superb views across the valley from the terrace and the picture windows of the dining-area. The welcoming owners and staff strike the perfect balance of attentive service without intrusion. Good, nourishing mountain food completes a happy picture.

Nearby skiing; Vallée de Manigod, Thônes (10 km); Annecy.

Rte du Col de la Croix-Fry, Manigod 74230 Thônes
Tel 04.50.44.90.16
Fax 04.50.44.94.87
Location at the col, 5 km NE of Manigod, on D16 6 km S of La Clusaz; in countryside, with garden; ample parking
Meals breakfast, lunch, dinner
Prices rooms 500F-1,500F; breakfast 80F; menus 140F-360F
Rooms 12 double with bath (4 whirlpool); all rooms have central heating, phone, satellite TV, balcony
Facilities dining-room, sitting-room, bar; heated swimming-pool, fitness room, tennis, ski bus **Credit cards** AE, MC, V
Children accepted **Disabled** no special facilities **Pets** not accepted in dining-room
Closed mid-Sep to mid-Dec, mid-Apr to mid-Jun
Proprietor Mme Marie-Ange Guelpa-Veyrat

Eastern France

Converted convent, Marcigny

Les Récollets

The Brionnais is a rural region, with gently rolling hills and lush meadows where Charollais cattle graze. It is a part of Burgundy that few foreigners bother with, which we hope explains why we get so few reports on this near-ideal combination of French chic and home comforts. More reports would be very welcome.

The small market town of Marcigny provides an excellent base for touring the region – it is close to the Loire, and not far from the famous cattle market of St-Christophe-en-Brionnais. It is also the location of this, one of the most delightful hotels in the region. We use the word 'hotel' loosely: this is really a private home open to guests.

Josette Badin, who runs the place with Burgundian *bonhomie*, has furnished the rooms superbly, from the dining-room with its hand-painted cupboards to the antique-laden bedrooms. There are log fires, home-made *brioches* for breakfast, hand-made chocolates by the bedside (along with sleeping tablets, indigestion pills and painkillers). Indeed, every need is catered for, and the only house-rule is 'do as you please'.

Officially, only breakfast is served, but ask in advance and Josette will be happy to prepare a simple meal: soup or omelette – even *foie gras*, followed by Charollais beef.

Nearby Mill Tower Museum; La Clayette (25 km); Charlieu Abbey (30 km); Château Drée (30 km).

Place du Champ de Foire
71110 Marcigny
Tel 03.85.25.05.16
Fax 03.85.25.06.91
Location on edge of small town 22 km S of Paray; in grounds with ample car parking
Meals breakfast; lunch and dinner on request
Prices rooms 330F-600F with breakfast; menus 170F-200F
Rooms 6 double (2 twin), all with bath; 3 family rooms, all with bath; all rooms have central heating, phone
Facilities TV room, library, breakfast/dining-room
Credit cards AE, V
Children accepted
Disabled one ground-floor bedroom
Pets accepted
Closed never
Proprietor Mme Josette Badin

Eastern France

Village inn, Mercurey

Hôtellerie du Val d'Or

Jean-Claude Cogny and his family keep standards as high as ever
in this early 19th-century coaching inn, on the main street of the
prestigious but rather dull wine village of Mercurey. It is easy to
see what brings the customers back: in a region of culinary excel-
lence and exorbitant prices, many are daunted by the formal (or
even pretentious) style of most hotels, and long to find some vil-
lage-inn simplicity. The friendly Val d'Or obliges, and combines
this with excellent cooking (Michelin-starred) and comfortable,
neatly decorated bedrooms – though some are rather small.
There is an attractive gravelled garden.
Nearby Château de Germolles (10 km); Buxy (20 km).

Grande-Rue 71640 Mercurey
Tel 03.85.45.13.70
Fax 03.85.45.18.45
Location in middle of village,
9 km S of Chagny; with
garden
Meals breakfast, lunch,
dinner
Prices rooms 350F-570F;
meals 163F-345F, children's
meals 85F
Rooms 10 double (3 twin),
one single, 2 family rooms; all
with bath or shower; all rooms
have central heating, phone,
TV
Facilities 2 dining-rooms,
lounge/bar
Credit cards MC, V
Children accepted
Disabled no special facilities
Pets not accepted
Closed Mon and Tue lunch
Proprietor Jean-Claude
Cogny

Eastern France

Auberge du Rostaing

We don't get many reports on this completely peaceful and relaxed *auberge* in an unspoiled area west of the Jura hills, but they are all positive. 'We are sure to return,' says the latest.

This is an area that is great for getting away from it all, with lovely walks (or bicycle rides) for the active. And this simple place, well run by a charming Franco-Swiss couple, seems entirely in harmony. It also has more to offer than most similarly simple competitors: an inviting sitting-room with music, games and books (and emphatically no TV), a shady courtyard garden where meals and drinks are served in summer, a large airy dining-room with an open fireplace and rustic furniture, and nine fresh, spacious and simple bedrooms – some of them in an adjacent building, reached by an outside staircase and a balcony decked with climbing vines and geraniums.

Madame Eckert does the cooking – good and wholesome, with lots of Swiss influences; *fondue* and *raclette* sometimes crop up, and there is a 'marvellous' daily cheese platter. Many of the guests come back year after year and it is easy to see why.

Nearby forest walks, bicycle rides, vineyards; Château-Chalon (5 km); Cirque de Ladoye (10 km); Poligny (10 km)

39230 Passenans
Tel 03.84.85.23.70
Fax 03.84.44.66.87
Location on outskirts of village, 11 km SW of Poligny on D57, follow Route des Vins; with garden
Meals breakfast, lunch, dinner
Prices rooms 132-248F; breakfast 25F, menus 62F-176F
Rooms 7 double (2 twin), 5 with shower; 2 family rooms with bath; all rooms have central heating
Facilities dining-room, sitting-room; bicycles for hire
Credit cards DC, MC, V
Children accepted; reductions by arrangement
Disabled no special facilities
Pets accepted
Closed Mon evenings except high season; Dec, Jan
Proprietor Félix Eckert

Eastern France

Town mansion, Vézelay

Le Pontot

Most visitors to this rambling fortified house – the only hotel inside the walls of the old town of Vézelay, just a short walk from the famous basilica – are captivated by its combination of character and luxury.

Rebuilt after the Hundred Years War, and added to in the 18th century, it has only recently become a hotel. Since 1984 the American owner, architect Charles Thum, and manager Christian Abadie have skilfully converted the building into a rather special bed-and-breakfast. (Who needs a restaurant when the famous Espérance lies just down the road?) The bedrooms include a large Louis XVI apartment, with canopied beds, fireplace and private dressing room; and another with stone paving, 16thC beamed ceiling and antique, country-style, furnishings.

Breakfast is quite a sumptuous affair, served as it is on gold-encrusted, royal blue Limoges porcelain. On cool days, it is eaten in front of a blazing fire in the handsome, panelled, Louis XVI salon; but in summer you sit outside in the delightful walled garden. A reader warns that bedrooms can be chilly in October.

Nearby St-Père-sous-Vézelay (2 km); Avallon (15 km); Auxerre (50 km); Chablis and Sancerre (50 km) – vineyards.

Place du Pontot 89450
Vézelay
Tel 03.86.33.24.40
Fax 03.86.33.30.05
Location in middle of town; with walled flower garden and car parking
Meals breakfast
Prices rooms 350F-1050F (child sharing room 100F); breakfast 50F
Rooms 9 double, one single, all with bath and shower (4 twin); all rooms have

phone, radio
Facilities sitting-room, bar, breakfast room
Credit cards DC, MC, V
Children accepted
Disabled not suitable for wheelchairs
Pets accepted; 50F charge
Closed Nov to Easter
Manager Christian Abadie

The East

Town hotel, Arnay-le-Duc

Chez Camille

Armand Poinsot's excellent cooking (traditional but light) is only
one attraction of this captivating little hotel. The mostly compact
bedrooms are tastefully decorated and cluttered with antiques –
and effectively double-glazed against noise from the RN 6. Much
cheaper rooms in the modern Clair de Lune annexe.

■ 1 Place Edouard-Herriot, 21230 Arnay-le-Duc (Côte-d'Or)
Tel 03.80.90.01.38 **Fax** 03.80.9 0.04.64 **Meals** breakfast, lunch, dinner
Prices rooms 400F-600F; menus 160F-4950F **Rooms** 14, all with bath,
central heating, phone, TV **Credit cards** AE, DC, V **Closed** never

---

Converted mill, Avallon

Moulin des Templiers

A recent report confirms our affection for this modest, captivating
stop-over on the way through Burgundy. Breakfast is served on
the riverside terrace on fine days, otherwise in a tiny room – there
may be a queue. The pretty bedrooms are mostly small, and the
smallest is minute. No alcohol is served.

■ Vallée du Cousin, Pontaubert, 89200 Avallon (Yonne) **Tel** 03.86.
34.10.80 **Meals** breakfast **Prices** rooms 250F-350F; breakfast 36F
Rooms 14, all with shower, phone **Credit cards** not accepted **Closed** Nov
to mid-Mar

Château hotel, Bagnols

Château de Bagnols

Some expensive château hotels are simply smart, or luxurious, or
full of character, or in exceptionally privileged settings. Bagnols is
entirely extraordinary – a medieval fortress restored and furnished
to be perfect in every detail. Send for the brochure before you dismiss the idea of paying the prices. 'Loved it; would certainly go
back,' says our ecstatic nominating reader.

■ 69620 Bagnols (Rhône) **Tel** 04.74.71.40.00 **Fax** 04.74.71.40.49
Meals breakfast, lunch, dinner **Prices** rooms 2,200F-3,000F; suites
4,000F-5,000F; breakfast 120F **Rooms** 20, all with bath, central heating,
phone, TV, hairdrier **Credit cards** AE, DC, MC, V **Closed** end-Oct to
mid-Apr

Converted mill, Bonnevaux-le-Prieuré

Le Moulin du Prieuré

Eight neat bedrooms are located in little modern chalets in the
garden of this converted watermill which offers complete peace,
wonderful scenery and competent cooking. You prepare your own
breakfast (an arrangement that suits trout-fishing guests).

■ 25560 Bonnevaux-le-Prieuré (Doubs) **Tel** 03.81.59.28.79
Fax 03.81.59.21.47 **Meals** breakfast, lunch, dinner **Prices** rooms 350F;
breakfast 30F, menus 280F-350F (at least one meal obligatory) **Rooms** 8,
all with bath or shower, phone, TV, minibar **Credit cards** AE, DC, MC, V
Closed mid-Nov to early Mar, Sun evening, Mon

The East

Country inn, La Celle-Saint-Cyr

La Fontaine aux Muses

'We absolutely loved it,' says a weary traveller refreshed by the 'delightful' pool of this creeper-covered rural auberge, which also offers golf, tennis and a music room where the family often play. Simple rooms opening on to the garden. Good simple cooking with an emphasis on fish; slow service.

■ Route de la Fontaine, 89116 La Celle-Saint-Cyr (Yonne)
Tel 03.86.73.40.22 **Fax** 03.86.73.48.66 **Meals** breakfast, lunch, dinner
Prices rooms 345F-650F; breakfast 38F, menu 185F **Rooms** 17, all
with bath or shower, central heating, phone **Credit cards** MC, V
Closed Mon; restaurant only, Tue lunch

Restaurant with rooms, Chablis

Hostellerie des Clos

You go here for the food; the modern, tasteful but unremarkable rooms are a bonus. The designer-decorated dining-room is light and stylish; the light, innovative cooking (one Michelin star, two toques from Gault-Millau) makes full use of the local white wines.

■ Rue Jules Rathier, 89800 Chablis (Yonne) **Tel** 03.86.42.10.63
Fax 03.86.42.17.11 **Meals** breakfast, lunch, dinner **Prices** rooms 250F-
530F; breakfast 60F, menus 175F-420F **Rooms** 26, all with bath, central
heating, phone, TV, radio, minibar **Credit cards** MC, V **Closed** 2 weeks
Christmas and New Year; Wed and Thu lunch from Oct to Apr

Château hotel, Chagny

Hostellerie du Château de Bellecroix

An approving report from a discriminating reader restores this creeper-covered château to the guide. It combines 12thC and 18thC architecture to magical effect. Comfortable bedrooms, some in the turrets, with plenty of antiques and views over the parkland. Large pool. 'Excellent' food.

■ Route Nationale 6, 71150 Chagny (Saône-et-Loire) **Tel** 03.85.87.13.86
Fax 03.85.91.28.62 **Meals** breakfast, lunch, dinner **Prices** rooms 600F-
1,000F; breakfast 63F, menus 260F-360F **Rooms** 21, all with bath or
shower, central heating, phone, TV, minibar **Credit cards** AE, DC, MC, V
Closed 20 Dec to 15 Feb; Wed, Oct to end May; restaurant only, Wed;
Jul, Aug

Town hotel, Chagny

Hôtel Lameloise

Jacques Lameloise maintains the reputation of this calm shuttered house, established by his father Jean, as one of the best restaurants in France. It is a comfortable hotel, too, with tastefully furnished bedrooms and solidly traditional public areas. Relais & Châteaux, but not at all snooty.

■ 36 Place d'Armes, 71150 Chagny (Saône-et-Loire) **Tel** 03.85.87.08.85
Fax 03.85.87.03.57 **Meals** breakfast, lunch, dinner **Prices** rooms 650F-
1,500F; menus 370F-600F **Rooms** 17, all with bath, phone, TV; some
have air-conditioning **Credit cards** AE, MC, V **Closed** Wed, Thu until
5 pm; mid-Dec to mid-Jan

The East

Chalet hotel, Chamonix

Hôtel du Jeu de Paume

Parisian chic comes to the mountains: this offshoot of the Jeu de Paume in Paris, newly built in traditional chalet style, has immediately become one of the most desirable places to stay in the Chamonix valley. Pine-panelled bedrooms. Small indoor pool and sauna.

■ 705, Route du Chapeau, Le Lavancher, 74400 Chamonix (Haute-Savoie) **Tel** 04.50.54.03.76 **Fax** 04.50.54.10.75 **Meals** breakfast, lunch, dinner **Prices** rooms 890F-1,390F; breakfast 65F, menus 165F-280F **Rooms** 22, all with bath, central heating, phone, TV, radio, minibar, hairdrier **Credit cards** AE, DC, MC, V **Closed** mid-May to mid-Jun, mid-Oct to mid-Dec

---

Town hotel, Charolles

Hôtel de la Poste

A prime example of an unassuming provincial hotel doing a sound job. The white-painted building is immaculately maintained, as is the smart bar-salon; and the dining-room has been made positively ritzy by small-town standards. It is also possible to dine in the lovely internal garden.

■ 2 Ave de la Libération, 71120 Charolles (Saône-et-Loire) **Tel** 03.85.24.11.32 **Fax** 03.85.24.05.74 **Meals** breakfast, lunch, dinner **Prices** rooms 270F-360F, 2 suites 340F-600F; breakfast 45F, menus 120F-260F **Rooms** 13, all with bath or shower, central heating, phone, TV **Credit cards** AE, MC, V **Closed** Sun evening, Mon; Nov

---

Village hotel, Chassignelles

Hôtel de l'Ecluse No. 79

The *écluse* is the nearby lock on the canal in front of this infant enterprise – a peaceful row of houses boldly but sympathetically converted to provide (at present) seven tastefully furnished bedrooms with smart bathrooms, as well as pleasantly rustic dining-rooms and a bar. Charming *patronne*, modest prices.

■ 89160 Chassignelles (Yonne) **Tel** 03.86.75.18.51 **Fax** 03.86.75.02.04 **Meals** breakfast, lunch, dinner **Prices** rooms 175F-300F; breakfast 25F, menus 75F-140F, children's 45F **Rooms** 7, all with bath or shower, central heating, phone, TV, hairdrier **Credit cards** DC, MC, V **Closed** never

---

Village hotel, Châteauneuf

Hostellerie du Château

The picturesque hostellerie, cleverly converted from a 15thC presbytery close to the château, is in keeping with the medieval village around it: old stone walls, quiet rustic rooms and terraced gardens. In the beamed restaurant wholesome Burgundian dishes are the order of the day. 'Very good value,' says a recent report.

■ Châteauneuf, 21320 Pouilly-en-Auxois (Côte-d'Or) **Tel** 03.80.49.22.00 **Fax** 03.80.49.21.27 **Meals** breakfast, lunch, dinner **Prices** rooms 270F-430F; menu 140F-220F **Rooms** 17, all with bath or shower, central heating, phone **Credit cards** AE, MC, V **Closed** Dec to mid-Feb

The East

Town inn, Châtillon-sur-Seine

Hôtel de la Côte d'Or

This creeper-covered family-run auberge in a leafy garden offers prettily decorated rooms at modest prices, friendly but proper service and food that is interesting and competently cooked (and served on the terrace when the weather permits).

■ Rue Charles-Ronot, 21400 Châtillon-sur-Seine (Côte-d'Or)
Tel 03.80.91.13.29 **Fax** 03.80.91.29.15 **Meals** breakfast, lunch, dinner
Prices rooms 320F-600F; breakfast 38F; menus 95F-180F **Rooms** 10, all with central heating, phone, TV **Credit cards** AE, DC, MC, V **Closed** Jan

---

Country house hotel, Chonas-l'Amballan

Domaine de Clairefontaine

Of the Girardons' two operations (see also the Marais St Jean) this has the higher reputation for food, with one Michelin star. The handsome old house in splendid, peaceful park-like grounds, is family-run without pretension, and offers entirely comfortable rooms at modest prices.

■ Chonas-l'Amballan, 38121 Reventin-Vaugris (Isère)
Tel 04.74.58.81.52 **Fax** 04.74.58.80.93 **Meals** breakfast, lunch, dinner
Prices rooms 150F-350F; breakfast 45F, menus 150F-350F **Rooms** 16, all with bath or shower, central heating, phone **Credit cards** AE, DC, MC, V **Closed** Dec, Jan; restaurant only, Sun evening and Monday lunch

---

Farmhouse hotel, Chonas-l'Amballan

Le Marais Saint-Jean

For some years now in the same ownership as the Clairefontaine, this neat farmhouse conversion has a private-home atmosphere, much of which has recently undergone redecoration. Modern comforts blend with the original timbered ceilings, beams and quarry tiles. Good food served in a beamed dining-room or on a sunny terrace.

■ Chonas-l'Amballan, 38121 Reventin-Vaugris (Isère)
Tel 04.74.58.83.28 **Fax** 04.74.58.81.9 6 **Meals** breakfast, lunch, dinner
Prices rooms 650F-700F; breakfast 60F, menus 150F-350F **Rooms** 10, all with bath, phone, satellite TV, minibar **Credit cards** AE, DC, MC, V
Closed Feb to mid Mar, Nov; restaurant only, Wed and Thurs lunch

---

Town hotel, Cluny

Hôtel de Bourgogne

The most comfortable and central hotel in Cluny, this attractive stone mansion, dating from 1817, is built around a garden and courtyard. The elegant setting and Burgundian specialities of the restaurant draw many non-residents

■ Place de l'Abbaye, 71250 Cluny (Saône-et-Loire) **Tel** 03.85.59.00.58
Fax 03.85.59.03.73 **Meals** breakfast, lunch, dinner **Prices** rooms 430F-990F; breakfast 55F, menus 200F-330F **Rooms** 15, all with bath, central heating, phone, TV **Credit cards** AE, DC, MC, V **Closed** mid-Nov to Feb, Tue; restaurant Tue, and Wed lunch

The East

Riverside hotel, Condrieu

Hôtellerie Beau Rivage

The 'beau rivage' is that of the Rhône – not an entirely appropriate description, given the nearby chemical works. But the immediate surroundings of this elegantly furnished place are 'most agreeable', the staff welcoming and the Michelin-starred food 'excellent'.

■ 69420 Condrieu (Rhône) **Tel** 04.74.59.52.24 **Fax** 04.74.59.59.36 **Meals** 20break fast, lunch, dinner **Prices** rooms 500F-820F; breakfast 65F, menus 170F-610F **Rooms** 24, all with bath or shower, central heating, phone **Credit cards** AE, DC, MC, V **Closed** never

---

Village hotel, Curtil-Vergy

Hôtel Le Manassès

What better way to spend an overnight stop in Burgundy than in the heart of a working vineyard in the Hautes Côtes de Nuits? The 'beautifully furnished' and well equipped rooms in a converted outbuilding offer remarkable value, and in the next-door wine museum Yves Chaley will treat you to a taste of his wines. Recommended restaurants nearby.

■ 21220 Curtil-Vergy (Côte-d'Or) **Tel** 03.80.61.43.81 **Fax** 03.80.61.42.79 **Meals** breakfast **Prices** rooms 400F; breakfast 50F **Rooms** 7, all with bath, central heating, air conditioning, phone, TV, minibar **Credit cards** AE, MC, V **Closed** Dec to Feb

---

Country hotel, Doussard

Marceau Hôtel

Recommended 'without reservation,' says a visitor of this plain-looking but welcoming family-run hotel, near lake Annecy. The beautiful mountain views are not the only attraction: bedrooms are spacious and dotted with antiques, there is a cosy sitting-room, a rambling garden and a panoramic dining terrace.

■ Bout du Lac, 74210 Doussard (Haute-Savoie) **Tel** 04.50.44.30.11 **Fax** 04.50.44.39.44 **Meals** breakfast, lunch, dinner **Prices** rooms 480F-680F; breakfast 50F, menus 130F-330F **Rooms** 16, all with bath or shower, central heating, phone, TV, radio **Credit cards** AE, DC, MC, V **Closed** Nov to 15 Feb

---

Château hotel, Fleurville

Château de Fleurville

Unlike so many château hotels, this is not a formal, luxury establishment – the atmosphere is pleasantly relaxed and it is reasonably priced. Many original 16thC features have been retained and, despite various modernizations, there is still a medieval atmosphere. Bedrooms are simply furnished. Tennis and swimming-pool.

■ 71260 Fleurville (Saône-et-Loire) **Tel** 03.85.33.12.17 **Fax** 03.85.33.95.34 **Meals** breakfast, lunch, dinner **Prices** rooms 420F, apartment 770F; breakfast 40F, menus 165F-250F **Rooms** 15, all with bath, central heating, phone **Credit cards** DC, MC, V **Closed** Nov to end Feb; restaurant only, Mon lunch

The East

Hôtel de la Halle

The façade and interior of this town-centre Logis are undergoing renovation as the guide goes to press, and we look forward to reports on its smarter appearance. What captivates British visitors and local regulars alike is the scrupulous housekeeping, excellent traditional Burgundian cuisine and exceptionally low prices.

■ Place de la Halle, 71640 Givry (Saône-et-Loire) **Tel** 03.85.44.32.45 **Fax** 03.85.44.49.45 **Meals** breakfast, lunch, dinner **Prices** rooms 210F-280F; breakfast 25F, menus 90F-180F **Rooms** 9, all with bath or shower, central heating, phone **Credit cards** AE, DC, MC, V **Closed** mid-Nov to early Dec

---

Chalet hotel, Goumois

Hôtel Taillard

A steady flow of readers approve of this pretty chalet in a wooded valley on the Swiss border. They like the wonderful views from the breakfast terrace, the delightful garden, the comfortable rooms, the friendly atmosphere and (not least) the food – 'delicious, if slightly repetitive'.

■ 25470 Goumois (Doubs) **Tel** 03.81.44.20.75 **Fax** 03.81.44.26.15 **Meals** breakfast, lunch, dinner **Prices** rooms 275F-480F; breakfast 52F; menus 135F-370F **Rooms** 24, all with bath or shower, central heating, phone, TV **Credit cards** AE, DC, MC, V **Closed** mid-Nov to mid-Mar

---

Château hotel, Igé

Château d'Igé

This turreted, creeper-covered castle retains its medieval atmosphere despite its conversion into a luxurious Relais & Châteaux hotel. Above-average food is served in front of a huge open hearth in the massively beamed dining-room – a marked contrast to the pleasant new conservatory.

■ 71960 Igé (Saône-et-Loire) **Tel** 03.85.33.33.99 **Fax** 03.85.33.41.41 **Meals** breakfast, lunch, dinner **Prices** rooms 480F-740F, suites 895F-1,100F; breakfast 70F, menus 195F-365F **Rooms** 13, all with bath, central heating, phone, TV, hairdrier **Credit cards** AE, DC, V **Closed** Dec to Mar

---

Bed and breakfast farmhouse, Levernois

Le Parc

Beaune has a dearth of reasonably priced accommodation but the Parc, 5 km away, offers excellent value and a pleasant rural setting. It is a simple hotel, converted from an old farmhouse, and run rather like a private home. Breakfast is served in a pretty courtyard.

■ Levernois, 21200 Beaune (Côte-d'Or) **Tel** 03.80.24.63.00 **Fax** 03.80. 24.21.19 **Meals** breakfast **Prices** rooms 180F-480F **Rooms** 25, all with bath or shower, central heating, phone, TV **Credit cards** MC, V **Closed** 10 days in early Dec

The East

Village hotel, Meursault

Hôtel les Charmes

This 18thC maison bourgeoise sits peacefully in a park-like garden with mature trees. A refined private-house atmosphere prevails: in the bedrooms the furniture is antique and elegant, the decorative schemes individual and harmonious. Secure parking. Fairly new to the guide – reports welcome.

■ 10 Place du Murger, 21190 Meursault (Côte-d'Or) **Tel** 03.80.21.63.53 **Fax** 03.80.21.62.89 **Meals** breakfast **Prices** rooms 390F-550F; breakfast 45F **Rooms** 14, all with bath, central heating, phone, TV, minibar **Credit cards** MC, V **Closed** Dec to Mar

---

Village bed-and-breakfast, Meursault

Les Magnolias

In a pleasantly quiet location, Les Magnolias is a polished and unusually stylish place – a group of old houses around a small courtyard, with spacious bedrooms that have been individually decorated with some panache. Expect to walk to a restaurant. New to the guide a few years ago; more reports, please.

■ 8 Rue Pierre Joigneaux, 21190 Meursault (Côte-d'Or) **Tel** 03.80. 21.23.23 **Fax** 03.80.21.29.10 **Meals** breakfast **Prices** rooms 380F-750F; breakfast 45F **Rooms** 12, all with bath or shower, central heating, phone; TV on request **Credit cards** AE, MC, V **Closed** Dec to Feb

---

Medieval inn, Pérouges

Ostellerie du Vieux Pérouges

The Ostellerie is at the heart of the perfectly preserved little medieval town of Pérouges. Excellent meals are served in the charming old dining rooms, while slices of *galette Pérougienne* (a sort of sugary pizza) are dispensed from the kitchen window. Bedrooms are in four other houses, the best splendidly old (and pricey).

■ Place du Tilleul, Pérouges, 01800 Meximieux (Ain) **Tel** 04.74.61.00.88 **Fax** 04.74.34.77.9 0 **Meals** breakfast, lunch, dinner **Prices** rooms 390F-950F; menus 190F-420F **Rooms** 29, all with bath, phone **Credit cards** V **Closed** never

---

Town hotel, St-Florentin

La Grande Chaumière

This attractive pink, turn-of-the-century building with a leafy garden makes a pleasant gastronomic stop-over on the route south. It's not strong on character: bedrooms are in an essentially modern style, the Michelin-starred restaurant light and smartly furnished.

■ 3 Rue des Capucins, 89600 St-Florentin (Yonne) **Tel** 03.86.35.15.12 **Fax** 03.86.35.33.14 **Meals** breakfast, lunch, dinner **Prices** rooms 350F-850F, breakfast 56F; menus 135F-275F **Rooms** 10, all with bath or shower, central heating, phone, TV **Credit cards** AE, DC, MC, V **Closed** first week Sep, mid-Dec to mid-Jan; Wed out of season

The East

Country inn, St-Lattier

Le Lièvre Amoureux

One reporter reckons the food at this old hunting lodge is of star quality. Michelin disagrees, but there are other attractions – not least the leafy garden and the pool, which is directly accessible from the pine-panelled rooms in the modern 'outbuildings'; in the main building there are more traditional alternatives.

■ La Gare, 38840 St-Lattier (Isère) **Tel** 04.76.64.50.67 **Fax** 04.76.64.31.21 **Meals** breakfast, lunch, dinner **Prices** rooms 320F-460F; breakfast 60F, menus 179F-290F **Rooms** 14, all with bath, central heating, phone, TV, hairdrier **Credit cards** DC, MC, V **Closed** Nov to mid-Feb

---

Converted abbey, Tonnerre

L'Abbaye Saint-Michel

Not everyone likes the way this ancient abbey has been elevated to Relais & Châteaux status – using plate glass or stainless steel as readily as stone and wood. But the innovative cooking deserves its toques and stars from gastronomic guides. One dining-room is a stone vault, the other gives views of the countryside.

■ Montée de Saint-Michel, 89700 Tonnerre (Yonne) **Tel** 03.86.55.05.99 **Fax** 03.86.55.00.10 **Meals** breakfast, lunch, dinner **Prices** rooms 590F-1,600F; suites 1,800F-1,900F; breakfast 55F-85F, menus 330F- 620F **Rooms** 14, all with bath, central heating, phone, TV, minibar **Credit cards** AE, DC, MC, V **Closed** never

---

Ski resort hotel, Val-Thorens

Fitz Roy

The ski resort of Val-Thorens is the highest Relais & Château in Europe. It is an exceptionally civilized and welcoming chalet-style hotel with light, pine-furnished bedrooms. Serious food – about the best in the resort. There is a classical music festival in January.

■ 73440 Val-Thorens (Savoie) **Tel** 04.79.00.04.78 **Fax** 04.79.00.06.11 **Meals** breakfast, lunch, dinner **Prices** DB&B 900F-1,650F **Rooms** 36, all with spa bath, central heating, phone, TV, radio, minibar, hairdrier **Credit cards** AE, DC, MC, V **Closed** early May to 2 Dec

---

Lakeside hotel, Veyrier-du-Lac

La Demeure de Chavoire

A splendid combination of traditional elegance and modern comfort, set in a pretty garden on the shores of lovely lake Annecy. Every room has been thoughtfully and richly furnished; the bedrooms are all individually decorated in romantic style, and named after local beauty spots and Annecy's famous writers.

■ Route d'Annecy-Chavoire, 74290 Veyrier-du-Lac (Haute-Savoie) **Tel** 04.50.60.04.38 **Fax** 04.50.60.05.36 **Meals** breakfast, snacks **Prices** rooms 650F-1,000F; suites 1,100F-1,550F; breakfast 68F **Rooms** 13, all with bath, central heating, phone, TV, radio, minibar, hairdrier **Credit cards** AE, DC, MC, V **Closed** never

The South-West

Area introduction

The Limousin hills represent the watershed between the basins of the Charente and the Loire, to the north, and that of the Garonne and its tributaries, to the south; and the start of our South-west region. For many British visitors, the valleys of the Dordogne and the Lot represent an ideal, not only of France but of life itself – life in a kind climate and a fertile landscape. And the concentration of our kind of hotel here is second only to that in Provence. To the west lie the peerless vineyards of Bordeaux, and the forests and limitless beaches of the Landes. To the south, Gascony and the Basque country of the Pyrenees.

Contenders in the South-west

Barcus, Chez Chilo 05.59.28.90.79 Idiosyncratic village hotel, smartly furnished; good food.

Cadéac-les-Bains, Hostellerie du Val d'Aure 05.62.98.60.63 Secluded Logis in wooded grounds with pool and tennis, near the ski resort of St-Lary.

Les Courrières, Les Murailles 05.53.05.58.09 English-run farmhouse B&B (option to dine with owners) tastefully restored; in large garden with pool.

Gramat, Château de Roumegouse 05.65.33.63.81 Prettily furnished mini-château surrounded by woods; pool.

Grenade-sur-l'Adour, Pain Adour et Fantaisie 05.58.45.18.80 Handsome riverside house with stylishly modern furnishings and knockout food – 2 stars, 4 *toques*.

Lascabanes, La Petite Auberge 05.65.31.82.51 A captivating group of stone farm buildings in a quiet country setting; charmingly simple stone-walled rooms.

Loubressac, Château de Gamot 05.65.38.58.50 Little 17thC château furnished in period, run as a B&B in summer by its Parisian owners; pool, but not available July and August.

Mussidan, Le Bastit 05.53.81.32.33 Carefully furnished country house in flowery garden (with pool) run by friendly Anglo-French couple.

Paulhiac, L'Ormeraie 05.53.36.45.96 Carefully converted farmhouse in lovely country setting, run in house-party style by retired publisher.

Port-de-Lanne, La Vieille Auberge 05.58.89.16.29 Warmly furnished village Logis with pleasant garden and pool.

St-Jean-de-Luz, Parc Victoria 05.59.26.78.78 Immaculate, elegantly furnished villa in leafy gardens with excellent pool.

St-Pierre-de-Côle, Domaine de Doumarias 05.53.62.34.37 Simply but tastefully furnished country B&B with pool in lush garden. **St-Robert, La Maison Anglaise** 05.55.25.19.58 Freshly decorated 19thC villa in peaceful setting with long views; carefully run by English proprietors.

Segos, Domaine de Bassibé 05.62.09.46.71 Small, intimate, comfortable hotel with lovely views and good chef.

Toulouse, Hôtel des Beaux Arts 05.61.23.40.50 Designer style in central Toulouse.

Valence-sur-Baïse, La Ferme de Flaran 05.62.28.58.22 Freshly decorated farmhouse with dining terrace and pleasant pool, in countryside; decent food.

The South-West

Hôtel Ohantzea

This is by some margin the cheapest of our main recommendations in the Pyrénées-Atlantiques, and accordingly simple – but no less charming for that.

The timbered and shuttered buildings is set on the road through the attractive mountain village of Cambo-les-Bains, which is renowned for its mild climate – Edmond Rostand, author of *Cyrano de Bergerac*, came her to take the spa waters and liked it so much that he built a house nearby – see below.

The house, has been in the Ithurria family for no less than three centuries, and dates from the 17thC. It was originally a farm, but it is now very much a family home with old furniture dotted about, satisfyingly rustic and tasteful throughout: uneven wooden floors, beamed ceilings and an unmatchable patina of age on well looked-after family possessions. The bedrooms are notably spacious, some with balconies.

The menus offer fair value and the dining-room is pleasant enough. "This is not a modern house," says Mme Ithurria in a pleasantly self-effacing way – "and we have no 'formula' – except to provide the atmosphere of a family home and fair prices."

Nearby Villa Arnaga, Rostand' house, on the D932 a short

Aïnhoa 64250 Cambo-les-Bains
Tel 05.59.29.90.50
Location in middle of village, 10 km SW of Cambo-les-Bains; with garden and car parking behind
Meals breakfast, lunch, dinner
Prices rooms 280F-315F; menus 120F-220F
Rooms 10 double, 9 with bath and shower (3 twin); all rooms have central heating, phone

Facilities sitting-room, dining-room
Credit cards AE, DC, MC, V
Children welcome
Disabled no special facilities
Pets accepted
Closed Dec and Jan
Proprietor M. Ithurria

The South-West

Le Chatenet

This lovely 17thC manor house has prompted a steady flow of approving reports from readers over the years of its inclusion in the guide, and the latest gives the clearest possible view: 'We left wanting to stay longer, and we will certainly go back.'

The appeal of the place stems not only from its rural surroundings – down a country track off the busy riverside road, blissfully far removed from the tourist bustle of Brantôme – but also from its informal atmosphere: despite evidently heavy investment in rich furnishings, the Laxtons attach importance to maintaining the family-home feel, and it shows. There are vases of fresh flowers on low tables, deep armchairs, and country antiques in both the sitting-room and breakfast room, which form part of the Laxtons' home. Bedrooms are spacious, with elegant decoration. In the cosy clubhouse there's an 'honesty' bar and room for wet-weather activities. Outside, deckchairs are scattered invitingly around the garden beneath shady trees, and there is plenty of space for children.

Breakfasts (Magdeleine has a repertoire of 10 sorts of home-made *confiture*) are served on a covered terrace in fine weather, and guests may have the use of an outdoor barbecue. If do-it-yourself doesn't appeal, there are several excellent restaurants nearby. The 'very cordial' welcome is 'enhanced by the dog'.

Nearby Brantôme – monks' garden, belfry, troglodyte caves; Bourdeilles (10 km) – château; Chancelade (30 km) – abbey.

24310 Brantôme
Tel 05.53.05.81.08
Fax 05.53.05.85.52
Location 1.5 km SW of town, off D78; in large grounds with ample car parking
Meals breakfast
Prices rooms 550F-590F, suites 800F
Rooms 8 double, all with bath (6 twin); 2 suites; one cottage with 2 double rooms; all rooms have central heating, phone; TV on request

Facilities sitting-room, breakfast room, clubhouse with billiards; heated swimming-pool, tennis
Credit cards MC, V
Children welcome if well behaved **Disabled** access easy; 2 ground-floor bedrooms, one specially equipped
Pets welcome if well behaved
Closed at times Nov to Apr – phone to check
Proprietors Philippe and Magdeleine Laxton

The South-West

Converted mill, Brantôme

Moulin de l'Abbaye

Our visits to this exquisite little mill have always left us wishing to stay longer; why, we wonder, do we not hear from more readers about it? Could the Relais & Châteaux prices be to blame?

The setting is the thing. The shady riverside terrace, illuminated in the evening, is an idyllic place for a drink or a meal while admiring Brantôme's unusual angled bridge, the tower of the abbey or the swans gliding by. Wonderful views over the river and the old houses of one of the prettiest villages in France are also to be had from many of the bedrooms – all beautifully decorated and comfortably furnished (some have four-poster beds and antiques, others are more modern).

Traditional Périgord dishes with a *nouvelle* touch earn the restaurant 3 *toques* from Gault-Millau and a star from Michelin. The dining-room is as pleasant a place to enjoy this excellent cuisine as the terrace it leads to, though we can raise no enthusiasm for the 'Monet-style' colour scheme. There are fresh flowers, sparkling glass and silverware, and soft lighting in the evening. Staff are correct and courteous; service is efficient.

Nearby Monk's garden, belfry; Antonne-et-Trigonant (3 km) – 15thC Périgord manor; Bourdeilles (10 km) – château.

1 Rte de Bourdeilles 24310 Brantôme
Tel 05.53.05.80.22
Location on edge of town, 20 km N of Périgueux; with garden, and ample car parking across road
Meals breakfast, lunch, dinner
Prices rooms 550F-950F, apartments 1,000F-1,350F; breakfast 75F, menus 220F-450F
Rooms 17 double,

3 apartments, all with bath; all rooms have central heating, TV, minibar
Facilities dining-room, sitting-room
Credit cards AE, DC, MC, V
Children welcome
Disabled no special facilities
Pets dogs accepted
Closed Nov to May; restaurant only, Mon lunch
Manager M. Dessum

The South-West

Manor house hotel, Le Buisson-de-Cadouin

Manoir de Bellerive

Our most recent report on this fine Napoléon III manor house sums up its attractions comprehensively: 'Magnificent rooms, spectacular grounds, very friendly staff'. Sadly our correpondent didn't sample dinner, which is the latest development in the Manoir's gradual progress towards full hotelhood.

The Manoir is set in lovely peaceful grounds which stretch down to the banks of the Dordogne. Sun beds and tables are liberally scattered over the lawns, and there is a swimming-pool and tennis court tucked away between the pine trees and flower borders. If you prefer to watch the world – and the slow-moving river – go by from a more elevated position, you can sit out on the balustraded first-floor terrace. Once you step inside the lofty entrance hall, you are transported back in time. The elegant staircase sweeps up to spacious and very comfortable designer-decorated bedrooms. Breakfast can be taken on the terrace or in a room with murals on the pale walls.

For six months of the year (mid-March to mid-June and mid-September to mid-November), the hotel is also used as a conference centre. At other times, peace reigns.

Nearby walking, golf; Lascaux – caves; Les Eyzies; Sarlat (35 km).

Route de Siorac 24480 Le Buisson-de-Cadouin
Tel 05.53.27.16.19
Fax 05.53.22.09.05
Location in countryside, 800 m SE of Le Buisson-de-Cadouin on D25; with grounds and ample car parking
Meals breakfast, dinner; lunch at weekends
Prices rooms 440F-800F; breakfast 55F-70F; menu 120F-190F

Rooms 16 double, 8 with bath, 8 with shower (6 twin); all rooms have central heating, phone, satellite TV, minibar **Facilities** sitting-room, breakfast room, sauna, jacuzzi, conference facilities; swimming-pool, tennis court
Credit cards MC, V
Children accepted
Disabled access difficult
Pets accepted
Closed Nov to mid-Apr
Proprietor Mme Huin

The South-West

Le Moulin du Roc

A steady flow of approving reports from readers confirm the attractions of this delectable old walnut-oil mill, one of that rare breed of hotels that give you the sensation of pampering without charging £100 a night for a room. 'Absolutely stellar,' says the most recent – although the Moulin is less stellar than it used to be (these days it rates 'only' one Michelin star).

The setting on the banks of the Dronne is wonderfully romantic; the waterside gardens are lush, secluded, shady and bursting with colour. Inside the rough-stone 17thC building, old beams, fireplaces, mill machinery, fine old carved furniture, rich fabrics and massive oil paintings – together with plenty of ornaments and flower arrangements – create a style that is highly individual, or even eccentric. Some may find it rather heavy. The same cannot be said of the food: in the land of *foie gras*, Alain Gardillou, who has taken over from his mother, manages to build on culinary traditions to produce remarkably light and inventive dishes. Breakfasts are a treat, with home-made rolls and jams, beautifully served. Bedrooms vary in size, but do not disappoint – pretty, cosy, with their full share of antiques.

Nearby Brantôme; Bourdeilles (15 km) – château.

24530 Champagnac-de-Belair
Tel 05.53.02.86.00
Fax 05.53.54.21.31
Location in hamlet, on D82 and D83, 6 km NE of Brantôme; with large garden and ample car parking
Meals breakfast, lunch, dinner
Prices rooms 380F-680F; breakfast 55F, menus 150F-280F, children's 100F
Rooms 10 double (2 twin), 4 suites; all with bath; all rooms have central heating,

phone, TV, minibar
Facilities sitting-room, dining-room; heated swimming-pool, tennis court, terrace
Credit cards AE, DC, MC, V
Children welcome
Disabled two ground-floor rooms
Pets accepted
Closed 2 Jan to 8 Mar; restaurant only, Tue, Wed lunch
Proprietors M. and Mme Gardillou

The South-West

Manor house, Coly

Manoir d'Hautegente

A reader describes this creeper-clad manor house as 'so good that I wouldn't tell you about it if it were not already in the guide'. We'll just have to hope that he doesn't mind our promotion of the Manoir – new to the guide a few years ago – to a full entry.

The house, set in beautiful wooded grounds, has been in the Hamelin family for about 300 years, and is now run by Edith Hamelin and her son Patrick. It was built as a forge in the 13th century, later became a mill (using the stream that runs beside it), was then embellished and turned into a family residence and was finally converted into a hotel – but with the private-home feel entirely intact. Public rooms and the spacious, comfortable bedrooms are imaginatively decorated with family antiques and paintings. Dinner in the pretty vaulted dining-room is a five-course affair – 'first-class cuisine' which inevitably includes home-produced *foie gras*, another of the Hamelins' commercial successes. Wines are reasonably priced.

In the pleasant grassy grounds there is a smart pool that gets plenty of sun. A warm welcome from the family awaits.

Nearby châteaux; Lascaux (15 km); Sarlat (25 km).

Coly 24120 Terrasson
Tel 05.53.51.68.03
Fax 05.53.50.38.52
Location in countryside, 6 km SE of Le Lardin on the D62; with grounds and car parking
Meals breakfast, dinner
Prices rooms 500F-950F; breakfast 60F, menus 200F-380F
Rooms 12 double, all with bath (2 twin); all rooms have central heating, phone; hairdrier, TV

Facilities dining-room, sitting-room; heated swimming-pool
Credit cards MC, V
Children welcome
Disabled one ground-floor room
Pets accepted if well behaved
Closed Nov to Easter
Proprietors Edith Hamelin and Patrick Hamelin

The South-West

Les Glycines

'I reckon it's the best in town now,' says a trusted reporter of this handsome 19th-century house – the 'town' being the touristy capital of the prehistory business. Les Glycines stands close to the station on the edge of Les Eyzies, in the lush and beautiful gardens that are one of the hotel's chief attractions; the name means wisteria, and that lovely flower is to be found here in abundance. There is also a swimming-pool and a terrace for drinks, so it's an excellent place for good weather.

Indoors there are also plenty of sitting-areas, well supplied with reading material, meaning this is also an hotel where it's not unpleasant to while away time in poor weather. The dining-room and covered terrace are very attractive, too. The bedrooms are comfortable but unremarkable – few are notably spacious; those at the back are superior. There are more rooms than we generally allow in a country hotel, but the hotel does not feel large, partly because some of the rooms are in a connected annexe.

The food is 'very good,' and Madame, although rather chic and cool at first, softens when she gets to know you.

Nearby Château de Fages (15 km); Sarlat (21 km); Lascaux caves (25 km); Beynac (30 km) – village and castle.

24620 Les Eyzies-de-Tayac
Tel 05.53.06.97.07
Fax 05.53.06.92.19
Location on edge of town, on main road; with large gardens and ample car parking
Meals breakfast, lunch, dinner
Prices rooms 355F-410F; breakfast 52F; DB&B 402F-450F; menus 140F-190F
Rooms 25 double, all with bath or shower (12 twin); all rooms have central heating, phone
Facilities 2 sitting-rooms, dining-room, bar; swimming-pool
Credit cards AE, MC, V
Children accepted
Disabled access possible
Pets accepted
Closed mid Oct to mid Apr; restaurant Sat lunch out of season
Proprietors M. and Mme Henri Mercat

The South-West

La Daille

Another Dordogne establishment that combines the best of France and Britain. The mellow stone, red-roofed buildings are surrounded by gardens with glorious herbaceous borders that could only be the work of British green fingers. Rich local produce is transformed into wonderful light dishes that stand in sharp contrast to the typical Périgord menu.

British *emigrés* Barbara and Derek Brown have been running this unusual establishment, in wonderful unspoilt and hilly countryside just south of the Dordogne, for nearly 20 years now – and have built up a regular local clientele for their afternoon teas and ambitious set dinners. La Daille is a small-scale *pension* catering for no more than 7 residents and 14 non-resident diners (half board obligatory, minimum stay three days unless you can sneak in a night or two between bookings). The double bed-rooms are in a modern single-storey building – thoroughly comfortable, with big bathrooms and terraces – across the garden from the original farmhouse, which contains the cool, rustic dining-room. The one (equally comfortable) single is in an old out-building.

Nearby golf, canoeing; Domme (15 km) – *bastide*; Sarlat (25 km)

Florimont-Gaumiers 24250 Domme
Tel 05.53.28.40.71
Location in countryside, 2 km S of Gaumiers (signposted from village); in large grounds with ample car parking
Meals breakfast, afternoon tea, dinner
Prices DB&B (with wine) 455F
Rooms 3 double (2 twin), one single, all with bath or shower; all rooms have central heating
Facilities dining-room, terrace
Credit cards not accepted
Children accepted over 7
Disabled access difficult
Pets not accepted
Closed Oct to 1 May
Proprietors Mr and Mrs Derek Vaughan Brown

The South-West

Château hotel, Lacave

Château de la Treyne

We've had our eye on this little château beside the Dorgogne since an inspector came back a few years ago with a report littered with emphatically underscored adjectives – 'gorgeous ... impeccable ... exceptionally comfortable'. Of course, it is not cheap; perhaps we should be grateful that elevation to Relais & Châteaux status has not pushed prices up further.

Michèle Gombert-Devals' house has made a splendid small hotel. It starts with the advantage of a beautiful position, in woods on a low cliff cut by the meandering river Dordogne. But the compelling attraction of the château is the near-ideal balance struck between the impressiveness of a fortified manor-house and the intimacy of a genuine home. The building dates from the early 14th century, but was substantially rebuilt in the 1600s; it is now tastefully equipped with a happy mix of furnishings – comfy sofas in front of an open fire, as well as grand antiques.

There are long walks to enjoy in the grounds, and a very beautiful formal garden before which you can take breakfast. Excellent regional food is served – on the delightful terrace perched above the river in good weather.

Nearby Souillac – abbey church; Rocamadour, Sarlat.

Lacave 46200 Souillac
Tel 05.65.27.60.60
Fax 05.65.27.60.70
Location 3 km W of village on D43, 6 km SE of Souillac; in large grounds beside river, with ample private parking
Meals breakfast, lunch, dinner
Prices rooms 700F-1,600F; apartments from 1,800F; DB&B 360F; breakfast 80F, menus 180F-280F
Rooms 14 double, all with bath; all rooms have central heating, air conditioning, phone, TV
Facilities 3 sitting-rooms, dining-room, bar, billiard room, meeting-room; sauna, swimming-pool, tennis
Credit cards AE, DC, MC, V
Children welcome
Disabled access difficult
Pets accepted if well behaved
Closed 15 Nov to Easter
Proprietor Mme Michèle Gombert-Devals

The South-West

Hostellerie Le Vert

Le Vert goes from strength to strength. The attractions of this secluded 17th-century farmhouse have been greatly increased by the construction of a swimming-pool. It will doubtless remain the kind of hotel you look forward to returning to at the end of the day; it also looks set to become the kind you're disinclined to leave at all.

There is just a small side door to lead you inside. Within, all is original stone walls and beams. The dining-room opens out on to a terrace with wide views; through an arch at one end is a small sitting-room – ideal for an aperitif. The bedrooms are all comfortably and tastefully modernized, and have lovely views. The largest are quite grand and furnished with antiques. But the most attractive are in the little annexe a couple of yards from the entrance – the lower one stone-vaulted, the upper one beamed, with a marble floor. The garden has chairs and tables, and is improving in colour despite dry summers. The Philippes are a friendly and hard-working couple – he cooks (interestingly and competently), she serves (and speaks excellent English).

Nearby Bonaguil (15 km) – château; Biron castle (35 km); Monpazier (50 km) – *bastide*; Cahors (50 km) – medieval bridge.

Mauroux 46700 Puy-l'Evêque
Tel 05.65.36.51.36
Location in countryside, off D5 10 km SW of Puy-l'Evêque; 10 km SE of Fumel; in garden, with ample private car parking
Meals breakfast, lunch, dinner
Prices rooms 230F-380F; breakfast 38F, menus 100F-160F
Rooms 7 double, all with bath or shower; all have central heating, phone, TV

Facilities dining-room, sitting-room, terrace, swimming-pool
Credit cards AE, MC, V
Children welcome – children's menu 50F
Disabled no special facilities
Pets welcome at extra charge
Closed mid Nov to mid Feb
Proprietors Eva and Bernard Philippe

The South-West

Au Bon Coin du Lac

We see no sign of slippage in the high standards of Jean-Pierre Caule, the third generation of his family to run Au Bon Coin, or indeed the exacting standards of Mme Caule, who oversees things front of house.

The two-storey, stone and painted-wood house has a superb lakeside setting, with neat little footpaths inviting you to walk around the grounds. But the hotel's *raison d'être* is its Michelin-starred restaurant, and M. Caule's culinary skill as head chef (seafood is his speciality). The generally expensive feel of the place is reflected in the menu – and the prices. The dining-room has an uncluttered view of the lake and is charmingly furnished: round tables, white table-cloths, floral china and floral-covered chairs. The service is formal, as you would expect in a restaurant in this price range, but nevertheless friendly.

The bedrooms are large and luxurious; not impersonal, but rather uniform. Despite the many activities on the lake – sailing, fishing – the swings nearby and the special children's menu, this is not really a place for a family holiday. But it is ideal for those who want four-star treatment, a relaxed and friendly atmosphere and excellent food.

Nearby Lakes; beaches (5 km); Landes forest (30 km); Sabres (40 km) – railway to Marquèze Ecomuseum.

34 Ave du Lac, Mimizan
40200 Landes
Tel 05.58.09.01.55
Fax 05.58.09.40.84
Location amid forests, 2 km N of Mimizan; on edge of lake, with garden and car parking
Meals breakfast, lunch, dinner
Prices rooms 360F-650F; menus 160F-350F; reduced rates for children
Rooms 5 double, all with bath and shower; 4 suites, all with bath and shower; all rooms have central heating, phone, TV, radio, minibar
Facilities sitting-room, dining-room
Credit cards AE, V
Children welcome; special meals, baby-listening available
Disabled ground-floor bedrooms
Pets not accepted
Closed Feb; restaurant only, Sun dinner, and Mon out of season
Proprietor Jean-Pierre Caule

The South-West

Château Cordeillan-Bages

This is a château in the Bordeaux manner – not a Loire-style extravagance, but a harmoniously proportioned, single-storey stone mansion dating from the 17th century, with an associated five-acre expanse of vineyard (formerly an important one, and nowgradually gaining in stature again). The house was completely restored in 1989 and the decoration is stylish and restful. There is something of the feel of an English country house about the intimate sitting-rooms and elegant dining-room, – until you walk out on to the terrace to be confronted by vines. The bedrooms are very comfortable, with the sure hand of the interior designer given full rein.

Chef Thierry Marx, who has taken over the kitchen at Château Cordeillan-Bages, uses his skills to create new dishes based on seasonal produce, as well as traditional regional food, and of course, the wine-list is long.

The *Ecole du Bordeaux*, based within Château Cordeillan-Bages, organizes a wide choice of courses for both professional and amateur wine lovers, with visits to other châteaux in this famous wine-growing region.

Nearby Château Mouton-Rothschild (museum) (5 km).

Route des Châteaux, 33250 Pauillac
Tel 05.56.59.24.24
Fax 05.56.59.01.89
Location in wine village on D2, 40 km N of Bordeaux; in own grounds, with ample car parking
Meals breakfast, lunch, dinner
Prices rooms 720F-990F; junior suite 915F-1100F; breakfast 65F-95F, menus 180F-290F
Rooms 25 double, all with bath; all rooms have central heating, phone, TV, radio, minibar, hairdrier, safe
Facilities sitting-rooms, bar, dining-room, breakfast room
Credit cards AE, DC, V
Children welcome; babysitting available **Disabled** lift/elevator, access ramp, ground-floor rooms, toilets **Pets** small ones accepted **Closed** 10 Dec to end Jan; restaurant only, Mon and Sat lunch
Manager Alain Rabier

The South-West

Converted stables, Rocamadour

Domaine de la Rhue

Curiously, we have no reports from readers recently on this lovely little hotel, peacefully set amid rolling countryside out of sight of any other building, yet only a few kilometres away from touristy Rocamadour. But we have great confidence in the charming young proprietors, Eric and Christine Jooris.

You might be somewhat disappointed to discover that the hotel does not occupy the magnificent family-owned château, but is set in the adjoining stable block. But your disappointment would be short-lived; this superb 19th-century stone building has been imaginatively converted into a dozen pretty, spacious bedrooms. Several are suitable for families – some with discreet kitchenettes, and their own garden entrance. Breakfast is served in a pleasant salon (stone-flagged, with an open fireplace), and the Joorises are happy to make snack lunches, which can be eaten beside the glorious swimming-pool in front of the hotel.

You might also want to take advantage of Eric's other passion; he is a qualified hot-air balloon pilot and offers his guests the chance to see Rocamadour from the air – 'an experience not to be missed'.

Nearby hot-air ballooning; walks; Rocamadour (7 km); Padirac (10 km), Loubressac (20 km); Carennac (20 km).

La Rhue 46500 Rocamadour
Tel 05.65.33.71.50
Fax 05.65.33.72.48
Location in countryside, 55 km S of Brive La Gaillarde on N20 towards Cressenssac, then N140. Turn right 1 km before crossing with D673 (Racamadour-Padirac); with grounds and ample car parking
Meals breakfast
Prices rooms 380F-580F; breakfast 45F-65F

Rooms 11 double, one suite, several suitable for families, all with bath; all rooms have phone
Facilities sitting-room; swimming-pool
Credit cards MC, V
Children accepted
Disabled access easy
Pets accepted
Closed Nov to Easter
Proprietors Eric and Christine Jooris

The South-West

Village hotel, St-Cirq-Lapopie

La Pélissaria

Recent reports leave us in no doubt that the Matuchets' distinctive little hotel is as compelling as ever. And the chances of finding a room vacant have increased since they bought an old house next door to the main one, providing three additional large bedrooms (two double beds in each).

The 13th-century house clings to the steep hillside on the edge of the lovely medieval hilltop village of St-Cirq-Lapopie. It was lovingly restored by the Matuchets themselves, and its quirky character is such that you descend the stairs to the bedrooms, which look out on to the tiny garden and enjoy stunning views over the Lot valley. The bedrooms – two of them detached from the house, down the garden – are light, airy and comfortable, with close attention to detail in the furnishings.

Dinner, served in the elegant and intimate beamed dining-room (with roaring log fire on cold nights) is adventurous and delicious; Madame does all the cooking, so the choice of dishes is naturally limited. M. Matuchet is a musician, and tapes of his music provide a background to dinner. Breakfast is served *al fresco* or in your room if you prefer.

Nearby Pech-Merle caves and museum; Cahors (35 km).

St-Cirq-Lapopie 46330
Cabrerets
Tel 05.65.31.25.14
Fax 05.65.30.25.52
Location in village, 30 km E
of Cahors; with garden;
parking difficult
Meals breakfast, dinner
Prices rooms 400F-600F, suite
650F; breakfast 50F, dinner
from 150F
Rooms 8 double, 6 with bath,
2 with shower (4 twin);
2 suites with bath; all rooms
have phone, TV
Facilities dining-room, sitting-
room; small swimming-pool
Credit cards MC, V
Children welcome
Disabled one adapted
bedroom
Pets accepted
Closed mid-Nov to Apr;
restaurant only, Thu and Fri
Proprietor Marie-Françoise
Matuchet

The South-West

Arcé

Oh dear. 'The car-park was full of GB plates,' commented one reporter, 'so we beat a hasty retreat.' Bad news for those who like to escape while on their travels, but not entirely surprising: we're not the only British guide to list this delightful hotel – now run by the fifth generation of the Arcé family – and it does not face a lot of competition, here in the Basque foothills of the Pyrenees.

The setting – by a river in a typical Basque village – is a magical one, best appreciated from the dining terrace, which juts out over the water and is sheltered by a canopy of chestnut trees. The food is almost as good as the view, featuring plenty of local specialities (game, fish) – though Michelin withdrew its star a few years ago. Inside the shuttered building are spacious public rooms – a beamed sitting-room with assorted furniture and a brick fireplace, a library with books in all languages, and a smart dining-room with picture windows. Some of the bedrooms are impressively large, with an apartment-sized sitting area; others open on to small terraces with mountain views. There is a smart swimming-pool across the river.

Nearby walking, fishing, bicycling; Pyrenees; Spanish border; Atlantic coast – beaches.

64430 St-Etienne-de-Baïgorry
Tel 05.59.37.40.14
Fax 05.59.37.40.27
Location in village 10 km W of St-Jean Pied-de-Port; with garden and car parking
Meals breakfast, lunch, dinner, snacks
Prices rooms 335F-715F; suite 915F-1,080F; breakfast 50F, menus 110F-260F
Rooms 22 double, 1 single, 20 with bath, 3 with shower; 6 family rooms with bath; 1 suite; all rooms have central heating, phone, TV, hairdrier
Facilities dining-room, sitting-rooms, games room; terraces, swimming-pool, tennis court
Credit cards MC, V
Children welcome
Disabled no special facilities
Pets accepted
Closed mid-Nov to mid-Mar
Proprietor M. Arcé

The South-West

Hostellerie St-Jacques

The more we learn about the Babayous' enterprise, the more thoroughly impressed we are by their sure understanding of holiday-makers' needs and priorities.

The front of the creeper-clad 18thC building gives little clue to what lies within – or, more to the point, what lies behind: the Babayou's 'summer sitting-room', which consists of lovely sloping gardens, with masses of colourful flowers, a fair-sized pool, tennis court and plenty of shade and space for children. Inside there is an unusually large dining-room/bar decorated in fresh summery colours, with big windows which open on to the terrace above the garden. All the bedrooms are comfortable, spacious and attractively decorated; several can accommodate families.

The food is rich and varied; even the basic menu is probably enough to satisfy most appetites. A buffet breakfast/brunch is served in the garden or by the pool. Occasionally there are lively evenings with dancing and games, or communal dinners devoted to exploration of regional cuisine. Not your cup of tea? Just give it a try; you might be surprised.

Nearby Montbrun (15 km) – fortress; Brantôme (30 km) – monks' garden, château de Richemont; Rochechouart (45 km).

24470 Saint-Saud-Lacoussière
Tel 05.53.56.97.21
Fax 05.53.56.91.33
Location in quiet village, 30 km N of Brantôme; with garden and car parking
Meals breakfast/brunch, lunch, dinner
Prices rooms 250F-450F, suites 750F; DB&B 255F-285F; breakfast 45F, menus 97F-217F
Rooms 22 double (7 twin), 2 suites, all with bath or shower; all rooms have central heating, phone; 10 have TV and minibar
Facilities 2 dining-rooms, bar, TV room; swimming-pool, tennis **Credit cards** MC, V
Children very welcome
Disabled no special facilities
Pets accepted
Closed mid-Oct to Mar; restaurant closed to non-residents Sun dinner and Mon
Proprietor Jean-Pierre Babayou

The South-West

Hôtel Arraya

We received a glowing report in 1996 about the Arraya, from a well-travelled couple whose own château features in this guide. Praise indeed.

With its timbered, white-painted houses, Sare can claim to be the prettiest of all the extremely pretty Basque villages. In the heart of the village, this 16th century house was once a hostel for pilgrims on their way across the Pyrenees to Santiago.

Behind the slightly severe frontage on the main square lies a country-style hotel of great character, where much 'flair and talent' has gone into the decoration. The sitting-room, bar and dining-room – not to mention every nook and cranny on stairways or landings – are filled with glorious old Basque furniture; sofas and chairs are comfortable and inviting, and flowers are everywhere. There are more antiques in the individually decorated bedrooms (not especially spacious, but bright and beautiful); some look out over the fine garden. As if all this is not enough, the cooking is good – 'refined and interesting' was one comment – and there is a particularly well-chosen wine list; and there is even a splendid Gâteau Basque.

Nearby Cog railway up La Rhune; Aïnhoa (10 km) – Basque village; Ascain (5 km) – Basque church; St-Jean-de-Luz (14 km).

64310 Sare
Tel 05.59.54.20.46
Fax 05.59.54.27.04
Location in middle of village, 14 km SE of St-Jean-de-Luz; with garden and ample public car parking (private parking nearby)
Meals breakfast, lunch, dinner
Prices rooms 385F-530F; breakfast 50F; menus 130F-195F
Rooms 20 double, 17 with bath, 3 with shower (14 twin); one single with shower; all rooms have central heating, phone; TV on request
Facilities sitting-room, bar, dining-room
Credit cards AE, MC, V
Children welcome; special menu available
Disabled no special facilities
Pets accepted in restaurant only
Closed Nov to Apr
Proprietor Paul Fagoaga

The South-West

Village hotel, Trémolat

Le Vieux Logis

We continue to list this glorious old hotel, for our money one of the most civilized in a region with many attractive hotels, despite the fact that (to judge by our postbag) precious few readers are inclined to pay its prices. (If you decide to treat yourself to a stay here, do let us have a report.)

The Giraudel-Destords have lived in this complex of farm and village houses for nearly 400 years. The part which is now the dining-room once held pigs and wine barrels. Now, all has been designer-decorated to produce comfort of a high degree. The bedrooms are particularly delightful: individually furnished and very cosy in a sophisticated rustic style, with fine materials and furniture; some have four-poster beds. Public rooms are elegant and comfortable, and there are plenty of quiet nooks; the small salon has an open fire, and there are fine antiques throughout. The galleried dining-room is very attractive, and looks out on to the green and flowery garden, where you can have breakfast. The classic and modern cooking of Pierre-Jean Duribreux is excellent (two *toques* from Gault-Millau).

Nearby Les Eyzies-de-Tayac (25 km) – National Prehistoric Museum; Monpazier (30 km) *bastide* ; Beynac (30 km).

24510 Trémolat
Tel 05.53.22.80.06
Fax 05.53.22.84.89
Location in village 15 km SW of Le Bugue; with garden and private car parking
Meals breakfast, lunch, dinner
Prices rooms 740F-1,545F; breakfast 75F, menus 180F-370F, children's 85F
Rooms 24 double (13 twin), all with bath; all rooms have central heating, phone, TV, minibar
Facilities 2 dining-rooms, 3 sitting-rooms, bar, conference room, swimming-pool
Credit cards AE, DC, MC, V
Children welcome
Disabled one adapted room; easy access to dining-room
Pets welcome
Closed never
Proprietor M. Bernard Giraudel

The South-West

Village hotel, Carennac

Hostellerie Fénelon

This jolly-looking Logis – all red roofs and window boxes – in a lovely old village comes strongly recommended for Mme Raynal's warm welcome, the friendly and unobtrusive service of her staff, the 'very good home-style' cooking and the excellent value for money. There is a small pool with tables around it, and another terrace for dining.

■ 46110 Carennac (Lot) **Tel** 05.65.10.96.46 **Fax** 05.65.10.94.86 **Meals** breakfa st, lunch, dinner **Prices** rooms 280F-300F; breakfast 40F; DB&B 290F-310F; menus 88F-300F **Rooms** 16, all with bath or shower, central heating, phone, TV **Credit cards** MC, V **Closed** early Jan to mid-Mar

---

Town hotel, Condom

Hôtel des Trois Lys

You will receive a warm welcome from Jeannette Manet, and the opening of a new restaurant, 'le Dauphin', has added to the delight of staying in this lovely 17th-century house, with its sandy stone walls and white shutters, and restrained elegant decoration within. The bedrooms are spacious and smart, with tasteful antique or reproduction furniture and fresh flowers. Swimming-pool.

■ 38 Rue Gambetta, 32100 Condom (Gers) **Tel** 05.62.28.33.33 **Fax** 05.62.28.41.85 **Meals** breakfast **Prices** rooms 260F-560F; breakfast 42F **Rooms** 10, all with bath or shower, central heating, phone, TV, hairdrier **Credit cards** AE, MC, V **Closed** Feb

---

Village inn, Dégagnac

Auberge sans Frontière

The recent proprietors of this simple auberge offer a 'professional but sincere' welcome, says our latest reporter. It is an integral part of sleepy Dégagnac, and not at all touristy – the dining-rooms also serve as a bar and sitting-room. Bedrooms are small-ish but comfortable and inviting. The food offers 'superb' value.

■ Dégagnac, 46340 Salviac (Lot) **Tel** 05.65.41.52.88 **Meals** breakfast, lunch, dinner **Prices** DB&B 220F-240F; menus 58F-140F **Rooms** 8, all with central heating **Credit cards** MC, V **Closed** never

---

Village hotel, Domme

Hôtel de l'Esplanade

In a busy tourist village with splendid views over the Dordogne, this three-fireplace Logis is well furnished with taste and flair. Housekeeping is immaculate, service efficient – and particularly praised by a visitor who needed medical attention. Some bedrooms in annexes. Michelin-starred cuisine. Difficult car parking.

■ 24250 Domme (Dordogne) **Tel** 05.53.28.31.41 **Fax** 05.53.28.49.92 **Meals** breakfast, lunch, dinner **Prices** rooms 300F-590F; breakfast 50F, menus 160F-350F **Rooms** 25, all with bath or shower, central heating, phone, TV, hairdrier **Credit cards** AE, MC, V **Closed** Nov to mid-Feb; restaurant only, Mon and Sun dinner out of season

The South-West

Village hotel, Escos

Relais des Voyageurs

This former presbytery – its pretty flower-filled garden used to be the cemetery of the next-door church – has been sympathetically converted. Some of the bedrooms are cramped – but the best are spacious and the dining-room is light and warm. 'We liked the informal atmosphere,' enthuse recent visitors.

■ Place de l'Église, 64270 Escos (Pyrénées-Atlantiques) **Tel** 05.59. 38.42.39 **Meals** breakfast, lunch, dinner **Prices** rooms 110F-230F; menus 60F-150F **Rooms** 8, all with bath or shower, central heating, phone **Credit cards** MC, V **Closed** never

---

Converted mill, Les Eyzies-de-Tayac

Moulin de la Beune

This little mill on the bank of the river Beune is a peaceful place to stay, despite the bustle of the town. Bedrooms are excellent, with bright colour schemes. There's a simple breakfast room and an inviting restaurant ('very good value') in another mill building in the garden.

■ 24620 Les Eyzies-de-Tayac (Dordogne) **Tel** 05.53.06.94.33 **Fax** 05.53.06.98.06 **Meals** breakfast, lunch, dinner **Prices** rooms 260F, DB&B 320F; breakfast 40F, menus 85F-315F **Rooms** 20, all with bath or shower, central heating, phone **Credit cards** AE, MC, V **Closed** Nov to Mar; Tue lunch

---

Village hotel, Gluges

Hôtel les Falaises

This good-value family-run Logis enjoys an enviable position – huddled below a fine cliff, on the edge of a tiny medieval village beside the Dordogne – with a restful garden. Bedrooms are simple, light and well decorated.

■ Gluges, 46600 Martel (Lot) **Tel** 05.65.37.33.59 **Fax** 05.65.37.34.19 **Meals** breakfast, lunch, dinner **Prices** rooms 220F-310F **Rooms** 15, all with bath or shower, central heating, phone **Credit cards** MC, V **Closed** Nov to Mar

---

Restaurant with rooms, Hossegor

Les Huitrières du Lac

Primarily a restaurant, specializing (as you might expect) in fish and seafood – though there are alternatives. The large dining-room and the best bedrooms share a view over the adjacent lake. Bedrooms are plain but spacious; some have balconies. Pleasant setting, good value.

■ 1187 Ave du Touring Club, 40150 Hossegor (Landes) **Tel** 05.58. 43.51.48 **Fax** 05.58.41.73.11 **Meals** breakfast, lunch, dinner **Prices** rooms 300F-400F, DB&B 390F-490F; menus 95F-135F **Rooms** 9, all with bath, central heating, phone **Credit cards** AE, MC, V **Closed** Jan to early Feb

The South-West

Riverside hotel, Lacave

Hôtel du Pont de l'Ouysse

The *raison d'etre* of this peaceful, small auberge is its stunning dining terrace overlooking the river, shaded by trees . The cooking makes use of local produce, including eel from the Ouysse. Prettily decorated rooms, smart new swimming-pool.

■ Lacave, 46200 Souillac (Lot) **Tel** 05.65.37.87.04 **Fax** 05.65.32.77.41 **Meals** breakfast, lunch, dinner **Prices** rooms 400F-700F; breakfast 60F, menus from 160F **Rooms** 12, all with bath, phone, TV **Credit cards** V **Closed** mid-Nov to end Feb

---

Riverside hotel, Lalinde

Le Château

His reputation for cooking established, Guy Gensou has turned to the building – an extraordinary little turreted affair, perched above the Dordogne; bedrooms and bathrooms have been refurbished and a cosy new sitting area designed. 'Service personal, friendly and welcoming' enthuses a recent visitor. Pool.

■ Rue de Verdun, 24150 Lalinde (Dordogne) **Tel** 05.53.61.01.82 **Fax** 05.53.24.74.60 **Meals** breakfast, lunch, dinner **Prices** rooms 250F-850F, demi-pension obligatory in high season 320F-620F; breakfast 60F, menus 160F-220F **Rooms** 7, all with bath or shower, phone, TV **Credit cards** MC, V **Closed** Jan; Mon out of season, Mon lunch Jul and Aug

---

Country inn, Lestelle-Bétharram

Le Vieux Logis

Smart modern additions have taken this thriving hotel in the foothills of the Pyrenees out of our normal size range. But the garden and pool are still very attractive, the cooking is well above average and the rooms are a bargain, even if they do lack character. Accommodation is in the main hotel or in wooden chalets dotted about the garden.

■ Rte des Grottes, 64800 Lestelle-Bétharram (Pyrénées-Atlantiques) **Tel** 05.59.71.94.87 **Meals** breakfast, lunch, dinner **Prices** rooms 210F-270F; menus 75F-210F **Rooms** 40, all with bath or shower, central heating, phone, TV **Credit cards** AE, MC, V **Closed** end Oct, Feb

---

Country hotel, Montfort-en-Chalosse

Aux Tauzins

A reader's firm recommendation brings this three-fireplace Logis into the guide. With white walls, green shutters and low-pitched tiled roof, the building is typical of the area. The large dining-room has excellent country views, and many of the bedrooms have balconies. 'Friendly, efficient service, excellent food.' Pool and mini-golf.

■ 40380 Montfort-en-Chalosse (Landes) **Tel** 05.58.98.60.22 **Fax** 05.58.98.45.79 **Meals** breakfast, lunch, dinner **Prices** rooms 220F-260F; breakfast 30F, menus 95F-140F **Rooms** 16, all with bath or shower, central heating, phone, TV **Credit cards** MC, V **Closed** first 2 weeks Oct, last 3 weeks Jan

The South-West

Village hotel, Plaisance

Le Ripa Alta

'Booked for one night, stayed for three,' says a report on this simple hotel. It revolves around the restaurant and the superb cooking of the 'hugely entertaining' Maurice Coscuella. Excellent breakfasts.

■ 3 Place de l'Eglise, 32160 Plaisance (Gers) **Tel** 05.62.69.30.43 **Fax** 05.62.69.36.99 **Meals** breakfast, lunch, dinner **Prices** rooms 170F-460F; breakfast 32F, menus 77F-278F, children's 50F **Rooms** 13, all with bath or shower, central heating, phone; most have TV **Credit cards** AE, DC, MC, V **Closed** Nov

---

Converted mill, Poudenas

Auberge à la Belle Gasconne

A detour to this pretty village to sample Marie-Claude Garcia's splendid cooking is highly recommended. The cosy bedrooms are in the lovingly converted 14th-century watermill next door to her miller's house, jutting out into the Gélise river and there is a romantic terrace and a large garden. Swimming pool.

■ 47170 Poudenas (Lot-et-Garonne) **Tel** 05.53.65.71.58 **Fax** 05.53.65.87.39 **Meals** breakfast, lunch, dinner **Prices** rooms 520F-650F; breakfast 55F, menus 180F-285F **Rooms** 7, all with bath or shower, central heating, phone **Credit cards** AE, DC, MC, V **Closed** 7 Jan to 10 Feb; Sun evening and Mon except Jul to Aug

---

Village hotel, Puymirol

Les Loges de l'Aubergade

The Agenais is not noted for its gastronomic highlights; but Michel Trama's cooking – and especially his patisserie – is among the best in France. The 10 spacious bedrooms are highly individual, in a restrained modern Italian style.

■ 52 Rue Royale, 47270 Puymirol (Lot-et-Garonne) **Tel** 03.53.95.31.46 **Fax** 03.53.95.33.80 **Meals** breakfast, lunch, dinner **Prices** rooms 750F-1,450F; menus from 280F **Rooms** 10, all with bath or shower, central heating, air-conditioning, phone, TV **Credit cards** AE, DC, V **Closed** 2 weeks in Feb; restaurant only, Mon out of season.

Country hotel, Razac d'Eymet

La Petite Auberge

Opened by its English owners in 1990, but run in a thoroughly French style, this converted farm – set in tranquil open countryside south of Bergerac – retains an informal 'family' atmosphere and is popular with foreign visitors and locals alike. Comfortable bedrooms. Outdoor giant chess set, swimming-pool.

■ 24500 Razac d'Eymet (Dordogne) **Tel** 05.53.24.69.27 **Fax** 05.53.27.33.55 **Meals** breakfast, lunch, dinner **Prices** rooms 180F-450F; breakfast 32F, menus 70F-200F **Rooms** 7, all with heating, phone; 2 two-bedroomed apartments **Credit cards** MC, V **Closed** restaurant only Sun and Mon

The South-West

Town hotel, Ribérac

Hôtel de France

A classic two-fireplace Logis de France – an old flower-decked inn at the heart of a bustling market town, with a pretty and warmly inviting restaurant and modest but spacious bedrooms which can accommodate families, offering excellent value.

■ 3 Rue Marc Dufraisse, 24600 Ribérac (Dordogne) **Tel** 05.53.90.00.61 **Fax** 05.53.91.06.05 **Meals** breakfast, lunch, dinner **Prices** rooms 170F-265F; breakfast 30F, menus 70F-200F **Rooms** 20, all with bath or shower, TV, phone **Credit cards** MC, V **Closed** never

---

Country hotel, Rocamadour

Les Vielles Tours

A beautifully restored stone building, dating from the 13th and 17th centuries, with its medieval atmosphere largely preserved. The cosy sitting-room occupies the first floor of an interesting circular turret-wing. Spacious, attractively furnished bedrooms. Proprietor Roger Zozzoli's paintings (for sale) are hung throughout the hotel. Madam cooks. Mixed reader reports.

■ Lafage, 46500 Rocamadour (Lot) **Tel** 05.65.33.68.01 **Fax** 05.65.33.68.59 **Meals** breakfast, lunch by arrangement, dinner **Prices** rooms 210F-460F; HB 310F-440F breakfast 41F-61F, menus 115F-300F **Rooms** 18, all with bath or shower, phone, TV on request **Credit cards** MC, V **Closed** 12 Nov to 22 Mar

---

Country hotel, Sabres

Auberge des Pins

The combined efforts of the Lesclauze family provide an excellent example of unpretentious French hotelkeeping – a three-fireplace Logis in a chalet-style building offering satisfactory accommodation and food in well-cared-for surroundings at moderate prices. The rustic restaurant caters as much to locals as to travellers.

■ Route de la Piscine, 40630 Sabres (Landes) **Tel** 05.58.07.50.47 **Fax** 05.58.07.56.74 **Meals** breakfast, lunch, dinner **Prices** rooms 280F-650F; menus 100F-350F **Rooms** 22, all with bath or shower, central heating, phone, cable TV **Credit cards** AE, V **Closed** Jan

---

Village hotel, St-Cyprien

L'Abbaye

There is a captivating atmosphere about this friendly, constantly improving hotel. In the rustic, stone-flagged sitting-room you can see the old pastry oven and potager. The best bedrooms (first floor of newer annexe) are spacious and very attractive.

■ 24220 St-Cyprien (Dordogne) **Tel** 05.53.29.20.48 **Fax** 05.53.29.15.85 **Meals** breakfast, lunch, dinner **Prices** rooms 300F-680F; menus 95F (lunch); 140F-320F **Rooms** 24, all with bath or shower, phone **Credit cards** AE, MC, V **Closed** mid-Oct to Apr

The South-West

Town hotel, St-Émilion

Hostellerie de Plaisance

'Delighted to confirm your recommendation,' says a reader of this converted monastery, superbly positioned in the middle of St-Émilion – on top of a small cliff with captivating views, not least from the plush dining-room. Bedrooms are smart and comfortable. Good food, with a 'particularly good-value' three-course menu.

■ Place du Clocher, 33330 St-Émilion (Gironde) **Tel** 05.57.24.72.32 **Fax** 05.57.74.41.11 **Meals** breakfast, lunch, dinner **Prices** rooms 500F-790F, suites 1,350F; breakfast 56F, menus 140F-270F **Rooms** 12, all with bath, central heating, phone; most have air-conditioning **Credit cards** AE, DC, MC, V **Closed** Jan

---

Village inn, St-Félix-Lauragais

Auberge du Poids Public

This thoroughly well run inn offers impressive views in all directions over the rolling uplands of the Lauragais. The dining-room is rustic and jolly; the bedrooms are rather grander in style. 'Food delicious, staff most helpful,' enthuses a visitor.

■ 31540 St-Félix-Lauragais (Haute-Garonne) **Tel** 05.61.83.00.20 **Fax** 05.61.83.86.21 **Meals** breakfast, lunch, dinner **Prices** rooms 250F-300F; menus 135F-305F **Rooms** 13, all with bath or shower, central heating, phone, TV, minibar **Credit cards** AE, V **Closed** Jan; Sun evening out of season

---

Seaside hotel, St-Jean-de-Luz

La Fayette

This little family-run hotel occupies a prime spot in the pedestrianised heart of the animated port and resort of St-Jean. The building is in Dutch style, all arches and red brick, and it has a street terrace for outside meals. Small, simple but cheerful bedrooms.

■ 18-20 Rue de la République, 64500 St-Jean-de-Luz (Pyrénées-Atlantiques) **Tel** 05.59.26.17.74 **Fax** 05.59.51.11.78 **Meals** breakfast, lunch, dinner **Prices** rooms 200F-350F; DB&B 450F **Rooms** 18, all with central heating, phone, TV **Credit cards** AE, DC, MC, V **Closed** never

---

Country hotel, Sarlat

Hostellerie de Meysset

'Splendid room, very good food, pleasant owners, good views,' ran the reader's report that introduced this creeper-covered, typically Perigordian country house a couple of years ago. Its style is traditional and unpretentious, though without floral excesses. The food leans towards traditional regional elements, too.

■ Rte des Eyzies, 24200 Sarlat (Dordogne) **Tel** 05.53.59.08.29 **Fax** 05.53.28.47.61 **Meals** breakfast, lunch, dinner **Prices** rooms 320F-450F; suites 590F-770F breakfast 45F, menus 98F-250F **Rooms** 26, all with bath or shower, phone **Credit cards** AE, DC, MC, V **Closed** Mon, Wed lunch

The South-West

Country villa, Soustons

La Bergerie

Mme Clavier has made her immaculate whitewashed house – built in southern single-storey style – a calm and civilized haven where the slow pace of life is infectious. The (obligatory) set dinner is based on whatever is fresh and good at the time. The bedrooms look on to the neat gardens.

■ Ave du Lac, 40140 Soustons (Landes) **Tel** 05.58.41.11.43
Meals breakfast, dinner **Prices** rooms 260F-380F; DB&B 360F-400F
Rooms 12, all with bath, central heating, phone **Credit cards** DC, MC, V
Closed Nov to Mar

Converted mill, Touzac

La Source Bleue

An enthusiastic reader persuaded us to restore this old paper-mill, to the guide. There is now a new fishing lake and a giant bamboo forest, though the beautiful and peaceful position beside the Lot remains a key attraction. The rustic dining-room and the best of the bedrooms are charming. Pool. More reports, please.

■ Moulin de Leygues, Touzac, 46700 Puy-l'Evêque (Lot)
Tel 05.65.36.52.01 **Fax** 05.65.24.65 .69 **Meals** breakfast, lunch, dinner
Prices rooms 295F-460F; breakfast 35F, menus 105F-220F **Rooms**16,
all with bath, central heating, phone; some have TV **Credit cards** AE,
MC, V **Closed** Jan to Mar; restaurant only, Wed lunch

Medieval manor, Vézac

Manoir de Rochecourbe

This rustic manor-house has been in the Roger family for genera-tions. A round tower housing the staircase gives the house a touch of grandeur, and the great beams and massive fireplaces inside do not disappoint.

■ Vézac, 24220 St-Cyprien (Dordogne) **Tel** 05.53.31.09.84
Fax 05.53.28.59.07 **Meals** breakfast, dinner **Prices** rooms 260F-490F;
breakfast 35F **Rooms** 6, all with bath or shower, central heating, phone
Credit cards AE, DC, MC, V **Closed** 5-31 Jan

Château hotel, Vieux-Mareuil

Château de Vieux Mareuil

Behind the thick, ivy-clad stone walls of this 15th-century fortified house lies a stylish little hotel, prettily decorated with plenty of attention to detail. Spacious bedrooms, home-like sitting-room, acres of parkland to explore. Well above-average food and outside dining. Pool. A recent change of ownership means that reports would be welcome.

■ Route Angoulème-Périgueux, 24340 Vieux-Mareuil (Dordogne)
Tel 05.53.60.77.15 **Fax** 05.53.56.49.33 **Meals** breakfast, lunch, dinner
Prices rooms 550F; breakfast 60F, menus 180F-250F **Rooms** 14, all with
bath, central heating, phone, TV, hairdrier **Credit cards** AE, MC, V **Closed**
end Oct to Apr; Mon, Sun dinner out of season

Massif Central

For many British visitors, the Massif is 'unknown France' – the high, remote area between Périgord on the west and the Rhône valley on the east. For guidebook purposes, it is a rather problematic region, particularly if (like all our regions) it is defined in terms of *départements*. The points where you might consider the physical Massif to begin and end don't always coincide happily with governmental boundaries (the *département* of Ardèche, for example, falls in our South of France region, but includes territory that is physically very much part of the Massif).

There is also a good case for considering this as 'unspoilt France'. Of course, tourism has had an impact, but it is slight compared with the impact on the much better-known areas to the west, east, north and south. There are bargains to be found as a result.

Boisset, Auberge de Concasty 04.71.62.21.16 Jolly little converted farmhouse with pool in grassy garden; country cooking.
Champagnac, Château de Lavendès 04.71.69.62.79 Simple but satisfactory Logis in countryside; basic pool.
Conques, Hostellerie de l'Abbaye 04.65.72.80.30 Comfortably furnished ancient house with beautiful country views.
Meyrueis, Château d'Ayres 04.66.45.60.10 Shuttered medieval house in leafy grounds with pool.

Reporting to the guide

We're very keen to hear from readers about their hotel-going experiences. We can't visit every hotel in the guide every year; even if we could, we wouldn't be staying in them all. And it's only when you stay in a place that you find out how the plumbing deals with the demand for hot water, what that much-vaunted 70F breakfast is really like, and what happens when you request something extraordinary like an extra pillow. So please do let us know how you get on next time you're travelling in France.

In particular, please do write when you like a small hotel, whether or not you've chosen it with our help. People are pretty good at letting us know when we've got a place wrong (usually, we hope, because the place has gone downhill). Places that come up to expectations don't always trigger a reaction.

It doesn't have to be a detailed, feature by feature description of the hotel (though highly detailed reports are always very welcome). The key thing is to let us know what you felt about the place, as a customer. We've suggested a structure for readers' reports on page 11, but you certainly don't have to stick to that; if you'd find it easier to dash off a few lines in whatever order they come to mind, please do just that.

Massif Central

Manor house hotel, Castelpers

Château de Castelpers

If our calculations are correct, Yolande Tapié de Celeyran has now been at the helm (and the stove) of this family-home-turned-hotel for more than 30 years – and she shows no sign of weakening. Her house makes a relaxing retreat. It dates from the 17th century and ranges from the purely rustic to the Gothic in style, with a tower, arched windows and rooms of character furnished comfortably with antiques. But it is not a château hotel in the grand manner; families can feel at ease, with swings and spacious lawns (dotted with ancient trees) for children to play on and trout streams to explore, and prices that reflect the modest size of some of the bedrooms. Good food, served in front of an open fire in winter. More reports would be very welcome.

Nearby Château du Bosc (10 km); Sauveterre-de-Rouergue (20 km).

Castelpers 12170 Requista
Tel 05.65.69.22.61
Fax 05.65.69.25.31
Location in countryside 9 km SE of RN88, 10 km S of Naucelle; in wooded park with private car parking
Meals breakfast, lunch, dinner
Prices rooms 285F-485F; menu 135F
Rooms 6 double (4 twin), 2 family rooms; 3 with bath, 5 with shower; all rooms have phone, 5 have TV
Facilities sitting-room, 2 dining-rooms; fishing
Credit cards AE, MC, V
Children welcome if well behaved **Disabled** one specially equipped ground-floor bedroom **Pets** accepted, but not in dining-room
Closed Oct to Mar; restaurant occasional evening or days only
Proprietor Mme de Saint Palais

Massif Central

Grand-Hôtel Sainte-Foy

Promotion to a full entry was long overdue for this delectable hotel in a lovely old village; as it is, we are somewhat behind the French tourist authorities, who in 1993 promoted the Sainte-Foy to four-star status – the first hotel in Aveyron to achieve the rating. Marie-France and Alain Garcenot, proprietors since they took over from an aunt in 1987, are justifiably proud of their achievement, but the facilities that are required for star-ratings are not the basis of the hotel's appeal.

Hôtel Sainte-Foy is a lovingly restored, partly timbered old house which takes its name from the great abbey church directly opposite. The house has been beautifully furnished with close attention to detail and to the character of the building. The warm glow of wood is everywhere. The large two-part sitting-room is particularly well furnished with antiques. Bedrooms are highly individual, tasteful and large, with views either over the church or the flowery courtyard garden. You can dine here or in the intimate but pleasantly spacious rooms inside. The increasingly inventive cooking (daily changing menus) gets good reviews.

Nearby Church of Ste-Foy (remarkable tympanum and treasury).

Conques 12320 St-Cyprien-sur-Dourdou
Tel 05.65.69.84.03
Fax 05.65.72.81.04
Location in heart of village, 40 km N of Rodez; with private car parking
Meals breakfast, lunch, dinner
Prices rooms 390F-990F, suites 1,100F to 1,200F; breakfast 58F; menus 160F-330F; lunch 100F
Rooms 15 double, 2 suites, all with bath; all rooms have central heating, phone
Facilities 3 dining-rooms, sitting-room, bar, interior patio, conference room; 2 terraces; exercise room
Credit cards AE, MC, V
Children accepted
Disabled no special facilities
Pets accepted
Closed end Oct to Easter
Proprietors Marie-France and Alain Garcenot

Massif Central

Le Grand Écuyer

One reporter reckons that the cooking of Yves Thuriès is less impressive than it was a few years ago. But he still gets a star from Michelin and two *toques* from Gault-Millau, and the other attractions of this ancient hunting lodge in the glorious medieval village of Cordes are undiminished.

Le Grand Écuyer is a classified historic monument, transformed into a comfortable, elegant and atmospheric hotel. The dining-room is medieval in style, with old stone walls and tiled floors, dark beamed ceiling, old prints and so on, blending well with the lacy white table-cloths, shining silver, painted plates and tapestry chairs. The sitting-room and 'rather gloomy' bar are more domestic, with deeply upholstered armchairs, low tables and potted plants. Bedrooms (varying in size) are inviting – beamed ceilings, monumental stone fireplaces, rugs on expanses of polished floor – and are beautifully furnished with antiques. Bathrooms are modern. M. Thuriès and his friendly staff ensure that a graciously informal atmosphere prevails.

Nearby Rue Droite (14thC houses); Fôret Grésigne (15 km) – marked trails; Albi – *la ville rouge*.

Rue Voltaire 81170 Cordes
Tel 05.63.56.01.03
Fax 05.63.56.18.83
Location in middle of village, 25 km NW of Albi; with public car parking nearby
Meals breakfast, lunch, dinner
Prices rooms 600F-850F, suite 1,400F; menus 170F-420F
Rooms 12 double, one suite, all with bath; all rooms have central heating, phone, radio
Facilities 2 dining-rooms, breakfast room, sitting-room, bar
Credit cards DC, MC, V
Children accepted
Disabled no special facilities
Pets accepted
Closed Nov to Easter
Proprietor Yves Thuriès

Massif Central

Le Chalet

Reviewing the entry of this Logis deep in the Bourbonnais countryside always raises an editorial smile, and not only because of the proprietor's name. We first visited it on a summer evening when its secluded, wooded garden (park-like in style and set out some 100 years ago) seemed idyllic. The big fish pond (where guests may fish) was perfect for strolling around, drink in hand, before pausing a while on the little raised terrace and then proceeding in to dinner.

It's a modest, traditional place. Rooms (in the chalet-style building itself, and in converted outbuildings) vary in style and size; none is notably stylish, but the best are cheerfully comfortable (with exposed beams and bright wallpaper). Some interesting regional specialities are served in the traditional-style dining-room, and the service is amiable. Saint-Pourçain and Sancerre are special features of the wine list. In fine weather, meals are served outside on the terrace, which has views of the countryside.
Nearby Moulins – timbered houses, cathedral; Souvigny's abbey, Balaine Arboretum; the oak forest of Tronçais; Romanesque churches.

03000 Coulandon
Tel 04.70.44.50.08
Fax 04.70.44.07.09
Location in countryside 6 km W of Moulins, off D945; with large grounds and ample car parking
Meals breakfast, lunch, dinner
Prices rooms 290F-460F; breakfast 45F, menus 110F-230F
Rooms 19 double, 5 with bath, 14 with shower (5 twin); 9 family rooms, 6 with bath, 3 with shower; all rooms have central heating, phone, TV
Facilities dining-room, sitting-room; fishing, swimming-pool
Credit cards AE, DC, MC, V
Children accepted
Disabled 6 ground-floor bedrooms
Pets accepted
Closed mid-Dec to end Jan
Proprietor M. H. Hulot

Massif Central

Country hotel, Lacabarede

Demeure de Flore

A new shop, *L'Insolite*, selling antiques, has been added to this exceptionally charming hotel, in the foothills of the mountains of Haut-Languedoc. It was opened by Monike and Jean-Marie Tronc in 1992, and they have created something close to our ideal hotel. Their 19th-century *maison de maitre* may be an undistinguished building, but it sits prettily in a mature, wooded *jardin anglais*, far enough from the passing RN112 to feel quite secluded. And within, there is a delightful ambience. None of your traditional French clashes of patterns here: stylish floral prints are set against warm, plain backgrounds. The house has lots of floor-to-ceiling windows, and the general effect is light and fresh. Carefully chosen antiques and ornaments give the feel of a lived-in but cared-for family home. The eleven bedrooms are individually furnished in the same careful way.

In good weather meals are served out on the terrace, and 'a bite of lunch' can be had by the smart little pool. We haven't tried the food – *cuisine 'maison bourgeoise'*, says Monike – so reports on this entry would be particularly welcome. **Nearby** Castres (35 km), Albi (60 km), Toulouse (100 km); Mediterranean beaches within reach.

106 Route Nationale, 81240 Lacabarede
Tel 05.63.98.32.32
Fax 05.63.98.47.56
Location opposite service station on outskirts of village on RN 112 between St-Pons and Mazamet; in gardens with ample car parking
Meals breakfast, lunch, dinner
Prices rooms 400F-500F; breakfast 55F, menus 100F-150F

Rooms 10 double, one suite, all with bath; all rooms have central heating, phone, TV, hairdrier
Facilities sitting-room, dining-room; swimming-pool
Credit cards MC, V
Children accepted
Disabled one adapted room
Pets not accepted except by special arrangement
Closed Feb
Proprietor Monike Flore Tronc

Massif Central

Farmhouse hotel, Moudeyres

Le Pré Bossu

This remote little place prompts more reports from readers than just about anywhere else in the guide – and they tell different stories. 'Absolutely delightful', says one; 'over-rated', another. A common reservation is an occasional lack of warmth, physical and metaphorical. But the latest is wholehearted: 'Excellent; comfortable; food outstanding and beautifully served; worth every franc – we will go again.'

Moudeyres is a remote village high (1,200 metres) in the volcanic Mézenc massif, surrounded by fields of wild flowers (in the spring) and mushrooms (in the autumn). The village consists of thatched rough-stone houses, many beautifully restored. The Pré Bossu is no exception, although it was built as recently as 1969, with old materials. The Flemish owners have worked hard to create an attractive and comfortable house. Starting with beams, wood floors and ingle-nook fireplace, they have added fine antique dressers, lace curtains, wild flowers, plants and books. It is all fresh and well-kept. Bedrooms are rustic, too – clean and simple, with good shower rooms; tranquillity is assured. Food is ambitious and reliable, earning a Michelin star.

Nearby Restored 18thC farm; Le Puy – volcanic rock formations.

43150 Moudeyres
Tel 04.71.05.10.70
Fax 04.71.05.10.21
Location on edge of village, 25 km SE of Le Puy, beyond Laussonne; in garden, with ample car parking
Meals breakfast, lunch, dinner
Prices rooms 365F-490F; breakfast 55F, menus 168F-295F
Rooms 10 double, 5 with bath, 5 with shower (4 twin); one family room; all rooms have central heating, phone
Facilities bar, TV room, dining-room (smoking not allowed)
Credit cards AE, MC, V
Children accepted
Disabled no special facilities
Pets accepted in bedrooms, but not in dining-room
Closed mid-Nov to Easter
Proprietor Carlos Grootaert

Massif Central

Longcol

This splendid turreted medieval farmhouse is immersed in woods a few miles from Najac. 'Farming hamlet' might be a more accurate description, since the hotel consists of multiple stone buildings, mostly grouped around the central swimming-pool and all equipped with distinctive bell-shaped slate roofs and neat small-paned windows.

The *long col* is a loop in the river Aveyron, which meanders through gorges below this secluded spot. The Luyckx family bought the original farm in 1982, and spent six years restoring it before opening for business. Since then they have gone from strength to strength, doubling the number of rooms without altering the atmosphere of a polished but welcoming home. They are keen antique collectors, and it shows; the low-beamed rooms are full of beautiful pieces of furniture, tapestries and Asian artefacts. Bedrooms are equally original and comfortable, but vary in size. Meals are served in the light, airy dining-room, or on the little walled terrace in summer – or by the angular swimming-pool, which shares the woody views. Food is taken seriously, and there is an excellent wine list.

Nearby Najac – medieval houses and castle.

La Fouillade 12270 Najac
Tel 05.65.29.63.36
Fax 05.65.29.64.28
Location in large wooded grounds NW of village, NE of Najac; with garden and car parking
Meals breakfast, lunch, dinner
Prices rooms 550F-800F; meals 135F-290F
Rooms 17 double, 15 with bath, 2 with shower; all rooms have central heating, phone, TV, radio, minibar
Facilities dining-room, sitting-room, billiard room, terrace; swimming-pool, tennis court
Credit cards AE, V
Children welcome; baby-sitting available
Disabled no special facilities
Pets welcome
Closed mid-Nov to Easter; restaurant only, Tue out of season
Proprietors Luyckx family

Massif Central

Hôtel du Midi-Papillon

Every year we receive a long hand-written bulletin from Jean-Michel Papillon, the fourth generation of Papillons to run this lovable old post inn, spelling out the latest improvements. And practically every year we receive enthusiastic reports, underlining the fact that the essential appeal of the place is unchanged. Readers say 'wonderful' food, 'faultless' welcome, 'outstanding' value.

The Midi is the rural Logis at its best: a village inn amid grand countryside, offering welcoming rooms (of varying sizes) and excellent food at irresistible prices. It is very much a family-run place, with Mme overseeing the dining-room while Jean-Michel cooks. Vegetables come from the garden, poultry is home-raised, jams and croissants home-made.

The dining-room is divided into three sections, so that although the Papillon family try to accommodate their diners as fairly as possible, some will have the pleasure of dining on the terrace with a splendid river view, while others may find themselves in the intimate *salon* with leather furniture. Perhaps worth expressing a preference.

Nearby Gorges de la Dourbie (10 km); Montpellier-le-Vieux.

12230 St-Jean-du-Bruel
Tel 05.65.62.26.04
Fax 05.65.62.12.97
Location by river, in village on D991, 40 km SE of Millau; with garden and garages
Meals breakfast, lunch, dinner
Prices rooms 81F-200F; menus 74F-204F
Rooms 12 double, 8 with bath (5 twin); 1 suite; 1 single; 5 family rooms, 3 with bath, 2 with shower; all rooms have central heating, phone
Facilities 3 dining-rooms, bar, sitting-room, TV room; swimming-pool, jacuzzi
Credit cards MC, V
Children welcome; special menus available
Disabled access to dining-room only
Pets accepted
Closed mid-Nov to Easter
Proprietors Papillon familily

Massif Central

Hostellerie de la Maronne

This 19th-century country house, set in a beautiful peaceful valley in the Auvergne, has had its critics in the past but these days earns nothing but praise from readers. Or nearly so: our latest reporter notes that the place has quite a formal air, but this is more to do with the elegant style of furnishing than the style of operation – she also commends the owners and staff as 'very welcoming and friendly.'

With its small modern swimming-pool and tennis court surrounded by lovely gardens and sweeping countryside, the *hostellerie* makes a fine retreat whether you are in search of peace or of outdoor exercise. Much has changed during Alain de Cock's tenure: a smart dining-room has been built into the hillside; newly built bedrooms have replaced the least attractive of the old ones; and the sitting-room and breakfast room have recently received new lighting, carpets and seating.

Food is taken seriously, with 'excellent' results. There is now a range of menus (reaching up to *gastronomique* levels), each offering no choice, as well as a reasonable *carte*. The wine list is quite wide-ranging. Gault-Millau awards a *toque*.

Nearby Salers (10 km); Anjony (20 km) – château.

Le Theil 15140 St-Martin-Valmeroux
Tel 04.71.69.20.33
Fax 04.71.69.28.22
Location in countryside 3 km E of St-Martin, on D37; with gardens, ample car parking
Meals breakfast, lunch, dinner
Prices rooms 460F-580F; DB&B 355F-455F; breakfast 60F; menu 150F-250F
Rooms 21 double, all with bath; all rooms have central heating, phone, minibar; 10 have balcony or terrace
Facilities dining-room, sitting-room, breakfast room, seminar room; swimming-pool, tennis, *pétanque*, sauna, garden
Credit cards MC, V
Children welcome; baby-sitting by arrangement
Disabled lift/elevator
Pets accepted but not in dining-room
Closed Nov to Mar
Proprietor Alain de Cock

Massif Central

Château hotel, Target

Château de Boussac

Increased public exposure – now in other British hotel guides as well as this one – does not seem to have affected the delicate balancing act conducted by the Marquis and Marquise de Longueil, who continue to welcome guests into their home with captivating charm.

The Château de Boussac lies between Vichy and Moulin, tucked away in the Bourbonnais – quite difficult to find. Solid, turreted and moated, the château could be a tourist sight in its own right; it is built around a courtyard, and the main reception rooms, furnished with Louis XV antiques and chandeliers, open on to a vast terrace with an ornamental lake and formal gardens.

But the château is very much lived-in. By day the Marquis dons his overalls and works on the estate, but comes in to cook at least one course of the evening meal and chat to his guests. His wife looks after the rooms with care – there are fresh flowers everywhere, and the antiques are highly polished. Dinner *en famille* can be a rather formal affair, but the food is hard to fault and the Marquis, who speaks English, will make you feel at home.
Nearby Souvigny (35 km) – Gothic/Romanesque church; Vichy (40 km) – spa town; Moulins (50 km) – half-timbered houses.

Target 03140 Chantelle
Tel 04.70.40.63.20
Fax 04.70.40.60.03
Location in countryside, off D42, 12 km NW of Chantelle, 50 km W of Vichy; in large park, with enclosed car parking
Meals breakfast, dinner
Prices rooms 600F-1,100F; breakfast 55F, menus 220F-320F with wine
Rooms 4 double (3 twin), one suite, all with bath; all rooms have central heating
Facilities dining-room, sitting-room
Credit cards AE, MC, V
Children accepted if well behaved
Disabled no special facilities
Pets accepted if well behaved
Closed Nov to Feb (except by reservation in advance)
Proprietors Marquis and Marquise de Longueil

Massif Central

Château hotel, Ydes

Château de Trancis

We should welcome reports from readers who leave the beaten tourist track to find this impressive place – a classic little Loire-style château on the 500-metre-high fringes of the Auvergne regional park. This unlikely thing is more easily understood when you know that the Italianate architectural flourishes are of 20th-century origin. And its opening as an elegant hotel is perhaps more easily understood when you discover that it is run by an English couple, travel writers Innes and Fiona Fennell.

They have refurbished it to create the kind of harmonious and stylish ambience that is distinctly rare in and around the Massif Central. Bedrooms are well equipped and individually decorated, with antique furniture and rugs on polished floors. Public rooms embrace an ornate Louis XIV salon, a 'German' dining-room and an 'English' library. The view from the terrace across the smart little pool, where candlelit dinners are served in summer, is pleasant and soothing.

A house-party atmosphere prevails, with the Fennels' five-course dinners served only to residents. Note that they do not normally accept children.

Nearby Dordogne gorges, Parc Régional des Volcans d'Auvergne.

15210 Ydes
Tel 04.71.40.60.40
Fax 04.71.40.62.13
Location on D15, off D22, 2 km N of village of Saignes, 3 km E of Ydes; in countryside, with car parking in grounds
Meals breakfast, dinner
Prices rooms 560F-950F, suite 1,300F, including breakfast; DB&B 580F-900F; menu 280F
Rooms 6 double (one twin), one suite, all with bath or shower; all rooms have central heating, phone, TV, minibar, tea/coffee kit, hairdrier, electric fan
Facilities 3 sitting-rooms, 2 dining-rooms; 2 terraces, park, swimming-pool
Credit cards AE, MC, V
Children not accepted
Disabled difficult access
Pets no dogs
Closed mid-Oct to end Mar
Proprietors Innes and Fiona Fennell

Massif Central

Medieval inn, Cordes

Hostellerie du Vieux Cordes

A simpler base than the Grand Ecuyer, this stone-built 13thC building is set at the top of the old hill town giving long views, notably from the grassy terrace. Inside, furniture is generally simple and rustic, except in the plush little sitting-room. 'Friendly service, excellent food, good value,' says a recent report.

■ Rue St-Michel, 81170 Cordes (Tarn) **Tel** 05.63.56.00.12 **Fax** 05.63.56.02.47 **Meals** breakfast, lunch, dinner **Prices** rooms 265F-420F; breakfast 40F, menus 80F-160F **Rooms** 21, all with bath or shower, central heating, phone, TV **Credit cards** AE, DC, MC, V **Closed** Jan

---

Country hotel, Cuq-Toulza

Cuq en Terrasses

A full entry in the making, if ever there was one: opened in 1993 after three years of restoration by its British designer owners, Tim and Zara Whitmore, this old presbytery is beautifully and sympathetically done out, with lots of hand-made tiles and natural materials. 'Beautiful terrace, with breathtaking views stretching as far as the Pyrénées', enthuses a recent visitor; flowery garden, pool.

■ Cuq-le-Château, 81470 Cuq-Toulza (Tarn) **Tel** 05.63.82.54.00 **Fax** 05.63.82.54.11 **Meals** breakfast, lunch, dinner **Prices** rooms 400F-900F; breakfast 55F, menus 130F-150F **Rooms** 5, 2 suites, 1 apartment, all with bath or shower; all with central heating, phone, TV; **Credit cards** DC, MC, V **Closed** 4 Jan to 6 Feb

---

Manor house hotel, La Malène

Manoir de Montesquiou

'Good-sized room, good food, very good views,' says a contented reader of this attractive castle-like 15th-century manor house. Your bedroom may be in one of the turrets; it may have a grand four-poster; it is sure to be comfortable and well looked after. Family run with care and good humour.

■ 48210 La Malène (Lozère) **Tel** 04.66.48.51.12 **Fax** 04.66.48.50.47 **Meals** breakfast, lunch, dinner **Prices** rooms 430F-760F; breakfast 60F, menus 165F-250F **Rooms** 12, all with bath or shower, central heating, air-conditioning, phone; some have TV **Credit cards** DC, MC, V **Closed** mid-Oct to early Apr

---

Village inn, Montsalvy

Auberge Fleurie

The two attractive dining-rooms – polished wood dressers, gleaming copper, red-check tablecloths – are the focal point of this delightful creeper-covered auberge. We last visited after it changed hands a few years ago; reports on the now-well-established new regime are welcome.

■ Place du Barry, 15120 Montsalvy (Cantal) **Tel** 04.71.49.20.02 **Meals** breakfast, lunch, dinner **Prices** rooms 120F-160F; breakfast 25F, menus 50F-180F **Rooms** 13, all with central heating **Credit cards** AE, DC, MC, V **Closed** restaurant only, mid-Jan to mid-Feb

Massif Central

Village hotel, Najac

L'Oustal del Barry

This spick-and-span little Logis, in the same family for five generations, will not be the same after Jean-Marie Miquel's tragic death in 1994, but the charming Catherine will doubtless continue to offer the genuine welcome, excellent food and notably good value for which it is known. Rooms are spacious but ordinary.

■ Place du Bourg, 12270 Najac (Aveyron) **Tel** 05.65.29.74.32 **Fax** 05.65.29.75.32 **Meals** breakfast, lunch, dinner **Prices** rooms 350F-550F with breakfast; menus 98F-320F **Rooms** 22, all with central heating, phone, TV, hairdrier **Credit cards** AE, MC, V **Closed** Nov to Mar

---

Farmhouse hotel, Pont-de-L'Arn

La Métairie Neuve

The Metairie is a tastefully renovated old farm with its heritage properly respected – exposed beams, stone walls, polished tiled floors – and with a relaxed atmosphere. Mme Tournier is a charming hostess who keeps the antique-furnished public areas looking immaculate.

■ Pont-de-L'Arn, 81660 Mazamet (Tarn) **Tel** 05.63.61.23.31 **Fax** 05.63.61.94.75 **Meals** breakfast, dinner **Prices** rooms 340F-450F; menus 100F-250F **Rooms** 11, all with bath, central heating, phone, TV **Credit cards** DC, MC, V **Closed** 15 Dec to 20 Jan; restaurant only, Sun

---

Riverside hotel, St-Sernin-sur-Rance

Hôtel Carayon

Well outside our upper size limit, but perenially a favourite with readers ('excellent' says the latest report). It is a white-painted, shuttered building with café tables in front; most of the rooms are in a smart modern extension. Pierre Carayon's cooking is outstanding. What is more, the menu prices are modest, earning a prized red *repas* rating from Michelin. And the Carayons are an attractive and friendly couple.

■ Place du Fort, 12380 St-Sernin-sur-Rance (Aveyron) **Tel** 05.65. 99.60.26 **Fax** 05.65.99.69.26 **Meals** breakfast, lunch, dinner **Prices** rooms 179F-349F; suites 500F-600F; menus 70F-300F **Rooms** 26, all with bath or shower, central heating, phone, TV, minibar **Credit cards** AE, DC, MC, V **Closed** Sun dinner and Mon, out of season

---

Village inn, Vitrac

La Tomette

'This hotel has all the qualities of peace, welcome, attractive setting and very good food that characterise your selections,' a reader says of the Tomette – a jolly inn, much expanded and improved over the last 16 years, evidently without the loss of its essential appeal. Pleasant garden, pool.

■ 15220 Vitrac (Cantal) **Tel** 04.71.64.70.94 **Fax** 04.71.64.77.11 **Meals** breakfast, lunch, dinner **Prices** rooms 230F-440F; breakfast 40F, menus 65F-185F **Rooms** 18, all with bath or show er, central heating, phone, TV **Credit cards** AE, MC, V **Closed** Jan to Mar

The South

Mediterranean France: sea, sun, wine, flowers, fruit, mountains, Roman remains. Heaven on earth – and with more guide entries and potential entries (listed below) than any other region.

Contenders in the South

Aigues-Mortes, Les Arcades 04.66.53.81.13 Characterful restaurant with individually decorated rooms in ancient building.

Aix-en-Provence, Hôtel des Augustins 04.42.27.28.59 Converted monastery in centre of Aix; garden for breakfast.

Aix-en-Provence, Hôtel des Quatre-Dauphins 04.42.38.16.39 Prettily designer-decorated little place in Mazarin quarter.

Avignon, Hôtel de la Mirande 04.90.85.93.93 Extravagantly elegant town hotel, opened in 1990.

Montfavet, Les Frênes 04.90.31.17.93 Elegant mansion, beautiful garden, and superb pool. Good food.

Les-Baux-de-Provence, Mas de l'Oulivie 04.90.54.35.78 Newly built, in traditional *mas* style, with attractive pool among olives.

Les-Baux-de-Provence, La Cabro d'Or 04.90.54.33.21 Starred restaurant, with lovely pool/gardens and comfortable rooms.

Bonnieux, Hostellerie Le Prieuré 04.90.75.80.78 Delightful 17thC abbey in small hillside village.

Castillon-du-Gard, Le Vieux Castillon 04.66.37.00.77 Luxurious and stylish conversion of old houses in ancient hilltop village.

Collias, Hostellerie Le Castellas 04.66.22.88.88 Stylish, slightly slick little place in centre of old village; small garden, pool.

Coursegoules, Auberge de l'Escaou 04.93.59.11.28 Simple, tastefully modernized inn, in quiet, isolated hill village.

Gordes, Les Romarins 04.90.72.12.13 Tastefully furnished house overlooking the village; pool.

Gordes, Les Bories 04.90.72.00.51 Expensive picturesque restaurant with rooms overlooking valley in medieval village.

Joucas, Mas des Herbes Blanches 04.90.05.79.79 Very attractive old *mas* with fine views; well-equipped rooms; pool; good food.

Joucas, Le Phebus 04.90.05.78.83 Stylishly decorated, welcoming farmhouse-style place, good food, attractive pool.

Malemort-du-Comtat, Château Unang 04.90.69.91.37 18thC house in formal gardens surrounded by vineyards, elegantly furnished but informally run as a B&B.

Montpellier, Hôtel le Guilhem 04.67.52.90.90 Tastefully done out old house in old town, with lovely terrace; B&B only.

Pernes-les-Fontaines, Hôtel l'Hermitage 04.90.66.51.41 Elegant, patchily furnished Logis in pleasant gardens with pool.

Le-Puy-Ste-Reparade, Domaine de la Cride 04.42.61.96.96 Home-like restored farmhouse in a leafy garden with pool.

Roquebrune-sur-Argens, La Maurette 04.94.45.46.81 Hilltop farmhouse with views; rooms open on to the garden.

Russamp-Est, Mas des Aigras 04.90.34.81.01 Simple but stylish farmhouse B&B in leafy gardens with pool, tennis.

St-Remy, Mas de la Tour 04.90.92.61.00 Traditional-style house with rooms opening on to flowery garden and pool.

Ste-Maxime-sur-Mer, La Croisette 04.94.96.17.75 Pastel coloured villa with secluded garden and good views; seafood specialities. **Vence, Château du Domaine St Martin** 04.93.58.02.02 Elegantly furnished Relais & Châteaux place, in splendid high setting; terrace, lovely pool, tennis.

The South

Farmhouse hotel, Aix-en-Provence

Mas d'Entremont

This farmhouse-style hotel just outside Aix, has a blemish-free record of reports from readers (including one who has been going there for over a decade) and impressed a recent inspector mightily.

The hotel consists of low red-roofed buildings clustered around a courtyard – modern constructions, but using lots of old materials. Within are wooden beams and pillars, rustic furniture, tiled floors and open fireplaces. Bedrooms are also rustic, comfortable and quite stylish. Five (relatively small, but all with terrace or balcony) are in the main building, the rest (bigger) spread around the gardens in bungalows. The setting is peaceful, and the gardens are a delight – with a big swimming-pool shielded by cypresses, plenty of secluded corners, and a pond with fountain, lilies and lazy carp. Overlooking this is a beautiful summer dining-room, with windows that slide away, effectively creating a roofed terrace.

Cuisine is classic in style, with a strong Provençal influence, and excellent in quality, attracting a full house for Sunday lunch. The Marignanes create a relaxed family atmosphere.

Nearby Aix-en-Provence; Abbaye de Silvacane (25 km).

Montée d'Avignon 13090 Aix-en-Provence
Tel 04.42.23.45.32
Fax 04.42.21.15.83
Location in countryside just off N7, 2 km NW of Aix; with large grounds and car parking
Meals breakfast, lunch, dinner
Prices rooms 640F-840F, suite 960F; breakfast 70F; DB&B 1,200F-1,400F (for two); menus 200F-230F
Rooms 17 double (7 twin) all with bath; all rooms have

air-conditioning, phone, satellite TV, minibar, safe, private terrace
Facilities dining-room, sitting-areas; swimming-pool, tennis
Credit cards MC, V
Children accepted; some rooms have side-rooms
Disabled lift/elevator
Pets accepted
Closed Nov to mid-Mar; restaurant only, Sun dinner and Mon lunch
Proprietors Marignane family

The South

Town villa, Aix-en-Provence

Villa Gallici

This is certainly one of the most expensive and one of the smallest hotels in Aix; from where we stand it is absolutely the best. We've called it a town villa; suburban villa might be more accurate, while country villa might convey more of the feel of the place, set in a beautiful garden just north of the centre.

It is a deliciously peaceful, relaxing place, where distinctions between indoors and out seem to blur. A shady terrace is converted to an outdoor sitting-room by deep-cushioned sofas and chairs; breakfast can be had here. Indoors, bright fabrics and light paintwork bring the sun into the welcoming sitting-rooms. Bedrooms are prettily sumptuous, with extravagant use of draped fabrics; furniture is in elegant 18th-century style throughout, but the decorative themes vary widely.

Light meals can be had by the hotel's pool, surrounded by trees and flowery shrubs. For more serious eating, the hotel's restaurant, the Clos de la Violette, does not let the side down, with a Michelin star and three *toques* from Gault-Millau. Not only the best hotel in Aix, but the best restaurant. No wonder the Villa Gallici offers 'courses for getting back into shape'.

Nearby Aix-en-Provence; Abbaye de Silvacane (25 km)

Avenue de la Violette 13100 Aix-en-Provence
Tel 04.42.23.29.23
Fax 04.42.96.30.45
Location just north of city centre, 500m from cathedral; in gardens with secure parking
Meals breakfast, lunch, dinner
Prices rooms 900F-2,800F; breakfast 95F, menu 300F
Rooms 19 double with bath; all rooms have central heating, air-conditioning, phone, TV, radio, minibar, hairdrier
Facilities sitting-room, bar, dining-room; terrace, swimming-pool
Credit cards AE, DC, MC, V
Children not accepted
Disabled one ground-floor bedroom
Pets accepted (50F charge)
Closed never; restaurant only, Thu (in winter)
Proprietors M. Dez, M. Montemarco, M. Jouve

The South

La Terrasse au Soleil

This mainly modern Catalan-style hotel has gradually moved upmarket over its years in the guide, and is now of four-star status, and has now added even its own helicopter landing space. It has expanded, too, and falls outside our usual size limits. But choice in the Pyrenees-Orientales is limited, and an approving reader's report encourages us to stick to the view that this is one of the most appealing places in the region.

A key part of the appeal is the lovely setting, with the splendid Mont Canigou as backdrop on a fine day (320 days of sun per year are claimed, so you should be lucky). As you might expect, it has a terrace, where you can eat out or just observe the view (as Picasso is said to have done); and there are good facilities for the more active. Inside, a relaxed and casual atmosphere prevails despite the modern comforts. The best of the bedrooms – all of which are well equipped – are very spacious and smart.

The restaurant has recently been given a separate identity – La Cerisaie. At lunchtime there is a tempting *carte brasserie* as a lighter alternative to the more serious food that for years has merited a Gault-Millau *toque*.

Nearby Perpignan; beaches (30 km); Castelnou (30 km).

Rte de Fontfrède 66400 Céret
Tel 04.68.87.01.94
Fax 04.68.87.39.24
Location in Pyrenean foothills above town, 26 km SW of Perpignan; with gardens and car parking
Meals breakfast, lunch, dinner; room service
Prices rooms 595F-795F, suites 1,100F-1,200F; breakfast 80F
Rooms 25 double, all with bath; 1 suite, with bath; all rooms have air-conditioning, phone, TV, minibar, hairdrier
Facilities dining-room, sitting-room, bar; ping-pong, helipad, swimming-pool, tennis-court, petanque, golf practice area **Credit cards** MC, V **Children** accepted
Disabled facilities
Pets accepted
Closed end Oct to end Feb
Proprietor M. Leveille-Nizerolle

The South

La Bonne Etape

'Exceptional food, impeccable service, beautiful pool and rooms – worth every franc' says a very satisfied recent visitor to this long-established 'good stopover'.

The setting (on a busy road in an unremarkable town) is not auspicious, and the outside gives little hint of what lies within – one of the most satisfactory blends of refinement and hospitality to be found in France. Where to start? Perhaps in the kitchen, where Pierre and Jany Gleize (father and son) make innovative and stylish use of largely home-grown ingredients, earning a star from Michelin and 18/20 from Gault-Millau. Among their specialities is Sisteron lamb (raised on fragrant Provençal pastures). The light, warm dining-room is a supremely comfortable and relaxing place, with well-spaced round tables.

But this is no restaurant-with-rooms. Bedrooms are more than comfortable – beautifully decorated and furnished with a tasteful mix of modern and antique pieces; bathrooms, too, are individual, 'spacious, with double basins and film star mirrors and lights' reports a delighted guest. The pool is a superb sun-trap, with an attractive terrace surround. To cap it all, the Gleize family are warmly welcoming hosts, happily committed to their work.

Nearby Les Mées (10 km); Sisteron – citadel; hill-walking.

Chemin du Lac 04160 Château-Arnoux
Tel 04.92.64.00.09
Fax 04.92.64.37.36
Location in country town, on main RN 85 14 km SE of Sisteron (motorway 3 km); with car parking, garage and garden
Meals breakfast, lunch, dinner
Prices rooms 600F-900F, suites 900F-1,300F; breakfast 85F; menus 220F-520F
Rooms 11 double, 7 suites, all with bath; all rooms have air-conditioning, phone, TV, radio, minibar
Facilities 2 dining-rooms, sitting-room, bar, conference room; heated swimming-pool
Credit cards AE, DC, MC, V
Children accepted
Disabled no special facilities
Pets accepted
Closed Jan to mid-Feb; Sun night and Mon from Nov to Mar
Proprietors Gleize family

The South

La Vieille Fontaine

Built within the walls of the ruined chateau of a medieval forti-fied village, with cobbled streets and ivy-clad ramparts, this little hotel is full of charm. *Patron* and chef, M Audibert, is a Marseillais; his *gratinée de langoustines* and *chou farci à la provençale*, accompanied by the local Tavel *rosé*, have long been the restaurant's attractions. The hotel is the creation of Mme Audibert, a native of this once semi-abandoned village. Inspired by the Louvre pyramid, she has, with great flair, clad the exterior circular staircase to the bedrooms with an elegant glass structure, at which one can gaze in wonder over breakfast in the courtyard. Her decorating style is simple and pretty; tiled bathrooms, Provençal fabrics, furniture from local *antiquaires*. One room contains a great chunk of the old château wall. Most have terraces; numbers 7 and 8 have views way over the top of the castle wall to the south. A steep flight of stone steps through terraced gardens leads to the pool: water gushes down from the hillside, and it is like bathing in a mountain stream. The welcome is spontaneous and warm; dinner on the terrace looking over the hills and vineyards of the Gard is a delight.

Nearby Orange; Avignon; the Gorges of the Ardèche.

30630 Cornillon
Tel 04.66.82.20.56
Fax 04.66.82.33.64
Location well into the village, with limited vehicular access
Meals breakfast, lunch, dinner
Prices 550F-950F; breakfast 45F
Rooms 8 double, all with bath and shower; all rooms have TV, phone, electric heating and entrance hall; 6 with terraces
Facilities sitting-room; dining-room; courtyard terrace; terraced garden; swimming-pool;
Credit cards AE, MC, V
Children welcome
Disabled not suitable
Pets accepted: 55F a day
Closed Jan and Feb
Proprietors M and Mme Audibert

The South

Hostellerie de Crillon le Brave

'Delightful,' enthuses one satisfied visitor to this luxurious hotel occupying the old vicarage in the hilltop village of Crillon-le-Brave. 'Very good restaurant, excellent service, a lovely setting and a charming *patron*.'

The rambling 16thC stone-built house is solid and calm, but most of the credit for the resounding success of the hotel – open only since late 1989 – must go to the aforementioned *patron*, Peter Chittick, a Canadian lawyer with exceptionally clear ideas about hotelkeeping. A considerable share goes also to the perched location, giving uninterrupted views of a heavenly landscape of olive groves and vineyards.

The central trick that Mr Chittick and his collaborator Craig Miller have pulled off is to provide luxury without erasing character. Despite the designer fabrics, fitted carpets and smart bathrooms, the exposed beams, white walls and rustic furniture dominate both in the sitting-rooms and the spacious bedrooms. You eat beneath stone vaults, or out on the pretty terrace. Chef Philippe Monti produces refined Provençale food that is in perfect harmony with this blissful setting.

Nearby Mont Ventoux; Orange (35 km); Avignon; Gordes.

Place de l'Eglise, 84410 Crillon-le-Brave
Tel 04.90.65.61.61
Fax 04.90.65.62.86
Location in hilltop village 35km NE of Avignon, on D138 off D974, with garden, private car parking and garages
Meals breakfast, lunch (Sat and Sun only), dinner, snacks
Prices rooms 750F-1,250F, suites 1,450F-2,300F; breakfast 80F, dinner about 350F
Rooms 19 double (7 twin), 18 with bath, one with shower; 5 suites; all rooms have central heating, phone, minibar, hairdrier
Facilities 3 sitting-rooms, dining-room; swimming-pool
Credit cards AE, MC, V
Children welcome; babysitting available **Disabled** access difficult **Pets** accepted
Closed Jan to Mar; restaurant, lunch, Mon-Fri
Proprietors Peter Chittick and Craig Miller

The South

Converted castle, Dieulefit

Les Hospitaliers

Readers continue to be impressed by this distinctive hotel, a former stronghold in a dominating position above the perched medieval village of Le Poët-Laval. Apart from the views, especially from the terrace (where meals are served in fine weather) and pool area, the warm welcome and the comfortable top-floor sitting-room are singled out. The restaurant has an interesting collection of paintings; Yvon Morin is a former art dealer. Tables are laid with fine china, white linen or lace, and candles; service is hard to fault, and the food is excellent – the daily changing menu is particularly recommended. Bedrooms are furnished with antiques; size varies along with price.

Nearby Montélimar (20 km); Viviers (30 km) – medieval town.

Le Poët-Laval, 26160 La Bégude-de-Mazenc
Tel 04.75.46.22.32
Fax 04.75.46.49.99
Location at top of old village, 5 km W of Dieulefit; with gardens; car parking nearby
Meals breakfast, lunch, dinner
Prices rooms 375F-1,100F; menus 160F-450F
Rooms 21 double, 20 with bath, one with shower (8 twin); 3 family rooms, all with bath; all rooms have central heating, phone
Facilities 2 dining-rooms, 2 sitting-rooms, bar; swimming- pool
Credit cards AE, DC, MC, V
Children accepted
Disabled no special facilities
Pets cats and dogs accepted
Closed mid-Nov to Feb (except Fri and Sat eve and Sun lunch)
Proprietors M. and Mme Yvon Morin

The South

Country hotel, Les Essareaux

La Manescale

The King of Belgium has slept here. No doubt, like so many others, he was charmed by all he found in this remote former shepherd's house up in the hills. The thoughtfulness of owners, M and Mme Warland, permeates what could be described as a pocket-sized hotel with every comfort. The smallest details are attended to here, from towels for the swimming-pool to a small library for serious readers and helpfully labelled light switches. Mme Warland, in her apron, cooks in the kitchen and gathers fresh flowers before meals for the tables; M Warland prints out the menu on his fax machine and delivers her delicious dishes, such as *magret de canard* with apples and bilberries, to diners. Stone steps and pathways connect the main building to garden rooms, each giving privacy and views of the forest and hillsides. Two rooms are named after M Warland's favourite painters – Tiepolo and Dali.A place for lovers of quiet and of nature, there are numerous paths through the woods for long walks. Classical music plays on the terrace at *aperitif* time; the views across vineyards and valleys to Mont Ventoux in the distance are superb. It's a steep walk from parking to hotel: a luggage trolley is provided.
Nearby Vaison-la-Romaine 7 km; Côtes du Rhône vineyards.

Route de Faucon
Les Essareaux,
84340 Entrechaux
Tel 04.90.46.03.80
Fax 04.90.46.03.89
Location in the hills
Meals breakfast, dinner
Prices 425F-850F; breakfast 65F
Rooms 5; 2 with bath, 3 with shower; all rooms have phone, TV, central heating, minibar
Facilities terrace, gardens; swimming-pool; secure parking
Credit cards AE, DC, EC, MC, V
Children welcome if well-behaved
Disabled not suitable
Pets dogs permitted
Closed end Oct to Easter
Proprietors M and Mme Warland

The South

Moulin de la Camandoule

We stick to this restored olive-mill year after year. We have received nothing but praise for the Rillas' deeply relaxing country hotel. As a rule, a minimum stay of three nights is required in the busy season, but this should prove no hardship, as an inspection visit confirms this to be one of the most captivating hotels in these pages.

The mill lies in extensive private grounds divided in half by the low Roman aqueduct which used to bring water to the mill. The existing building dates from the 19th century, and was rescued from ruin some thirty years ago. Shirley and Wolf Rilla (an English/German couple) moved here in 1986.

Food is a highlight for most visitors. Meals are served outside in summer – on a terrace overlooking the cherry orchard, or by the pool – or in the delightfully rustic dining-room decorated with original mill trappings. Between this and the lofty, beamed sitting-room (with its adjoining 'snuggery') is the ancient water wheel, now preserved behind glass. Bedrooms differ widely in size and style. Books, family paintings, ornaments and fresh flowers add to the welcoming (not at all smart) atmosphere.

Nearby Grasse (23 km) – perfumes; Cannes (30 km).

Chemin Notre-Dame-des-Cyprès 83440 Fayence
Tel 04.94.76.00.84
Fax 04.94.76.10.40
Location at foot of village, 30 km NW of Cannes; in large grounds with ample parking
Meals breakfast, lunch, dinner
Prices rooms 250F-700F, DB&B 455F-580F (obligatory 25 Mar to 15 Oct); breakfast 51F, menu 185F-265F
Rooms 10 double, 8 with bath, 2 with shower, (4 twin); 2 single with shower; all rooms have central heating, phone; most with TV
Facilities dining-room, sitting-room with bar; swimming-pool with bar, barbecue
Credit cards MC, V
Children accepted
Disabled no special facilities
Pets accepted (40F)
Closed never
Proprietors Wolf and Shirley Rilla

The South

Converted mill, Fontvieille

La Régalido

We continue to be fond of this 19th-century oil mill, a Relais & Chateaux place which manages to remain informal and friendly despite its elegant furnishings and high prices – largely thanks to the presence at all hours of the welcoming and helpful Jean-Pierre Michel, chef-proprietor.

The Régalido has been converted into a fine auberge in a thoroughly Provençal style, decorated with great flair by Madame Michel. There is a charming sitting-room full of flowers, and a log fire lit on chilly days. Tables are beautifully set in the elegant, peaceful, stone-vaulted dining-room, and there is an atmosphere of well-being which suits the excellent cooking of Jean-Pierre. His style is classic, but he has a penchant for Provençal dishes (seafood, olive oil, herbs and garlic) – and terracotta or cast iron pots appear alongside the silver salvers.

Bedrooms are individually decorated, and very comfortable, with lots of extras in the well equipped bathrooms. Friendly staff and a pretty, flowery garden – with a terrace surrounded by mimosa and shaded by fig and olive trees – complete the picture. **Nearby** Montmajour Abbey; Arles; the Camargue (10 km) – flamingoes, white horses; Tarascon (15 km) – château.

Rue Frederic-Mistral 13990 Fontvieille
Tel 04.90.54.60.22
Fax 04.90.54.64.29
Location in middle of village, 9 km NE of Arles; with gardens and ample car parking
Meals breakfast, lunch, dinner
Prices rooms 660F-1,510F; breakfast 98F, menus 260F-410F
Rooms 15 double, 12 with bath, 2 with shower; all rooms have central heating, air-conditioning, phone, minibar
Facilities dining-room, 2 sitting-rooms, bar
Credit cards AE, DC, MC, V
Children accepted
Disabled one specially equipped ground-floor bedroom
Pets accepted (at a charge)
Closed Jan; restaurant only, Mon and Tue lunch, Mon dinner in low season
Proprietor Jean-Pierre Michel

The South

Relais de la Magdeleine

'If only there were more hotels like this,' begins our latest enthusiastic reader's report on this lovely old *bastide*. We share the sentiment: for those of us who can't or won't pay the prices (or don't like the style) of Relais & Châteaux places, a gracious country house like this is quite a find. It is a family affair. Daniel Marignane's mother opened the hotel in 1932, he and his wife now run the hotel with great charm and good humour, and their son is now in charge of the kitchen – and achieving great things.

An acid test of a hotel is visitors' reactions to flaws. When they reveal them to us grudgingly, in a favourable light, we know we are on to a winner. 'A touch of shabbiness here and there only adds to the charm,' says one report otherwise full of praise.

The great trick that the Marignanes pull off is that of steering a sensitive middle course. The public rooms are elegant, but lived-in. The bedrooms too are home-like, but the best have posh bathrooms. The hotel pampers grown-ups, but is welcoming to children. Prices are at exactly the level that many comfortably-off British travellers in France will find bearable. If only there were more like this, indeed.

Nearby Cassis (15 km) – coastal inlets; La Ste-Baume massif.

13420 Gémenos
Tel 04.42.32.20.16
Fax 04.42.32.02.26
Location on outskirts of town, 23 km E of Marseilles; with garden and ample car parking
Meals breakfast, lunch, dinner
Prices rooms 395F-750F; menu 250F
Rooms 24 double, 20 with bath, 4 with shower (12 twin); 4 family rooms, all with bath; all rooms have central heating, phone, TV
Facilities sitting-rooms, dining-rooms; swimming-pool
Credit cards MC, V
Children accepted
Disabled no special facilities
Pets not accepted
Closed Dec to mid-Mar
Proprietors M. and Mme Marignane

The South

Le Coteau Fleuri

Our files contain a pretty solid record of support for this attractive stone house, built into the hillside at the edge of the fashionable perched village of Grimaud, and run by Jacques Minard (previously manager of the Mas de Chatelas) since 1988. Our most recent reporter had not only 'a good time' in general, but 'the best meal of the holiday.'

The house is about a hundred years old and retains a simple Provençal style. There is a rambling garden with olive trees, and a small flowery terrace in front of the hotel. The spotless bedrooms have pretty furnishings and prints, and smart tiled bathrooms; most are rather small, but many have a splendid view of vineyards and the Maures massif (others look out over the garden and the ruins of Grimaud castle and chapel). The public rooms are attractive and relaxing: there is a small bar, a dining-room in two parts (both of which extend on to the terrace and benefit from the view), and a spacious sitting-room with tiled floor and grand piano. Throughout the hotel are masses of fresh flowers. In winter there are log fires.

Food is a highlight; *nouvelle* in style but not in quantity, theatrically presented by attentive staff. The *mousse au chocolat* is acquiring cult status

Nearby St-Tropez (10 km); Pampelonne (15 km).

Place des Pénitents, Grimaud 83310 Cogolin
Tel 04.94.43.20.17
Fax 04.04.94.43.33.42
Location in middle of village behind chapel; with car parking in front
Meals breakfast, lunch, dinner
Prices rooms 300F-550F; breakfast 45F, menus from 190F
Rooms 13 double, 8 with bath, 5 with shower (4 twin); one family room with bath; all rooms have phone
Facilities dining-room, sitting-room, bar
Credit cards AE, DC, MC, V
Children welcome
Disabled no special facilities
Pets accepted if well behaved
Closed 3 weeks Dec, 2 weeks Jan; restaurant only, Tue (except Jul and Aug)
Proprietors Jacline and Jacques Minard

The South

Le Verger

'Glad to see Le Verger appearing in your guide,' says a reader, in response to its inclusion for the first time a few years ago. 'I've known this pleasant little spot for some years, and often thought it was your kind of hotel – that is, a very unhotel-like hotel.' Indeed: the Zacharys have kept the scale and feel of the private house they converted in 1987. It is a typical Provencal building – low, with shallow roofs of pale tiles.

'Our friends call this place 'Little Normandy' because it is so green, unlike most of the Côte d'Azur,' says Anne Zachary, highlighting just one attractive aspect of Le Verger. The 'French windows' of harmonious, freshly decorated bedrooms open directly on to the lawn, and so the pool. Meals are served outside in summer, on a partly covered terrace looking across the pool to woods and hills, or before an open fire in a large dining-room in cooler weather. M. Zachary – an experienced chef, with quite a local following – cooks varied and satisfying dishes in the Mediterranean style, with no pretensions. And while you're at dinner your bed will be turned down – one of the little things that Anne insists on, in order to make your stay entirely restful.

Nearby Provence countryside; St-Tropez (12 km).

Route de Collobrières 83360 Grimaud
Tel 04.94.43.25.93
Fax 04.94.43.33.92
Location in countryside 1 km W of Grimaud, on D14 off D558, 12 km W of St-Tropez; in spacious gardens with private car parking
Meals breakfast, lunch, dinner
Prices rooms 500F-850F; breakfast 60F, menus 100F-150F
Rooms 6 double, all with bath; 2 single, one with bath, one with shower; all rooms have central heating, phone, TV
Facilities sitting-room, dining-room; swimming-pool
Credit cards MC, V
Children accepted, but no special facilities
Disabled not very suitable
Pets welcome
Closed Nov to Easter; restaurant also Christmas and New Year
Proprietor Mme Zachary

The South

Le Cagnard

A reader's report raised some doubts about this lovely hotel, perched along the ramparts of an old hill village – specifically about standards of service in the Michelin-starred restaurant. It is far from the most expensive hotel in the Relais & Châteaux group, but it is pricey enough for expectations in this department to be high. Off went an inspector; happily, all was well.

Le Cagnard has been sensitively converted from a series of medieval houses, most with separate street entrances. In the main house there is a stunning medieval vaulted dining-room where you eat by candlelight. But the real knockout is the upper dining-room, leading out on to the terrace: its elaborate painted ceiling slides away at the touch of a button, opening the room to the sky. The bedrooms vary widely; most retain a medieval feel, thanks to the preservation of features such as stone floors, and are furnished with style, but incongruous exceptions remain. Three rooms in one house have a lovely flowery garden. Access in anything other than a small car is tricky, and getting to some rooms involves a bit of awkward suitcase-lugging.

Nearby Château Grimaldi – modern art museum, with Renaissance courtyard; Nice (15 km); Grasse (30 km) – perfumes.

Rue Pontis-Long, Haut-de-Cagnes 06800 Cagnes-sur-Mer
Tel 04.93.20.73.21
Fax 04.93.22.06.39
Location in middle of hill village, 2 km above main town of Cagnes; car parking 300m away at entrance to village
Meals breakfast, lunch, dinner
Prices rooms 400F-1,050F, suites 1,300F-1,500F; breakfast 80F, menus 300F-500F

Rooms 18 double, 10 apartments, all with bath; all rooms have central heating, phone, TV, minibar; most have air-conditioning
Facilities dining-room, bar
Credit cards AE, DC, MC, V
Children accepted
Disabled no special facilities
Pets accepted
Closed restaurant only, Thu lunch and Nov to mid-Dec
Proprietors Barel Laroche family

The South

Auberge Atalaya

The Toussaints' delightful little rustic inn continues to impress, although recent reports are few, and more would be welcome. Llo is an attractive village high up in the Pyrenees, and is typical of the Cerdagne – a high sun-drenched plateau of pastures and pine forests, popular for summer and winter sports. The Atalaya, in a prime spot in the village, was expertly converted from an old farmhouse in 1969. The bedrooms are quiet, comfortable and intimate, with romantic fabrics and soft lighting. Local specialities are served either in the rustic dining-room – gleaming antiques against stone walls – or on a charming flowery terrace.
Nearby Odeillo (10 km) – solar furnace; Font-Romeu (15 km).

Llo 66800 Saillagouse
Tel 04.68.04.70.04
Fax 04.68.04.01.29
Location in middle of village, 2 km E of Saillagouse and 10 km E of Bourg-Madame; ample car parking
Meals breakfast, lunch, dinner
Prices rooms 490F-750F; breakfast 60F, menus 155F-195F
Rooms 12 double, 10 with bath, 2 with shower (3 twin); one suite; all rooms have central heating, phone, TV, minibar, safe
Facilities sitting-room, bar, dining-room; swimming-pool
Credit cards MC, V
Children welcome if well behaved
Disabled no special facilities
Pets accepted in bedrooms only
Closed 5 Nov to 20 Dec
Proprietors M. and Mme H Toussaint

The South

Château hotel, Madières

Château de Madières

This magnificently sited 14th-century fortress. perched above the Vis river gorge, was upgraded a few years ago to four-star status. More importantly, the refurbishments have given the interior a new vitality, shifting the hotel from the 'historic and adequately comfortable' category to the distinctly compelling.

The château was rescued from decay by the Brucys in 1982. They opened for business in 1986, having restored it to its former glory – creating comfortable rooms within the existing framework of medieval walls and arches. No two bedrooms are alike, though all have modern bathrooms and most have good views. The best are very spacious and delightfully furnished, with bold, colourful fabrics against plain white walls and oriental rugs on tiled floors. Key attractions are the public rooms – a galleried sitting-room with a vast Renaissance fireplace, and the vaulted dining-room, jutting out of the main building, with spectacular valley views. Above it is the main terrace.

Chef, Guy Bonafous, who gained a reputation for fine cooking at l'Oustal del Barry, Najac (page 170), has taken over the cooking from Madame Brucy. The *toque* from Gault Millau remains.

Nearby Cirque de Navacelles; Grotte des Demoiselles; Ganges.

Madières 34190 Ganges
Tel 04.67.73.84.03
Fax 04.67.73.55.71
Location on hillside overlooking village, on crossroads of D48 and D25; with shady park and ample car parking
Meals breakfast, lunch, dinner
Prices rooms 585F-1,150F; breakfast 80F, menus 195F-380F, children's 130F
Rooms 7 double (one twin),
3 apartments, all with bath; all rooms have central heating, phone, TV, minibar
Facilities 3 sitting-rooms, bar, 2 dining-rooms, 3 terraces, swimming-pool, fitness room
Credit cards AE, MC, V
Children accepted
Disabled no special facilities
Pets accepted
Closed Nov to Easter
Proprietors Bernard and Françoise Brucy

The South

Les Muscadins

'It's really delicious!' Our latest reporter doesn't give us any clue as to whether this endorsement is a literal verdict confined to the food, or whether it is a metaphorical verdict on the whole of this lovely place.

It certainly could be the latter; if it's the former, our reporter is at odds with our colleagues at the Guide Michelin, who have withdrawn the star Les Muscadins gained a few years ago. This is part of a gastronomic earthquake that has shaken fashionable hill-top Mougins. Michelin withdrew stars from two other restaurants as well, leaving Roger Vergé's famous Moulin sitting tight with its two stars. Meanwhile, rival guide Gault-Millau suspended Vergé's *toques*. Make of that what you will.

Star or no star, Les Muscadins – a white-washed building surrounded by tropical vegetation – is irresistible. The American owner Edward Bianchini has filled it with memorable antiques, many from the lavish homes of 18thC fops called *Muscadins*. The luxurious bedrooms are highly individual and beautifully coordinated, and have impeccable bathrooms; most also have views of the coast. Elegantly furnished terrace.

Nearby Cannes; Grasse; Vallauris (10 km) – Picasso museum.

18 Bd Courteline 06250 Mougins
Tel 04.93.90.00.43
Fax 04.92.92.88.23
Location on E road into old village, 2 km N of A8 motorway, 6 km N of Cannes; with car parking
Meals breakfast, lunch, dinner
Prices rooms 750F-950F, suite 1,200F; breakfast 60F, menus 165F-290F
Rooms 7 double, one suite;

all rooms have central heating, air-conditioning, phone, TV, minibar
Facilities sitting-room, dining-room, bar
Credit cards AE, DC, MC, V
Children welcome
Disabled access difficult
Pets welcome
Closed 1 week in Dec, mid Feb to mid Mar
Proprietor Edward Bianchini

The South

Auberge de la Madone

A recent visitor described the setting of this hotel as 'stunning'. 'Delightful' was the one-word verdict offered by another reader reporting on this top-of-the-range Logis, which happily combines a sense of special hospitality with affordable (though not low) prices. And such is its appeal, that the Millos have just opened an annexe in the old part of the village – the Auberge du Pourtail. Rooms here are less expensive and you take your meals at the Madone.

You may think that you have taken a wrong turning as you first spy Peillon, perched impossibly above, with little sign of any road leading up. Time stands still here. The medieval village consists of a few dark cobbled alleys leading up to the church, and tall stone houses looking out over rocky crests and distant forests.

The *auberge* is set just outside the walled village itself. Behind, paths lead off into the hills, past the grazing sheep with their tinkling bells; in front is the village car park and *boules* area. Within, the rather small bedrooms (with equally small balconies) are attractive and comfortable with stylish all-white bathrooms. Meals are served on the pretty, sunny terrace, under a large awning, or in the welcoming Provençal-style dining-room. Cooking is above average (a *toque* from Gault-Millau), and the menus are fair value. An all-weather tennis court is another of the hotel's attractions.

06440 Peillon-Village
Tel 04.93.79.91.17
Fax 04.93.79.99.36
Location on edge of perched village, 19 km NE of Nice; with ample car parking
Meals breakfast, lunch, dinner
Prices rooms 460F-780F; breakfast 56F; DB&B 460F-680F; menus 130F-360F
Rooms 20 double, 15 with bath, 5 with shower; all rooms have central heating, phone, TV
Facilities bar, 2 dining-rooms; tennis court
Credit cards MC, V
Children very welcome
Disabled no special facilities
Pets accepted by arrangement
Closed mid-Oct to mid-Dec, 2 weeks Jan
Proprietors Millo family

The South

Mas des Brugassières

'Very relaxed atmosphere – an excellent place to unwind after the long drive south,' is the verdict of one visitor to this modern (1974) 'farmhouse', set in lush gardens surrounded by vineyards. Bedrooms (some non-smoking) have tiled floors and traditional furniture; some open out directly on to the garden and swimming-pool (and are ventilated only by leaving the door open). There is one public room – a sitting-room-cum-bar with simple wooden furniture and vast French windows – but from Easter to October most sitting will be done outside. Mas des Brugassières is basically a breakfast-only place, but in high season light lunches can be had by the pool.

Nearby Ste-Maxime – beach resort; Port-Grimaud (15 km)

Plan-de-la-Tour 83120
Ste-Maxime
Tel 04.94.43.72.42
Fax 04.94.43.00.20
Location in countryside 8 km NW of Ste-Maxime; with gardens and ample car parking
Meals breakfast
Prices rooms 420F-550F; breakfast 40F
Rooms 14 double, all with bath and shower (5 twin); all rooms have central heating, phone
Facilities sitting-room/bar; swimming-pool, tennis
Credit cards MC, V
Children accepted
Disabled ground-floor bedrooms
Pets dogs accepted at extra charge (60F)
Closed Nov to mid-Mar
Proprietors Steve and Annick Geffine

The South

Inn, Le Pontet

Auberge de Cassagne

Although this Provençal-style *auberge* in a leafy suburb of Avignon is at the top end of our size range, it is emphatically our kind of hotel. However, we look forward to hearing other opinions, so more reports please.

The mellow 18th-century house sits in lush gardens which are among the main attractions of the hotel. There is ample space for relaxing – a swimming-pool, a plane-shaded terrace for meals, manicured lawns and paved courtyards surrounded by peaceful bungalow-style bedrooms with traditional Provençal furniture and confidently colourful fabrics, as well as all modern conveniences. There are some bedrooms in the main building, along with a cosy sitting-room. The dining-room is a lofty, spacious affair with huge exposed beams, and 'French windows' overlooking the garden.

When chef Philippe Boucher first came to the Auberge de Cassagne he was advertised as an ex-disciple of Paul Bocuse and Georges Blanc; now, he has an established reputation of his own, recognised with a star from Michelin and two *toques* from Gault-Millau.

Nearby Avignon – Palais des Papes, Pont St-Bénèzet.

84130 Le Pontet – Avignon
Tel 04.90.31.04.18
Fax 04.90.32.25.09
Location in rural suburb of Avignon, 4 km NW of middle, 3 km W of A7; with gardens and ample car parking
Meals breakfast, lunch, dinner
Prices rooms 490F-1,180F; menus 230F-460F, children's 110F
Rooms 27 double, all with bath or shower; 5 family rooms, all with bath; all rooms have central heating, air-conditioning, phone, satellite TV, minibar, safe
Facilities dining-room, 2 sitting-rooms, bar; swimming-pool
Credit cards AE, DC, MC, V
Children welcome
Disabled no special facilities
Pets accepted; 60F charge
Closed never
Proprietors Jean-Michel Gallon, Philippe Boucher and André Trestour

The South

Country house hotel, Reillanne

Auberge de Reillanne

We don't get many reports on this lovely old *bastide* turned country auberge, but they are always positive, and sometimes verge on the ecstatic. Maurice Bellaiche, who took over the place just after its appearance in our first edition, is now firmly established.

Despite the grandeur of the building – mainly 18th-century, but with parts dating from the 12th – it is not a hotel of four-star sophistication. It's a peaceful place (surrounded by fields, with views towards the Lubéron massif) with a private-home feel, sparsely furnished with great style and individuality. There are seven very large bedrooms with stone walls and beamed ceilings, and rows of books take the place of the usual mod cons – there are no radios or TVs. In the dining-room, paintings and sculptures are in perfect harmony with the setting.

Maurice Bellaiche is also in charge in the kitchen and impresses visitors with his simple honest dishes. One reporter describes him as a 'brilliantly inventive self-taught cook'. More reports would be welcome.

Nearby Lubéron Park – marked trails; St-Michel observatory (10 km); Aix-en-Provence (70 km); Avignon (80 km).

04110 Reillanne
Tel 04.92.76.45.95
Location in countryside, 1 km from village, 19 km SW of Forcalquier; in garden, with car parking
Meals breakfast, dinner
Prices rooms 270F-370F; DB&B 370F; breakfast 45F; menus 135F-180F
Rooms 5 double, all with bath (2 twin); 2 family rooms, both with bath; all rooms have central heating, phone,
minibar
Facilities sitting-room, 2 dining-rooms
Credit cards MC, V
Children welcome
Disabled no special facilities
Pets welcome if well behaved
Closed never
Proprietor Maurice Bellaiche

The South

Country hotel, Roquefort-les-Pins

Auberge du Colombier

Yes, this attractive-looking hotel in Provence really does have rooms at 160F a night – but they are singles, without a garden view, in winter. Whether you'll judge the doubles with garden terraces to be good or bad value at around 600F-700F in summer will probably depend on your luck with the weather; the rooms are relatively plain, but the gardens and pool are 'wonderful' (to quote a recent reporter), which makes up for a lot.

This is an old *mas*, low and white, whose chief attraction is certainly the setting – amid tall, shady trees, with views over wooded hills towards the sea – and the outdoor facilities that go with it. There is an especially attractive terrace for summer eating, a tennis court, and plenty of space around the swimming-pool for lounging. Should the weather let you down, you'll find a pleasant dining-room with rustic furniture indoors.

We lack recent reports on the food in general, but breakfast is good, with 'some of the best pastries we've had.' This is a useful base for seeing the sights of the Côte d'Azur – though you may be tempted to stay put instead; the Wolffs and their young staff are charming hosts.

Nearby St-Paul (10 km); Grasse – perfumeries.

06330 Roquefort-les-Pins
Tel 04.93.77.10.27
Fax 04.93.77.07.03
Location in countryside off D2085, 15 km E of Grasse, 18 km N of Cannes; with large garden and car parking
Meals breakfast, lunch, dinner
Prices rooms 160F-650F, apartments 450F-800F; breakfast 50F; menus 125F-190F, children 60F
Rooms 18 double (7 twin), 2 apartments, all with bath; all rooms have phone, TV
Facilities 2 dining-rooms, sitting-room, bar, conference room; swimming-pool, tennis court, private night-club
Credit cards AE, DC, MC, V
Children accepted
Disabled no special facilities
Pets accepted
Closed Jan
Proprietor M. Wolff

The South

Mas de Garrigon

'We arrived without reservation and were willingly accommodated; the Provençal-style room was very comfortable, the bathroom large and well stocked; the pool was heavenly after a long drive, and the surrounding area pleasant for strolling; dinner was wonderful, with a wide selection and large portions.' A reader reports this ideal end to a day's touring, supporting our promotion of this farmhouse-style hotel to a full entry a few years ago.

The ochre-coloured building was purpose-built by the Rech-Druarts in the late 1970s, though you might not guess it: the traditional Provençal farmhouse style has been carefully reproduced, with a multiplicity of rough-tiled roofs facing this way and that, as if built at random over the years. The hotel stands isolated among pines and scrub, facing the Lubéron hills. In front of the house is a neat sheltered pool sharing country views with the sunny private terraces of the bedrooms – done out in restrained modern style, and thoroughly equipped.

The place is run on house-party rather than conventional hotel lines. Guests are encouraged to browse in the well-stocked library or listen to classical music in the comfortable salon – before an open fire in winter. A new chef, Sylvain Bourlet, has taken over the cooking, but Mme Rech-Druart continues to be much involved in the menu-planning and daily food shopping.

Nearby Gordes (7 km) – château; Village des Bories (5 km).

Rte de St-Saturnin d'Apt, Roussillon 84220 Gordes
Tel 04.90.05.63.22
Fax 04.90.05.70.01
Location in countryside, on D2 3 km N of Roussillon, 7 km E of Gordes; in grounds with ample car parking
Meals breakfast, lunch, dinner
Prices rooms 590F-960F; breakfast 85F, menus 185F-330F
Rooms 7 double (2 twin), two family rooms, all with bath; all rooms have phone, TV, minibar, terrace
Facilities 3 dining-rooms, bar, library, sitting-room; swimming-pool
Credit cards AE, DC, V
Children older ones accepted if well behaved **Disabled** ground-floor bedrooms
Pets accepted by arrangement
Closed restaurant only, Mon; mid-Nov to Mar
Manager Mme Christiane Rech-Druart

The South

Country villa, St-Paul-de-Vence

Le Hameau

It's a standard pattern among readers reporting on Le Hameau that they stay longer than they planned to, which is about as clear a recommendation as you can get. Not only is it a captivating place, but also it offers very good value.

St-Paul-de-Vence is a perfectly preserved hill village. Its ramparts, rising above green terraces of vineyards and bougainvillea, provide panoramic views of the Alpes-Maritimes, and its old streets are lined by galleries, workshops and chic boutiques. Of the few hotels in and around the village, Le Hameau is certainly one of the most desirable – an unusually stylish and notably relaxed place run by a friendly and eager-to-please young couple.

It consists of a cluster of red-roofed Provençal villas, surrounded by orange, lemon and other fruit trees. Bedrooms are rustic in style, with beams, dark-wood furniture and rugs on red-tiled floors; they vary in size and price considerably – many have their own terrace or balcony. There is a cool, neat breakfast room, but you will be hoping to have no need of it – one of Le Hameau's great delights is breakfast (with home-made jam) taken in the large terraced garden, which accommodates a small but smart pool.

Nearby Maeght Foundation – contemporary arts; Cagnes-sur-Mer (5 km); Nice (15 km); Grasse (25 km) – perfumes.

528 Rte de la Colle 06570 St-Paul-de-Vence
Tel 04.93.32.80.24
Fax 04.93.32.55.75
Location one km outside village, 20 km from Nice; with gardens and ample car parking
Meals breakfast
Prices rooms 400F-620F, suites 720F; breakfast 52F
Rooms 11 double (5 twin), one single, 3 suites; all with bath or shower; one children's room ; all rooms have central heating, air-conditioning, phone, minibar, safe
Facilities sitting-room, dining-room; swimming-pool
Credit cards AE, MC, V
Children accepted if well behaved
Disabled no special facilities
Pets accepted if well behaved
Closed mid-Nov to 24 Dec, mid-Jan to mid-Feb
Manager Xavier Huvelin

The South

Château hotel, St-Rémy-de-Provence

Château hotel, St-Rémy-de-Provence

Château de Roussan

The McHugo family, who took over this beautiful country house some six years ago, are now well into their stride, with necessary upgrading (of the kitchen, for example) and a larger restaurant, now behind them. The welcoming private-home atmosphere so carefully cultivated by the original Roussel family remains intact.

The château was built by a grandson of Nostradamus (Catherine de Medici's famous astrologer) at the beginning of the 18th century. An impressive avenue of trees leads to a gracious building with a mellow exterior and fine rooms carefully and beautifully furnished with antiques. The bedrooms vary in size but are all furnished in an appropriate style (though bathrooms are modern) and are enormously atmospheric. There is a formal library/salon in the oldest part of the house, and a vaulted breakfast room.

Meals and drinks can be had on the terrace. In the delicious, informal grounds there is plenty of room to sit in perfect solitude – overlooking a fountain, or perhaps the 16th-century farmhouse which belonged to Nostradamus himself.

Nearby Tarascon (15 km) – château; Avignon (30 km); Arles (30 km) and the Camargue.

Rte de Tarascon 13210 St-Rémy-de-Provence
Tel 04.90.92.11.63
Fax 04.90.92.50.59
Location in countryside, 2 km W of town; in large park, with ample car parking
Meals breakfast, lunch, dinner
Prices rooms 430F-750F; menus 75F Mon to Fri
Rooms 21 double (7 twin), 17 with bath, 4 with shower; all rooms have central heating,
phone
Facilities TV room, library
Credit cards AE, MC, V
Children welcome
Disabled 1 ground-floor bedroom
Pets accepted
Closed never
Proprietors Judy and Brian McHugo

The South

Town hotel, St-Tropez

La Ponche

You might not think St-Tropez would be our kind of town, but La Ponche is our kind of hotel, at least when we're feeling like a treat. Tucked away in a tiny square overlooking the small fishing port and tiny beach of La Ponche (where Vadim's *And God Created Woman* was filmed, starring Brigitte Bardot), this cluster of 17thC houses offers a compelling combination of sophistication and warmth. Margerite Barbier started her fishermen's bar in 1937; later her daughter, Simone Duckstein, steadily transformed it into a stylish, arty 4-star hotel, full of personal touches. Paintings by Mme Duckstein's first husband cover the walls.

You can eat on a terrace, looking across a square to the sea, or in one of several areas indoors, including the main dining-room – unpretentious but sophisticated. The food is memorable, particularly the seafood. Bedrooms are captivating and very comfortable. Many have recently been smartly re-vamped, with stylish colour schemes and slick bathrooms. A couple of noisier bedrooms facing the street may induce you to sleep with the double-glazed windows closed and the air-conditioning on.

Nearby Beaches: Les Graniers (100m); La Bouillabaisse (1 km); Tahiti (4 km).

3 Rue des Remparts 83990 St-Tropez
Tel 04.94.97.02.53
Fax 04.94.97.78.61
Location in heart of old town, overlooking Port des Pêcheurs; with private garage and valet parking
Meals breakfast, lunch, dinner
Prices rooms 500F-1,700F, suites 1,100F-2,300F; breakfast 60F, lunch 120F, dinner 180F

Rooms 11 double with bath; 2 family rooms with bath; 2 apartments; 3 suites; all have air- conditioning, central heating, phone, satellite TV, minibar, safe
Facilities TV room, bar, 2 dining-rooms
Credit cards AE, MC, V
Children accepted
Disabled access difficult
Pets accepted
Closed end Oct to end Mar
Proprietor Mme Barbier

The South

Seaside hotel, Les Stes-Maries-de-la-Mer

Mas de la Fouque

Prices at this casual but exclusive retreat in a lagoonside setting near the main resort of the Camargue are about as high as any in this guide. But the hotel 'provides every luxury and was well worth the money,' according to a recent visitor and his wife, who could find no fault. Its appeal lies in the peaceful, away-from-it-all atmosphere – 'from the room we could watch egrets wading and the famous white horses of the Camargue grazing'. Rooms throughout are smartly decorated – white walls, tiled floors, timbered ceilings – and the bedrooms are the epitome of comfort, with private terraces built over the lagoon. Despite the four-star luxuries, this is very much a family-run hotel with a friendly, relaxed atmosphere. Food is excellent, with regional dishes elegantly presented; many vegetables and herbs are home-grown.
Nearby The Camargue; Aigues-Mortes (25 km); Arles (38 km).

Rte du Petit Rhône 13460 Les Stes-Maries-de-la-Mer
Tel 04.90.97.81.02
Fax 04.90.97.96.84
Location in the Camargue, 4 km NW of Les Stes-Maries-de-la-Mer; with ample car parking
Meals breakfast, lunch, dinner
Prices rooms 980F-2,020F; lunch 170F-235F, dinner 235F-395F
Rooms 10 double, all with bath and terrace (4 twin);1 family room and 2 suites, with whirlpool bath and shower; all rooms have phone, TV, air-conditioning, minibar, fans
Facilities 2 sitting-rooms, bar, dining-room; tennis, swimming-pool, putting
Credit cards AE, DC, MC, V
Children welcome if well supervised **Disabled** access easy; all on ground floor
Pets dogs accepted
Closed 2 Nov to 25 Mar
Proprietor Jean-Paul Cochat

The South

Hôtel des Deux Rocs

A captivating hotel in a captivating hill village, the hotel's setting (it is an 18th-century mansion, just outside the medieval walls) remains one of its main attractions. The streets may be very steep and cobbled, and parking may be awkward, but for most visitors that counts for little compared to the pleasure of breakfast or an evening drink beside the fountain on the shady little square in front, looking across the green valley.

Inside there are two inviting little *salons*, one serving as a bar, and a long wood-and-stone dining-room. The food is traditional and excellent. Bedrooms vary in size and standard. Those at the back of the house are rather cramped, while some of those at the front are marvellously spacious and light, with vigorous colour schemes. The dynamic Mme Hirsch is ever-present, overseeing the scrupulous housekeeping – first-class linen and towels – taking the orders at dinner, advising on sightseeing excursions. Food is plentiful, with some regional-based dishes, and served in the light, Provençal-style dining-room. An elderly couple, who visited recently were delighted by the considerate and efficient staff.
Nearby Lac de Saint Cassien (15 km); Gorges du Verdon (40 km); Grasse (32 km); Cannes (47 km).

Place Font d'Amont 83440 Seillans
Tel 04.94.76.87.32
Fax 04.94.76.88.68
Location at top of small village, 30 km W of Grasse; with terrace
Meals breakfast, lunch, dinner
Prices rooms 260F-520F; breakfast 43F; DB&B 310F-440F; menus 140F-210F
Rooms 15 double (5 twin), all with bath or shower; all rooms have central heating, phone, minibar
Facilities dining-room, bar, sitting-room
Credit cards MC, V
Children accepted
Disabled no special facilities
Pets dogs accepted but not in dining-room
Closed Nov to mid-Mar
Proprietor Mme Hirsch

The South

Château de Trigance

For well over 20 years now, Jean-Claude Thomas and his wife have run this characterful and comfortable hotel in the remote limestone hills that surround the dramatic Gorges du Verdon, but they show no sign of flagging. Trigance remains a welcoming port of call in a region of few villages and even fewer hotels, and the cooking by young chef Philippe Joffroy is an added bonus.

On arrival, you might be taken aback. Is this fortress perched high on a rocky hilltop really your hotel? (Yes.) And if it is, how are you going to penetrate its defences? (By climbing a steep flight of rocky stairs – don't worry, your bags will be carried up.)

Once inside, you are in the Middle Ages. Stone by stone, M. Thomas has painstakingly rebuilt his 11thC castle (for many years it served as a quarry for the local villagers); he will be delighted to show you before-and-after photographs to prove it. The impressive stone-vaulted, candle-lit dining-room, and the sitting-room below, are windowless and highly atmospheric, furnished in medieval style. Most of the bedrooms (cut into the hill) are similar, with canopied beds, antique furniture, tapestries and banners – and fine views from their windows.

Nearby Verdon gorge – Europe's 'Grand Canyon'.

83840 Trigance
Tel 04.94.76.91.18
Fax 04.94.85.68.99
Location overlooking tiny village, 10 km NW of Comps-sur-Artuby; with terrace, and private car parking
Meals breakfast, lunch, dinner
Prices rooms 550F-750F, suites 900F; menus 200F-360F
Rooms 8 double, all with bath; 2 suites; all rooms have central heating, phone, TV

Facilities dining-room, sitting-room
Credit cards AE, DC, MC, V
Children welcome
Disabled access very difficult
Pets accepted
Closed Nov to mid-Mar
Proprietor Jean-Claude Thomas

The South

Village inn, Vallon-Pont-d'Arc

Le Manoir du Raveyron

It sounds grand, but is nothing of the sort: this is the sort of rustic village inn that is the bedrock of French hotelkeeping – a two-fireplace Logis offering simple but satisfactory accommodation, modest prices, a warm welcome and excellent wholesome food (visit the place on a Sunday and you'll find it bursting at the seams with lunching families.) The hotel faces an ugly modern building; but the surroundings do not intrude, because the old stone building is set well back from the street, behind gates and a large and leafy courtyard-cum-garden. We get occasional reports confirming our recommendation of the Manoir, but we would welcome more.

Nearby Gorges de l'Ardèche; Pont d'Arc (5 km); Marzal (20 km).

Rue Henri Barbusse 07150 Vallon-Pont-d'Arc
Tel 04.75.88.03.59
Fax 04.75.37.11.12
Location in village on D579, 33 km S of Aubenas, 51 km NE of Alés; with garden and car parking
Meals breakfast, lunch, dinner
Prices rooms 175F-275F; menus 98F-220F, children's 42F
Rooms 15 double, one single, all with shower; all rooms have central heating
Facilities dining-room, sitting-room/bar
Credit cards MC, V
Children welcome
Disabled no special facilities
Pets accepted
Closed mid-Oct to mid-Mar
Proprietors M. Bourdat and M. Gauthier

The South

Converted castle, Les Arcs

Le Logis du Guetteur

This 11thC fort still looks more or less as it must have done nine centuries ago. The modernised bedrooms are quiet, with lovely views, and there is a pleasant pool. But the main emphasis is on the medieval cellar restaurant and terrace, where satisfying classic dishes are served.

■ Place du Château, 83460 Les Arcs (Var) **Tel** 04.94.73.30.82 **Fax** 04.94.73.39.95 **Meals** breakfast, lunch, dinner **Prices** rooms 450F; breakfast 48F, menus 135F-280F **Rooms** 11, all with bath or shower, central heating **Credit cards** AE, DC, MC, V **Closed** mid-Jan to mid-Feb

---

Seaside hotel, Argelès-sur-Mer

Le Cottage

An enthusiastic readers' report restores the entry of this three-fireplace Logis, evidently much improved since its last appearance: 'We'd be pleased to go back. Bright, simple room; elegant, innovative and delicious dinner.' Pleasant garden, with pool.

■ 21 Rue Arthur-Rimbaud, 66700 Argelès-sur-Mer (Pyrénées-Orientales) **Tel** 04.68.81.07.33 **Fax** 04.68.81.59.69 **Meals** breakfast, lunch, dinner **Prices** rooms 290F-520F; breakfast 50F, lunch 80F, menus 150F-270F **Rooms** 32 (1 suite), all with central heating, phone, satellite TV, hairdrier, safe **Credit cards** MC, V **Closed** Nov to end-Mar

---

Country hotel, Auribeau

Auberge de la Vignette Haute

This extraordinary place has been virtually rebuilt since the disastrous fire of 1986, but has the feel of a medieval farmhouse. It is filled with gleaming rustic antiques, and bedrooms are spacious, and highly individual. Pool. There is a farm menagerie nearby. Caters for parties, so you might want to avoid weekends.

■ 06810 Auribeau (Alpes-Maritimes) **Tel** 04.93.42.20.01 **Fax** 04.93.42.31.16 **Meals** breakfast, lunch, dinner **Prices** rooms 750F-1,900F; breakfast 80F-110F, lunch 160F-350F, menus 360F-510F (drinks included) **Rooms** 12, all with bath, central heating, phone, TV, minibar **Credit cards** AE, MC, V **Closed** never; restaurant only, mid-Nov to mid-Dec

---

Country hotel, Baix

Hostellerie La Cardinale

The birthplace of the Relais & Châteaux chain. La Cardinale is a gloriously welcoming old house, with five beautiful bedrooms; the rest, along with a smart pool, are 3 km away at the Résidence.

■ Quai du Rhône, 07210 Baix (Ardèche) **Tel** 04.75.85.80.40 **Fax** 04.75.85.82.07 **Meals** breakfast, lunch dinner **Prices** rooms 700F-1,200F, suite 1,500F-1,800F; breakfast 100F **Rooms** 15, all with bath or shower, 9 with air-conditioning, TV, phone, minibar, **Credit cards** AE, DC, V **Closed** Jan to mid-Mar

The South

Village hotel, Le Barroux

Les Géraniums

Well off the beaten track, this is the sort of simple and peaceful *auberge* that is becoming increasingly hard to find. Comfortable rustic-style bedrooms and smart bathrooms (some separating walls are rather thin). Attractive beamed dining-room. Cooking is uncomplicated but 'excellent'. 'Bustling', 'friendly', 'good value for money' comment recent satisfied customers.

■ Le Barroux, 84330 Caromb (Vaucluse) **Tel** 04.90.62.41.08 **Fax** 04.90.62.56.48 **Meals** breakfast, lunch, dinner **Prices** rooms 210F-250F; breakfast 35F; menus 80F-250F **Rooms** 20, all with bath or shower, central heating, phone **Credit cards** AE, DC, MC, V **Closed** restaurant only, Jan-mid Feb

---

Country inn, Les Baux-de-Provence

Auberge de la Benvengudo

The Beaupied family's creeper-clad hotel remains compelling – and much more affordable than most places in the area. Rooms have the style of a private country house: a cosy sitting-room with beams, an intimate dining-room and bedrooms with pretty patterned curtains. Light lunches are served by the pool. Tennis.

■ Vallon de l'Arcoule, 13520 Les Baux-de-Provence (Bouches-du-Rhône) **Tel** 04.90.54.32.54 **Fax** 04.90.54.42.58 **Meals** breakfast, lunch, dinner **Prices** rooms 520F-670F, suites 800F-930F (reductions in Feb, Mar and Oct); menus 240F **Rooms** 20, all with bath, central heating, air-conditioning, phone, TV, safe **Credit cards** AE, MC, V **Closed** Nov to mid-Feb; restaurant only, Sun

---

Converted mill, Les Beaumettes

Le Moulin Blanc

An attractive (though not cheap) base for an extended stay: extensive lawns and a smart pool. Bedrooms are large, with restrained decoration and handsome antiques. The main dining-room is light and lofty, the sitting-room a rough-stone vault with rugs on a polished floor. Excellent classic cooking.

■ Les Beaumettes, 84220 Gordes (Vaucluse) **Tel** 04.90.72.34.50 **Fax** 04.90.72.25.41 **Meals** breakfast, lunch, dinner **Prices** rooms 450F-920F; breakfast 60F; menus 160F-250F **Rooms** 18, all with bath, phone, TV, radio alarm, minibar; some rooms have terrace **Credit cards** AE, DC, MC, V **Closed** never

---

Seaside hotel, Cap d'Antibes

La Gardiole

We have conflicting reports on this pink-washed hotel – one of the more modest places in this 'exclusive' area. It is furnished simply – dark-wood chairs and rugs on polished tiled floors. The regional cooking is 'not cheap but very good'. More reports, please.

■ Chemin de la Garoupe, 06600 Cap d'Antibes (Alpes-Maritimes) **Tel** 04.93.61.35.03 **Fax** 04.93.67.61.87 **Meals** breakfast, lunch, dinner **Prices** rooms 420F-650F; menus 99F-175F **Rooms** 21, all with bath or shower, central heating, air-conditioning, phone, minibar, safe; TV on request **Credit cards** AE, DC, MC, V **Closed** Nov to Feb

The South

Country house hotel, Carcassonne

Domaine d'Auriac

A relaxing country house of which the primary attractions are outdoors: golf and tennis on the doorstep, a pool surrounded by beautifully manicured gardens and a dining terrace with a blissfully verdant view. But conditions indoors are comfortable too – this, after all, is a member of Relais & Châteaux.

■ Route de Saint-Hilaire, 11009 Carcassonne (Aude) **Tel** 04.68.25.72.22 **Fax** 04.68.47.35.54 **Meals** breakfast, lunch, dinner **Prices** rooms 500F-1,500F; breakfast 80F, menus 190F-390F **Rooms** 27, all with bath or shower, central heating, air conditioning, phone, TV, minibar **Credit cards** AE,DC, MC, V **Closed** 10 Feb to 3 Mar, 17 Nov to 8 Dec; Sun, Mon out of season; restaurant 1 Oct to Easter, Sun eve; Mon lunch out of season

---

Country hotel, Céret

Le Mas Trilles

Two separate reports force this charming 17thC farmhouse to our attention – 'the hotel we enjoyed most in two very enjoyable weeks,' says one; 'like staying with friends, in a beautiful setting,' says the other. Simple, stylish furnishings in spacious rooms. Lush garden with a fair-sized heated pool. Enclosed car park.

■ Le Pont de Reynès, 66400 Céret (Pyrénées-Orientales) **Tel** 04.68. 87.38.37 **Fax** 04.68.87.4 2.62 **Meals** breakfast, dinner **Prices** rooms 440F-975F; breakfast 65F, menus 180F-220F **Rooms** 10, all with bath, central heating, phone, TV **Credit cards** AE, MC, V **Closed** Nov to end Mar

---

Village hotel, Cotignac

Lou Calen

The shady garden, dining terrace and pool are the key attractions of this shuttered house on the occasionally noisy village square of Cotignac. The house is furnished in a home-like blend of antique and rustic styles, and bedrooms vary considerably in size, style and price. Cooking is simple but hearty.

■ 1 Cours Gambetta, 83850 Cotignac (Var) **Tel** 04.94.04.60.40 **Fax** 04.94.04.76.64 **Meals** breakfast, lunch, dinner **Prices** 300F-550F; DB&B 480F-730F; FB 620F-870F (reductions for 2); menus 105F-245F **Rooms** 16, all with bath or shower, central heating, phone, TV **Credit cards** AE, DC, MC, V **Closed** Jan to late Mar; Wed except Jul and Aug; restaurant only Wed

---

Château hotel, Eygalières

Mas de la Brune

A typical Provençal *mas* – a superb Renaissance mansion, now a listed historic monument. In summer, meals are served on the terrace, overlooking the park. The dining-room and salon are both stone-vaulted; the bedrooms are furnished with colourful, harmonious fabrics. Recently under new ownership. Reports welcome.

■ 13810 Eygalières-en-Provence (Bouches-du-Rhône) **Tel** 04.90.95. 90.77 **Fax** 04.90.95.99.21 **Meals** breakfast, lunch, dinner **Prices** DB&B 845F-1,025F, including aperitif, wine and coffee **Rooms** 10, all with bath, central heating, air-conditioning, phone, hairdrier, TV, minibar, safe **Credit cards** MC, V **Closed** Jan-Mar

The South

Seaside hotel, Eze

Château Eza

Stunning views are only one attraction of this luxury hotel perched at the top of the precipitous medieval village of Eze. Bedrooms and suites are magnificent, with priceless antiques and marble bathrooms. Dishes, which have a Provençal and Italian influence, are served in the glass dining-room or outdoor terraces.

■ Rue de la Pise, 06360 Eze (Alpes-Maritimes) **Tel** 04.93.41.12.24 **Fax** 04.93.41.16.64 **Meals** breakfast, lunch, dinner **Prices** rooms 2,000F-3,000F, suites 2,500F-3,500F; lunch 250F (including wine and coffee), menus 350F-490F **Rooms** 10, all with bath, central heating, air-conditioning, phone, TV, radio, hairdrer, video recorders **Credit cards** AE, DC, MC, V **Closed** Nov to early Apr

---

Country hotel, La Favède

A l'Auberge Cévenole

Set in a circle of hills, it is peaceful and alluring. The building is a much-expanded 1950s villa in an exceptional garden with secluded corners, plus a fair-sized (unheated) swimming-pool. A rash of shepherds and shepherdesses covers many of the walls; bedrooms and bathrooms range from adequate to very comfortable.

■ La Favède, 30110 Les Salles-du-Gardon (Gard) **Tel** 04.66.34.12.13 **Fax** 04.66.34.50.50 **Meals** breakfast, lunch, dinner **Prices** rooms 300F-600F; breakfast 45F; menus 165F-265F **Rooms** 19, all with bath or shower, central heating, phone **Credit cards** MC, V **Closed** mid-Oct to Mar

---

Country inn, Gigondas

Les Florets   o'' 33

This small, family-run hotel is appropriately named: floral bedrooms, flowers on the tables and (at the right time of year) surrounded by a riot of blossom on the nearby hills. Food is excellent, and the patron is a winemaker.

■ Route des Dentelles, 84190 Gigondas (Vaucluse) **Tel** 04.90.65.85.01 **Fax** 04.90.65.83.80 **Meals** breakfast, lunch, dinner **Prices** rooms 350F-410F; breakfast 50F, lunch 95F, menus 120F-210F **Rooms** 15, all with central heating, phone; some have TV **Credit cards** AE, DC, MC, V **Closed** Jan, Feb; restaurant only, Wed

---

Farm guest-house, Gordes

La Ferme de la Huppe

'Very comfortable room in a converted stable. Beautiful pool and a lovely courtyard garden. Well run by a Dutch/Swiss family. Food very good.' So ran the reader's report that earned a place for this huddle of farm buildings. Furnishings are stylishly rustic, with some antiques and tasteful fabrics. More reports, please.

■ Les Pourquiers, 84220 Gordes (Vaucluse) **Tel** 04.90.72.12.25 **Fax** 04.90.72.01.83 **Meals** breakfast, lunch (Sun only), dinner **Prices** rooms 400F-650F with breakfast; menus 145F-200F, children's 110F **Rooms** 8, 4 with air-conditioning, all with bath, central heating, phone, TV, minibar, hairdrier **Credit cards** MC, V **Closed** early Nov to late Mar

The South

Country hotel, Gordes

Le Gordos

No restaurant, but few other drawbacks to this *mas de pierre seche*, just outside Gordes – especially if the Provençal sun shines. Most of the rooms are in outbuildings opening directly on to some part of the garden; there is tennis, as well as an attractive pool. 'Very good' service.

■ Rte de Cavaillon, 84220 Gordes (Vaucluse) **Tel** 04.90.72.00.75 **Fax** 04.90.72.07.00 **Meals** breakfast, snacks **Prices** rooms 390F-800F; breakfast 55F **Rooms** 19, all with bath or shower, phone, TV **Credit cards** AE, V **Closed** Nov to mid-Mar

---

Château hotel, Lamastre

Château d'Urbilhac

This fairy-tale château – 19thC but in Renaissance style, with round tower and steep roof – has a peaceful, elevated setting in a large park, with a good pool. The interior is rather ponderous but does not lack character or comfort. 'Good food' but 'atmosphere a little stilted' comments a visitor.

■ 07270 Lamastre (Ardèche) **Tel** 04.75.06.42.11 **Fax** 04.75.06.52.75 **Meals** breakfast, lunch, dinner **Prices** rooms 500F-700F; menus from 230F; DB&B (obligatory in season) 550F-625F **Rooms** 12, all with bath or shower, phone **Credit cards** AE, DC, MC, V **Closed** Oct to Apr

---

Town hotel, Lamastre

Hôtel du Midi

The restaurant is the heart of this hotel, serving a very successful blend of traditional and nouvelle dishes. The dining-rooms are rather plain but intimate, service helpful and friendly. Bedrooms, in a separate building a minute's walk away, are comfortably spacious and tastefully furnished.

■ Place Seignobos, 07270 Lamastre (Ardèche) **Tel** 04.75.06.41.50 **Fax** 04.75.06.49.75 **Meals** breakfast, lunch, dinner **Prices** rooms 300F-480F; menus 195F-400F **Rooms** 13, all with bath or shower, central heating, phone; some have TV **Credit cards** AE, DC, MC, V **Closed** Sun evening, Mon; mid-Dec to Feb

---

Seaside hotel, Le Lavandou

Auberge de la Calanque

This arcaded hotel overlooking the marina of Le Lavandou has no right to be here, but it comes strongly recommended by a reader – not only for the 'fantastic' view but also the 'very comfortable, airy' rooms and 'very helpful' manager. Restaurant in the hotel, but also lots of others nearby.

■ 62 Avenue du Général de Gaulle, 83980 Le Lavandou (Var) **Tel** 04.94.71.05.96 **Fax** 04.94.7 1.20.12 **Meals** breakfast, lunch, dinner **Prices** rooms 500F-1,050F; breakfast 55F, menu 180F **Rooms** 38, all with bath/shower, central heating, phone, TV **Credit cards** AE, DC, MC, V **Closed** Nov to mid- Mar; restaurant only, end-Oct, Wed out of season

The South

Village inn, Maussane-les-Alpilles

L'Oustaloun

This village hostellerie – a cheaper alternative to staying in nearby Les Baux – has abundant old-world charm and character. The restaurant occupies three 16thC stone-vaulted rooms, with a terrace for summer dining; food is honest, regional fare. Bedrooms are simple in style but furnished with handsome antiques. Reports welcome.

■ Place de l'Église, 13520 Maussane-les-Alpilles (Bouches-du-Rhône) **Tel** 04.90.54.32.19 **Fax** 04.90.54.45.57 **Meals** breakfast, lunch, dinner **Prices** rooms 280F-395F; breakfast 30F, menus 120F (Jan to Jun and Oct to Dec), 150F (Jun to Oct) **Rooms** 9, all with bath or shower, phone, TV **Credit cards** MC, V **Closed** Jan to mid-Feb; restaurant only, Wed, Jan to Jun, and Oct to Dec; Thu from Jun to Sep

---

Village hotel, Mirmande

La Capitelle

A rough-stone building in a backwater setting in a walled medieval village, yet only a few minutes' drive from the autoroute – La Capitelle makes an excellent stopover. It has an air of confident good taste, with a stylishly traditional feel to the individually and boldly decorated bedrooms, and the vaulted dining-room.

■ Le Rempart, 26270 Mirmande (Drôme) **Tel** 04.75.63.02.72 **Fax** 04.75.63.02.50 **Meals** breakfast, lunch, dinner **Prices** rooms 260F-550F, DB&B 327F-457F; breakfast 47F, menus 135F-260F, children's 55F **Rooms** 11, all with bath or shower, central heating, phone **Credit cards** AE, DC, MC, V **Closed** mid-Dec to mid-Feb; Tue and Wed lunch

---

Country hotel, Montferrat

La Calanco

The proprietor of one of our Burgundian entries suggests this new hotel in a 400-year-old house, tucked away from the crowds. Six 'lovely' bedrooms, tastefully decorated and thoughtfully equipped, and 'unobtrusive and considerate hospitality'.

■ Rue du docteur Rayol, 83131 Montferrat (Var) **Tel** 04.94.70.93.10 **Fax** 04.94.70.91.49 **Meals** breakfast, dinner on request **Prices** rooms 280F-450F with breakfast; dinner from100F **Rooms** 6, all with bath, central heating, hairdrier **Credit cards** MC, V **Closed** never

---

Country hotel, Mougins

Le Mas Candille

A charming old farmhouse that made a brief appearance in the guide in 1991. Since then it has been smartened up, and is now one of the most compelling hotels in (just outside, in fact) fashionable Mougins. Tiles, beams, ochre walls; pretty dining-terraces by the house and one of the two pools; extensive grounds.

■ Boulevard Rebuffel, 06250 Mougins (Alpes-Maritimes) **Tel** 04.93.90.00.85 **Fax** 04.92.92.85 .56 **Meals** breakfast, lunch, dinner **Prices** rooms 680F-980F, suites 2,100F; breakfast 85F, menus 165F-280F **Rooms** 24, all with bath or shower, phone **Credit cards** AE, DC, MC, V **Closed** Nov to mid-Mar; restaurant only, Tue, Wed lunch

The South

Château hotel, Nans-les-Pins

Domaine de Chateauneuf

For golfing bon viveurs, this takes some beating – a polished little Relais & Châteaux hotel beside the golf course of Sainte-Baume. The four-square 17thC house, white-painted and red-roofed, stands surrounded by pines. Inside, the style of the public rooms is grandly traditional; bedrooms have a fresh, designer style. If golf is not for you, there are tennis courts and a swimming-pool.

■ Au Logis de Nans, 83860 Nans-les-Pins (Var) **Tel** 04.94.78.90.06 **Fax** 04.94.78.63.30 **Meals** breakfast, lunch, dinner **Prices** rooms 620F-1,700F; breakfast 75F, menus 170F-230F **Rooms** 30, all with bath or shower, phone, satellite TV, minibar, hairdrier **Credit cards** AE, DC, MC, V **Closed** Dec to early Mar

---

Manor house hotel, Noves

Auberge de Noves

Luxurious and pricey (nothing like an *auberge*) isolated in the Provençal countryside. The bedrooms are beautiful and highly individual, the cooking exquisite (Michelin starred). The charming M. Lalleman displays a genuine interest in his guests despite what they are paying him.

■ 13550 Noves (Bouches-du-Rhône)**Tel** 04.90.94.19.21**Fax** 04.90.94.47.76 **Meals** breakfast, lunch, dinner **Prices** rooms 1,150F-1,500F; breakfast 100F, menus 210F-495F **Rooms** 19, 4 suites, all with bath, central heating, air-conditioning, phone,TV **Credit cards** AE, DC, V **Closed** never

---

Country hotel, Olargues

Domaine de Rieumegé

A reader alerted us to this peaceful, rustic 17thC house in the foothills of the Haut-Languedoc national park. Good food in the barn-like restaurant, antique furnishings in the cosy sitting-room and simple bedrooms. Pool and tennis in the lush grounds.

■ Rte de St-Pons, 34390 Olargues (Hérault) **Tel** 04.67.97.73.99 **Fax** 04.67.97.78.52 **Meals** breakfast, lunch, dinner, snacks **Prices** rooms 285F-510F; breakfast 55F; menus 100F-165F **Rooms** 14, all with bath or shower, central heating, phone; TV on request **Credit cards** AE, MC, V **Closed** Nov to Easter

---

Converted mill, Ornaisons

Relais du Val d'Orbieu

A carefully converted old mill encircled by trees, with simply but neatly furnished rooms, mostly at ground level and opening on to a grassy courtyard. The fixed-price menu is 'excellent', the carte 'fabulous', the welcome warm. Pool and tennis. More reports, please.

■ 11200 Ornaisons (Aude) **Tel** 04.68.27.10.27 **Fax** 04.68.27.52.44 **Meals** breakfast, lunch, dinner **Prices** rooms 420F-750F, suites 750F-1,100F; breakfast 70F, menus 195F-375F, children's 95F **Rooms** 20, all with bath, central heating, phone, TV, radio, minibar, hairdrier **Credit cards** AE, DC, MC, V **Closed** Jan; restaurant only, lunch Nov to Mar

The South

Country hotel, Pégomas

Le Bosquet

This modern hotel with a spacious garden but no restaurant has a special place in the affections of many British and other foreign visitors – probably due to the relaxed atmosphere, coupled with the the very un-Provençal prices. Pool, tennis. Our most recent reporter was 'very happy' here.

■ 74 Chemin des Perissols, 06580 Pégomas (Alpes-Maritimes) **Tel** 04.92.60.21.20 **Fax** 04.92.60.21.49 **Meals** breakfast **Prices** rooms 160F-320F, studios 340F-430F; breakfast 30F **Rooms** 24, all with bath or shower, central heating, phone **Credit cards** not accepted **Closed** 15 Feb to 4 Mar

---

Seaside hotel, Ile de Port-Cros

Le Manoir

This large green-shuttered 19thC manor house stands on a lush, secluded island (a nature reserve) a few km off the south coast and is run along house-party lines. White-walled bedrooms are furnished with 19thC pieces – simple but stylish and comfortable. Good seafood.

■ Ile de Port-Cros, 83400 Hyéres (Var) **Tel** 04.94.05.90.52 **Fax** 04.94.05.90.89 **Meals** breakfast, lunch, dinner **Prices** DB&B 690F-960F **Rooms** 23, all with bath or shower, central heating, phone **Credit cards** MC, V **Closed** Oct to Apr

---

Château hotel, Rochegude

Château de Rochegude

Despite the high cost of rooms here, we cannot resist including this sumptuous château because of its wonderful setting – overlooking the vineyards of the Rhône plain – and its equally wonderful food (one Michelin star). Bedrooms are palatial. Relais & Châteaux.

■ 26790 Rochegude (Drôme) **Tel** 04.75.97.21.10 **Fax** 04.75.04.89.87 **Meals** breakfast, lunch, dinner **Prices** rooms 500F-2,500F; breakfast 95F, menus 200F-490F **Rooms** 29, all with bath, central heating, air-conditioning, phone, TV, most have minibar **Credit cards** AE, DC, MC, V **Closed** Mid-Jan to mid-Mar

---

Seaside hotel, St-Clair

Hôtel Belle-Vue

This informal seaside hotel in lush, colourful gardens lives up to its name, with a wonderful view across the bay. It offers unpretentious but comfortable accommodation; bedrooms vary – the best are bright and spacious, with big new bathrooms; some have sea views. More reports welcome.

■ Blvd du Four des Maures, St-Clair, 83980 Le Lavandou (Var) **Tel** 04.94.71.01.06 **Fax** 04.94.71.64.72 **Meals** breakfast, lunch, dinner **Prices** rooms 350F-750F; menus 170F-250F **Rooms** 19, all with bath or shower, central heating, phone, TV **Credit cards** AE, DC, MC, V **Closed** Nov to Mar

The South

Villa guest-house, St-Jean-Cap-Ferrat

Clair Logis

It is not easy to find such a reasonably priced hotel in such an exclusive area, let alone one which has the charm of a private villa and is set in lush, secluded gardens. Bedrooms are simple (those in the annexe are not particularly spacious) and four can accommodate families. No restaurant.

■ 12 Ave Centrale, 06230 St-Jean-Cap-Ferrat (Alpes-Maritimes) **Tel** 04.93.76.04.57 **Fax** 04.93.76.11.85 **Meals** breakfast **Prices** rooms 290F-690F; breakfast 45F **Rooms** 18, all with bath, central heating, phone; most have TV, minibar **Credit cards** AE, DC, MC, V **Closed** 15 Jan to end Apr, mid-Nov to mid-Dec

---

Village hotel, St-Paul-de-Vence

La Colombe d'Or

A famous, chic small hotel, distinguished by a collection of modern art, but also a delightful place to stay. All is simple and in exquisite 'country' taste; outside there is a creeper-surrounded terrace. The food is unsophisticated, but that hardly matters.

■ Place de Gaulle, 06570 St-Paul-de-Vence (Alpes-Maritimes) **Tel** 04.93.32.80.02 **Fax** 04.93 .32.77.78 **Meals** breakfast, lunch, dinner **Prices** rooms 1,150F-1,400F; breakfast 60F, menus 250F-400F **Rooms** 25, all with bath, some with spa baths, central heating, air-conditioning, phone, TV, radio **Credit cards** AE, DC, MC, V **Closed** mid-Nov to mid-Dec

---

Country villa, St-Paul-de-Vence

Les Orangers

A traditional Provençal house in a fine hillside setting (good views), furnished with simple good taste and immaculately kept. In the sitting-room there are exposed beams, solid antiques, fresh flowers; most of the bedrooms have balconies or terraces. 'A lovely hotel despite the busy street,' enthuses a visitor.

■ Chemin des Fumerates, 06570 St-Paul-de-Vence (Alpes-Maritimes) **Tel** 04.93.32.80.95 **Fax** 04.93.32.00.32 **Meals** breakfast **Prices** rooms 410F-730F; breakfast 45F **Rooms** 10, all with bath, central heating, phone **Credit cards** MC, V **Closed** never

---

Country hotel, St-Pierre-dels-Forcats

Mouli del Riu

St-Pierre is in one of the Pyrenees' major ski areas, around Font-Romeu. The Mouli – a modern and undistinguished house, despite the traditional-sounding name – is a simple and rather quirky place. It has been in the guide since 1989, but we welcome more reports.

■ St-Pierre-dels-Forcats, 66210 Mont-Louis (Pyrénées-Orientales) **Tel** 04.68.04.20.36 **Fax** 04.68.04.20.25 **Meals** breakfast, lunch, dinner **Prices** rooms 230F-280F; menus 90F-165F **Rooms** 15, all with bath, central heating **Credit cards** AE, MC, V **Closed** Wed; Nov to mid-Dec

The South

Town hotel, St-Rémy-de-Provence

Hôtel des Arts

The shady pavement tables of this unpretentious place have long been a happy spot to sit and watch the Provençal world go by. The restaurant serves well cooked, reasonably priced, simple food (liberally laced with the region's herbs). Bedrooms seem secondary but are neatly done out in rustic style.

■ 30 Blvd Victor-Hugo, 13210 St-Rémy-de-Provence (Bouches-du-Rhône) **Tel** 04.90.92.08.50 **Fax** 04.90.92.55.09 **Meals** breakfast, lunch, dinner **Prices** rooms 190F-350F; menus 105F-140F **Rooms** 17, all with central heating, phone **Credit cards** AE, MC, V **Closed** Feb; restaurant, Tues

---

Château hotel, St-Rémy-de-Provence

Château des Alpilles

An elegant, upright 19thC manor house offering an atmosphere of gracious living combined with the facilities of a modern luxury hotel. Bedrooms are spacious and furnished with antiques, the bathrooms marble and modern. Food is served by the swimming-pool in summer.

■ Route Départmentale 31, 13210 St-Rémy-de-Provence (Bouches-du Rhône) **Tel** 04.90.92.03.33 **Fax** 04.90.92.45.17 **Meals** breakfast **Prices** rooms 860F-1,080F; suites 1,290F-2,000F; breakfast 78F, menu 190F **Rooms** 20, all with bath, central heating, phone, satellite TV, radio, minibar **Credit cards** AE, DC, MC, V **Closed** 7 Jan to 17 Feb

---

Country hotel, St-Rémy-de-Provence

Domaine de Valmouraine

The McHugos, who now manage the Château de Roussan, offer a rather more indulgent experience at their own charming farmhouse, stylishly converted into a hotel in the late 1980s. It is beautifully furnished in rustic style, and the flowery gardens contain a smart pool. Good, inventive food.

■ Petite Route des Baux, 13210 St-Rémy-de-Provence (Bouches-du-Rhône) **Tel** 04.90.92.44.62 **Fax** 04.90.92.37.32 **Meals** breakfast, lunch, dinner **Prices** rooms 590F-1,310F; breakfast 65F, menus 220F-3 30F **Rooms** 14, all with bath, central heating, air-conditioning, phone, TV, minibar, hairdrier **Credit cards** AE, DC, MC, V **Closed** never

---

Farm guest-house, St-Rémy-de-Provence

Mas des Carassins

One of the few hotels occupying an authentic mas: a farmhouse built in 1854, mellow and peaceful, set in large and rambling gardens. Almost all the bedrooms have views of the rocky Alpilles and there is a cosy sitting-room with books and plenty of local information.

■ 1 Chemin Gaulois, 13210 St-Rémy-de-Provence (Bouches-du-Rhône) **Tel** 04.90.92.15.48 **Fax** 04.90.92.63.47 **Meals** breakfast; simple evening meal on request **Prices** rooms 390F-550F; breakfast 50F **Rooms** 15, all with bath, central heating, phone **Credit cards** MC, V **Closed** Nov to Apr

The South

Village inn, St-Restitut

Auberge des Quatres Saisons

The vine-clad auberge is a fascinating conversion of ancient houses in a backwater perched village, preserving many of the old stone walls. Bedrooms are quiet, rather dark and cosy – with heavy patterns and furniture, in Provençal style. Good regional fare.

■ Place de l'Eglise, 26130 St-Restitut (Drôme) **Tel** 04.75.04.71.88 **Fax** 04.75.04.70.88 **Meals** breakfast, lunch, dinner **Prices** rooms 325F-450F; menus 130F-215F **Rooms** 10, all with bath or shower, phone **Credit cards** AE, DC, MC, V **Closed** Jan; Sat lunch

---

Seaside villa, St-Tropez

Le Yaca

This smart little hotel has been cleverly converted from three 200-year-old buildings, using a confusing mix of styles, but with 'rustic-chic' predominating. Bedrooms are furnished with antiques, simply decorated in a typical southern style, but with all the comforts.

■ 1 Blvd d'Aumale, 83990 St-Tropez (Var) **Tel** 04.94.97.11.79 **Fax** 04.94.97.58.50 **Meals** breakfast **Prices** rooms 1,900F-2,300F, suite 2,900F-3,400F; breakfast 85F **Rooms** 23, all with bath, central heating, air-conditioning, phone, TV, radio, minibar **Credit cards** AE, DC, MC, V **Closed** mid-Oct to Easter

---

Converted abbey, Salon-de-Provence

L'Abbaye de Sainte-Croix

A former monastery rescued from ruin in 1969 by the Bossard family. Superb views; cosy vaulted sitting-room with huge open fireplace; restrained solid furnishings. Bedrooms, some former monks' cells, vary in size. Food is a highlight – Michelin star.

■ Route du Val de Cuech, 13300 Salon-de-Provence (Bouches-du-Rhône) **Tel** 04.90.56.24.55 **Fax** 04.90.56.31.12 **Meals** breakfast, lunch, dinner **Prices** rooms 615F- 1,145F; breakfast 75F-110F; menus 190F-400F **Rooms** 19, all with bath or shower, central heating, phone, TV, minibar **Credit cards** AE, DC, MC, V **Closed** Nov-Mar; restaurant only, Mon lunch

---

Village hotel, Séguret

Table du Comtat

Built against the hillside above a tiny, unspoilt medieval village, this hotel enjoys wonderful views. The much modernized interior is light, airy and spacious, with attractive fabrics and furniture. Excellent, eclectic food, Michelin-starred. Pool.

■ Séguret, 84110 Vaison-la-Romaine (Vaucluse) **Tel** 04.90.46.91.49 **Fax** 04.90.46.94.27 **Meals** breakfast, lunch, dinner **Prices** rooms 450F-600F; menus 250F-450F **Rooms** 8, all with bath, central heating, phone, TV **Credit cards** AE, DC, MC, V **Closed** Feb, 23 Nov to 11 Dec; restaurant only, Tue eve, Wed (except Apr to end Dec)

The South

Restaurant with rooms, Tavel

Hostellerie du Seigneur

This congenial little restaurant-with-rooms is a cosy place, with a pleasant little terrace overlooking a square. Inside, a bar-cum-reception area leads into the hotel's hub: an intimate stone-vaulted dining-room where *cuisine bourgeoise* is offered. Bedrooms are old-fashioned but entirely adequate.

■ Place du Seigneur, 30126 Tavel (Gard) **Tel** 04.66.50.04.26 **Meals** breakfast, lunch, di nner **Prices** rooms 180F-300F; menus 95F-138F **Rooms** 7, all with central heating **Credit cards** MC, V **Closed** mid-Dec to mid-Jan

---

Country hotel, Tourtour

La Bastide de Tourtour

This modern but traditional-style hotel offers comfort and attentive service (it is in the Relais & Châteaux group), and the food is excellent, if not in the first rank. For many, the key attraction is the secluded setting, high up amid pine forests. Swimming-pool.

■ Rte de Draguignan, Tourtour, 83690 Salernes (Var) **Tel** 04.94.70.57.30 **Fax** 04.94.70.54.9 0 **Meals** breakfast, lunch, dinner **Prices** rooms 420F-1,400F; lunch 160F, menus 290F-360F **Rooms** 25, all with bath, central heating, phone, TV, minibar **Credit cards** AE, DC, V **Closed** Nov to mid-Mar

---

Manor house hotel, Tourtour

L'Auberge Saint-Pierre

This 16thC manor house is a peaceful, unpretentious retreat run as a welcoming hotel by the helpful Marcellins. The public rooms preserve something of a medieval feel; the spacious bedrooms are newly refurbished. Food relies heavily on produce of the home farm, and is served on the terrace in good weather. There is tennis, archery, cycling and fishing, as well as a pool and sauna.

■ Tourtour, 83690 Salernes (Var) **Tel** 04.94.70.57.17 **Fax** 04.94.70.59.04 **Meals** breakfast, lunch, dinner **Prices** rooms 400F-520F; breakfast 50F, menus 170F-200F **Rooms** 16, all with bath or shower, central heating, phone **Credit cards** V **Closed** Oct to end Mar; restaurant only, Wed

---

Restaurant with rooms, Valence

Pic

The food's the thing. Despite the death in 1992 of Jacques Pic, this remains (under son Alain) one of the best restaurants in the country – yet it is delightfully free of any snobby atmosphere. The good news is that the Pic family have recently added another small restaurant and 9 more comfortable bedrooms to this rarely vacant member of the Relais & Châteaux group.

■ 285 Ave Victor-Hugo, 26001 Valence (Drôme) **Tel** 04.75.44.15.32 **Fax** 04.75.40.96.03 **Meals** breakfast, lunch, dinner **Prices** rooms 700F-1,000F; breakfast 100F, menus 290F-660F **Rooms** 14, all with bath, central heating, phone, TV **Credit cards** AE, DC, MC, V **Closed** Sun evening; 2 weeks Aug

The South

Auberge la Fontaine

First an excellent restaurant, then five lovely suites, then in 1993 an alternative 'bistro' – the Soelkes show no sign of flagging. The rooms in this 18thC village house are decorated in rustic style – stone-flagged floors, wooden furniture, dried flowers.

■ Place de la Fontaine, Vénasque, 84210 Carpentras (Vaucluse) **Tel** 04.90.66.02.96 **Fax** 04.90.66.13.14 **Meals** breakfast, lunch (in bistro), dinner **Prices** rooms 800F; breakfast from 50F, lunch 90F, dinner 200F **Rooms** 5, all with bath, central heating, air-conditioning, phone, TV, radio, minibar, hairdrier **Credit cards** MC, V **Closed** restaurant only, Wed eve; bistro only, Sun eve, Mon

---

La Roseraie

This 'belle époque' villa has undergone considerable refurbishment over the past few years. Enthusiastic visitors describe the Ganiers as 'gracious and accommodating' hosts, the bedrooms, decorated in Provençal style, as 'rather small but comfortable'. Splendid views, and the place itelf is 'an oasis of peace'. Pretty pool.

■ Ave Henri Giraud, 06140 Vence (Alpes-Maritimes) **Tel** 04.93.58.02.20 **Fax** 04.93.58.99.31 **Meals** breakfast **Prices** rooms 395F-550F; breakfast 55F **Rooms** 12, all with bath, central heating, phone, TV, radio, minibar, hairdrier **Credit cards** AE, MC, V **Closed** never

---

Hôtel de l'Atelier

This old town house has been sympathetically restored – original stone walls much in evidence – with careful attention to detail. There is a picturesque courtyard at the back, enclosed by a jumble of old buildings – an ideal place in which to sit and drink muscat before dinner.

■ 5 Rue de la Foire, 30400 Villeneuve-lès-Avignon (Gard) **Tel** 04.90.25.01.84 **Fax** 04.90.25 .80.06 **Meals** breakfast **Prices** rooms 240F-450F; breakfast 38F-42F **Rooms** 19, all with bath or shower, central heating, phone; some have TV **Credit cards** AE, DC, MC, V **Closed** Nov to Dec

---

Hostellerie la Magnaneraie

Much up-graded in recent years, the Magnaneraie is a mellow stone house in a well-heeled residential corner of Villeneuve-lès-Avignon. The Prayals pride themselves on the place's easy-going elegance, but we don't rate this very high on personal approach.

■ Rue du Camp-de-Bataille, 30400 Villeneuve-lès-Avignon (Gard) **Tel** 04.90.25.11.11 **Fax** 04.90.25.46.37 **Meals** breakfast, lunch, dinner **Prices** rooms 500F-1,000F; breakfast 70F; menus 180F-350F **Rooms** 25, all with bath, central heating, phone, cable TV, minibar; some rooms have private terrace and/or air-conditioning **Credit cards** AE, DE, MC, V **Closed** never

Corsica

Corsica isn't our strong point. The reports we get from readers on Corsican hotels can be counted on the fingers of one hand.

Contenders in Corsica
Pioggiola, Auberge de l'Aghjola 04.95.61.90.48 Family-run creeper-clad inn; beams and painted furniture.
Porticcio, Le Maquis 04.95.25.05.55 Sophisticated fairly pricey (but special) hotel by water's edge.
St-Florent, Hôtel Bellevue 04.95.37.00.06 Chic, freshly decorated modern hotel with sea views and ambitious food.

Seaside hotel, Barcaggio

La Giraglia

The rooms in this simple creeper-covered stone building are no more than adequate, but the position overlooking the sea is superb and the atmosphere is relaxed and welcoming. This is a lovely and wild part of Corsica, well off the beaten tourist track. We would welcome more reports.

■ Barcaggio, 20275 Essa (Corse) **Tel** 04.95.35.60.54 **Fax** 04.95.35.65.92 **Meals** breakfast **Prices** rooms 320F-420F with breakfast **Rooms** 12, all with central heating, phone **Credit cards** not accepted **Closed** late Sep to mid-Apr

---

Country hotel, Calvi

La Signoria

A very welcome addition to our thin Corsica section – a 17thC country house in lush grounds, furnished and decorated with stylish simplicity. Inventive and excellent food is served in a beamed, ochre-washed room or beneath palms on the terrace overlooking the smart pool. There is also tennis and a steam room.

■ Route de la Forêt de Bonifato, 20260 Calvi (Corse) **Tel** 04.95.65.23.73 **Fax** 04.95.65.38.77 **Meals** breakfast, lunch (except Jul/Aug), dinner **Prices** rooms 450F-2000F; breakfast 70F; meals 300F-350F **Rooms** 10, all with bath, air-conditioning, phone, hairdrier, TV, minibar, safe **Credit cards** AE, MC, V **Closed** Nov to Mar

---

Village inn, Monticell

A Pasturella

Recent reports confirm the attractions of this modest little 'gem' on the square of a sleepy hill village, its bar at the very heart of local life. Bedrooms are pretty and mostly spacious, with terraces and balconies giving views. Food is wholesome and generous.

■ Monticello, 20220 l'Ile-Rousse (Corse) **Tel** 04.95.60.05.65 **Fax** 04.95.60.21.78 **Meals** breakfast, lunch, dinner **Prices** rooms 300F-320F; menu 140F **Rooms** 12, all with bath or shower, phone **Credit cards** DC , MC, V **Closed** Nov; restaurant only, Sun dinner Dec to Mar

Index of hotel names

In this index, hotels are arranged in order of the most distinctive part of their name; very common prefixes such as 'Auberge', 'Hôtel', 'Hostellerie' and 'Le/La/Les' are omitted, but more significant elements such as 'Château' are retained.

33 Rue Thiers, La Rochelle **97**

A
Abbaye, Annecy-le-Vieux **111**
Abbaye, Beaugency **103**
Abbaye, Le Bec-Hellouin **38**
Abbaye, Fontgombault **105**
Abbaye, Paris **47**
Abbaye, St-Cyprien **154**
Abbaye Saint-Michel, Tonnerre **130**
Abbaye de Ste-Croix,
  Salon-de-Provence **212**
Alisiers, Lapoutroie **88**
Angleterre, Paris **48**
Arcé, St-Étienne-de-Baïgorry **146**
Argouges, Bayeux **37**
Armes de Champagne, L'Épine **86**
Arraya, Sare **148**
Arts, St-Rémy-de-Provence **211**
Artzenheim, Artzenheim **86**
Atalaya, Llo **186**
Atelier, Villeneuve-lès-Avignon **214**

B
Banville, Paris **49**
Bas-Breau, Barbizon **70**
Bastide de Tourtour, Tourtour **213**
Beau Rivage, Condrieu **127**
Beaubourg, Paris **70**
Belle Gasconne, Poudenas **153**
Belle-Vue, St-Clair **209**
Benvengudo, Les
  Baux-de-Provence **203**
Bergerie, Soustons **156**
Bersoly's Saint-Germain, Paris **71**
Bois Joli, Bagnoles-de-l'Orne **37**
Bois Prin, Chamonix **116**
Bon Coin du Lac, Mimizan **142**
Bonne Étape, Château-Arnoux **175**
Bosquet, Pégomas **209**
Bourgogne, Cluny **126**
Bretonne, La Roche-Bernard **42**
Bretonnerie, Paris **50**

C
Cagnard, Haut-de-Cagnes **185**
Calanco, Montferrat **207**
Calanque, Le Lavandou **206**
Capitelle, Mirmande **207**
Carayon, St-Sernin-sur-Rance **170**
Cardinale, Baix **202**
Caron de Beaumarchais, Paris **71**
Cassagne, Le Pontet **191**
Castel, Mailly-le-Château **117**

Cathédrale, Rouen **43**
Cerf, Marlenheim **82**
Cévenole, La Favède **205**
Chaîne d'Or, Les Andelys **37**
Chalet, Coulandon **161**
Chambard, Kaysersberg **88**
Chapelle-Saint-Martin,
  St-Martin-du-Fault **108**
Charmes, Meursault **129**
Château, Châteauneuf **125**
Château, Lalinde **152**
Château des Alpilles,
  St-Rémy-de-Provence **211**
Château de Bagnols, Bagnols **123**
Château de Bellecroix, Chagny **124**
Château de la Beuvrière,
  St-Hilaire-de-Court **107**
Château de Boussac, Target **167**
Château de Castelpers, Castelpers **158**
Château de Chissay, Montrichard **106**
Château de Coatguélen, Pléhédel **42**
Château Cordeillan-Bages, Pauillac **143**
Château de Courcelles,
  Courcelles-sur-Vesle **86**
Château des Crayères, Reims **85**
Château Eza, Eze **205**
Château de Fleurville, Fleurville **127**
Château d'Igé, Igé **128**
Château de Locguénolé, Hennebont **39**
Château de Madières, Madières **187**
Château de la Menaudière,
  Montrichard **106**
Château de Montreuil,
  Montreuil-sur-Mer **84**
Château de Nieuil, Nieuil **96**
Château de Noirieux, Briollay **92**
Château de Pray, Amboise **102**
Château de la Râpée, Gisors **27**
Château de Remaisnil, Doullens **80**
Château de Rochecotte, St-Patrice **108**
Château de Rochegude,
  Rochegude **209**
Château de Roussan,
  St-Rémy-de-Provence **196**
Château de Trancis, Ydes **168**
Château de la Treyne, Lacave **140**
Château de Trigance, Trigance **200**
Château d'Urbilhac, Lamastre **206**
Château de la Vallée Bleue,
  St-Chartier **99**
Château de Vault-de-Lugny,
  Avallon **113**
Château de Vieux Mareuil,
  Vieux-Mareuil **156**

Index of hotel names

Chatenet, Brantôme **133**
Chaumière, Honfleur **40**
Cheval Blanc, Bléré **103**
Cheval Blanc, Sept-Saulx **89**
Chez Camille, Arnay-le-Duc **123**
Chez Pierre, Raguenès-Plage **42**
Chopin, Paris **71**
Christine, Paris **61**
Clair Logis, St-Jean-Cap-Ferrat **210**
Clarion, Aloxe-Corton **110**
Clé d'Or, Barbizon **70**
Cléry, Hesdin-L'Abbé **81**
Clos, Chablis **124**
Clos, Verneuil-sur-Avre **35**
Clos Fleuri, Belle-Ile-en-Mer **38**
Clos Médicis, Paris **71**
Clos du Montvinage, Etréaupont **87**
Clos Normand, Martin-Église **41**
Clos Saint-Vincent, Ribeauvillé **89**
Cochon d'Or et Petit Castel,
    Beuzeville **38**
Colombe d'Or, St-Paul-de-Vence **210**
Colombier, Roquefort-les-Pins **193**
Conquérant, Barfleur **37**
Côte d'Or, Châtillon-sur-Seine **126**
Coteau Fleuri, Grimaud **183**
Cottage, Argelès-sur-Mer **202**
Crillon le Brave, Crillon-le-Brave **177**
Croix Blanche,
    Chaumont-sur-Tharonne **104**
Croix Blanche,
    Souvigny-en-Sologne **108**
Croix-Fry, Manigod **118**
Cuq en Terrasses, Cuq-Toulza **169**

D

Daille, Florimont-Gaumiers **139**
Degrés de Notre-Dames, Paris **51**
Demeure de Chavoire,
    Veyrier-du-Lac **130**
Demeure de Flore, Lacabarède **162**
Désirade, Belle-Ile-en-Mer **38**
Deux Iles, Paris **72**
Deux Magots, La Roche-Bernard **43**
Deux Rocs, Seillans **199**
Diderot, Chinon **94**
Domaine d'Auriac, Carcassonne **204**
Domaine de Chateauneuf,
    Nans-les-Pins **208**
Domaine de Clairefontaine,
    Chonas-l'Amballan **126**
Domaine de la Rhue, Rocamadour **144**
Domaine de Rieumegé, Olargues **208**
Domaine de Valmouraine, St-Rémy-de-
    Provence **211**
Domaine deVilotte, Ardenais **102**
Donjon, Etretat **26**
Duc de St-Simon, Paris **52**

E

Eber Paris **53**
Ecluse No. 79, Chassignelles **125**
Ermitage, Paris **54**
Esplanade, Domme **150**
Essille, Bassac **102**

F

Falaises, Gluges **151**
Fayette, St-Jean-de-Luz **155**
Fénelon, Carennac **150**
Ferme de la Huppe, Gordes **205**
Ferme Saint-Siméon, Honfleur **40**
Fitz Roy, Val-Thorens **130**
Fleuray, Cangey **93**
Fleurie, Montsalvy **169**
Fleurie, Paris **55**
Florets, Gigondas **205**
Fontaine, Vénasque **214**
Fontaine aux Muses,
    La Celle-Saint-Cyr **124**
France, Ribérac **154**
France et des Fuschias,
    St-Vaast-la-Hougue **32**
Frontière, Auberge sans, Dégagnac **150**

G

Gardiole, Cap d'Antibes **203**
Géraniums, Le Barroux **203**
Giraglia, Barcaggio **215**
Globe, Paris **72**
Glycines, Les Eyzies-de-Tayac **138**
Gordos, Gordes **206**
Grand Écuyer, Cordes **160**
Grande Chaumière, St-Florentin **129**
Grandes Écoles, Paris **72**
Grandes Roches, Trégunc **44**
Grands Crus, Gevrey-Chambertin **115**
Grands Hommes, Paris **72**
Grenoullière, Montreuil-sur-Mer **83**
Gros Marronnier, Senlisse **69**

H

Halle, Givry **128**
Hameau, St-Paul-de-Vence **195**
Hauts de Montreuil,
    Montreuil-sur-Mer **88**
Haye-le-Comte, Louviers **40**
Hermitage, Buzançais **103**
Hospitaliers, Dieulefit **178**
Huitrières du Lac, **151**

J

Jabloire, Florent-en-Argonne **87**
Jardin des Plantes, Paris **73**
Jeanne de Laval,
    Les Rosiers-sur-Loire **98**
Jeu de Paume, Chamonix **125**
Jeu de Paume, Paris **56**

Index of hotel names

K
Kastell Dinec'h, Tréguier **44**
Korrigane, St-Malo **30**

L
Lameloise, Chagny **124**
Landes, Ouchamps **107**
Lenox, Paris **73**
Lièvre Amoureux, St-Lattier **130**
Loges de l'Aubergade, Puymirol **153**
Logis du Guetteur, Les Arcs **202**
Logis Saint-Martin,
   St-Maixent- l'Ecole **108**
Longcol, Najac **164**
Lord Byron, Paris **73**
Lou Calen, Cotignac **204**
Louvre, Paris **62**
Lyon D'or, Angles sur L'Anglin **102**
Lys, Paris **73**

M
Madone, Peillon **189**
Magdeleine, Gémenos **182**
Magnaneraie,
   Villeneuve-lès-Avignon **214**
Magnolias, Meursault **129**
Manassès, Curtil-Vergy **127**
Manescale, Les Essareaux **179**
Manoir, Fontenay-Trésigny **70**
Manoir, Ile de Port-Cros **209**
Manoir de Bellerive,
   Le Buisson-de-Cadouin **135**
Manoir du Butin, Honfleur **40**
Manoir du Grand Martigny,
   Fondettes **104**
Manoir d'Hautegente, Coly **137**
Manoir de Lan-Kerellec, Trébeurden **44**
Manoir du Lys, Bagnoles-de-l'Orne **21**
Manoir de Montesquiou, La Malène **169**
Manoir du Raveyron,
   Vallon-Pont-d'Arc **201**
Manoir de Rochecourbe, Vézac **156**
Manoir du Rodoir, La Roche-Bernard **43**
Mansart, Paris **57**
Marais, Coulon **104**
Marais Saint-Jean,
   Chonas-l'Amballan **126**
Marceau, Doussard **127**
Maronne, St-Martin-Valmeroux **166**
Mas des Brugassières,
   Plan-de-la-Tour **190**
Mas de la Brune, Eygalières **204**
Mas Candille, Mougins **207**
Mas des Carassins,
   St-Rémy-de-Provence **211**
Mas d'Entremont, Aix-en-Provence **172**
Mas de la Fouque,
   Les Stes-Maries-de-la-Mer **198**
Mas de Garrigon, Roussillon **194**

Mas Trilles, Céret **204**
Maurandière, Sourdeval **43**
Mayflower, Paris **74**
Métairie Neuve, Pont-de-L'Arn **170**
Métropole, Boulogne-sur-Mer **86**
Meysset, Sarlat **155**
Midi, Lamastre **206**
Midi-Papillon, St-Jean-du-Bruel **165**
Mouli del Riu,
   St-Pierre-dels-Forcats **210**
Moulin, Flagy **46**
Moulin, Loches **105**
Moulin de l'Abbaye, Brantôme **134**
Moulin de la Beune,
   Les Eyzies-de-Tayac **151**
Moulin Blanc, Les Beaumettes **203**
Moulin de la Camandoule, Fayence **180**
Moulin de Chaméron, Bannegon **91**
Moulins du Duc, Moëlan-sur-Mer **41**
Moulin de la Gorce,
   La Roche-l'Abeille **107**
Moulin d'Hauterive, Chaublanc **114**
Moulin de Marcouze, Mosnac **106**
Moulin de Mombreux, Lumbres **88**
Moulin du Prieuré,
   Bonnevaux-le-Prieuré **123**
Moulin du Roc,
   Champagnac-de-Belair **136**
Moulin des Templiers, Avallon **123**
Moulin du Vey, Clécy **23**
Moulin de Villeray, Villeray **36**
Muscadins, Mougins **188**

N
Nice, Paris **58**
Normandie, Caudebec-en-Caux **39**
Noves, Noves **208**

O
Ohantzea, Aïnhoa **132**
Orangers, St-Paul-de-Vence **210**
Orée du Bois, Futeau **87**
Oustal del Barry, Najac **170**
Oustaloun, Maussane-les-Alpilles **207**

P
Parc, Levernois **128**
Parc des Maréchaux, Auxerre **112**
Parc Saint-Séverin, Paris **59**
Pasturella, Monticello **215**
Pavillon de la Reine, Paris **60**
Pélissaria, St-Cirq-Lapopie **145**
Petit Coq aux Champs, Campigny **22**
Petite Auberge, Razac d'Eymet **153**
Pic, Valence **213**
Pins, Sabres **154**
Place des Vosges, Paris **74**
Plage, Ste-Anne-la-Palud **33**
Plaisance, St-Émilion **155**

Index of hotel names

Poids Public, St-Félix-Lauragais **155**
Ponche, St-Tropez **197**
Pont de l'Ouysse, Lacave **152**
Pontoise, Pons **107**
Pontot, Vézelay **122**
Porte Verte, Marans **105**
Poste, Charolles **125**
Pré Bossu, Moudeyres **163**
Prieuré, Ermenonville **87**
Prieuré, St-André-d'Hébertot **29**
Prieuré, Tonnay-Boutonne **101**
Prima-Lepic, Paris **74**
Prince Albert, Paris **74**

Q
Quatres Saisons, St-Restitut **212**

R
Récollets, Marcigny **119**
Régalido, Fontvieille **181**
Reillanne, Reillanne **192**
Repaire de Kerroc'h, Paimpol **41**
Riboutté Lafayette, Paris **75**
Ripa Alta, Plaisance **153**
Rivage, Gien **105**
Rivage, Olivet **106**
Rives de Notre Dame, Paris **75**
Roche Corneille, Dinard **39**
Roseraie, Chenonceaux **104**
Roseraie, Vence **214**
Rostaing, Passenans **121**

S
St-Dominique, Paris **75**
St-Germain, Paris **63**
St-Germain-des-Prés, Paris **75**
St-Grégoire, Paris **64**
St-Jacques, Cloyes-sur-le-Loir **24**
St-Jacques, St-Saud-Lacoussière **147**
St-Louis, Paris **76**
St-Louis Marais, Paris **76**
St-Merry, Paris **65**
St-Paul, Paris **66**
St-Pierre, La Bouille **39**
St-Pierre, Le Mont-St-Michel **41**
St-Pierre, St-Pierre-du-Vauvray **31**
St-Pierre, Tourtour **213**
Ste-Beuve, Paris **67**
Ste-Catherine, Montbron **95**
Ste-Foy, Conques **159**
Sts-Péres, Paris **76**
Sarthe, Châteauneuf-sur-Sarthe **103**
Seigneur, Tavel **213**
Sélune, Ducey **25**
Signoria, Calvi **215**
Solférino, Paris **68**
Solognote, Brinon-sur-Sauldre **103**
Source Bleue, Touzac **156**
Sphinx, Perros-Guirec **42**

T
Table du Comtat, Séguret **212**
Taillard, Goumois **128**
Tauzins, Montfort-en-Chalosse **152**
Terrasse au Soleil, Céret **174**
Thoumieux, Paris **76**
Ti Al-Lannec, Trébeurden **34**
Tomette, Vitrac **170**
Tonnellerie, Tavers **100**
Tour du Roy, Vervins **89**
Trois Lys, Condom **150**
Trois Mousquetaires, Aire-sur-la-Lys **79**
Tuileries, Paris **77**

U
Université, Paris **77**

V
Val d'Or, Mercurey **120**
Val d'Orbieu, Ornaisons **208**
Verger, Grimaud **184**
Verneuil-St-Germain, Paris **77**
Vert, Mauroux **141**
Verte Campagne, Trelly **44**
Vielle Fontaine, Cornillon **176**
Vieilles Tours, Rocamadour **154**
Vieux Cordes, Cordes **169**
Vieux Logis, Lestelle-Bétharram **152**
Vieux Logis, Trémolat **149**
Vieux Pérouges, Pérouges **129**
Vieux Puits, Pont-Audemer **28**
Vignette Haute, Auribeau **202**
Villa Gallici, Aix-en-Provence **173**
Vosges, Ribeauvillé **89**
Voyageurs, Escos **151**

Y
Yaca, St-Tropez **212**

Index of hotel locations

In this index, hotels are arranged by the name of the city, town or village they are in or near. Hotels located in a very small village may be indexed under the name of a larger place nearby.

A

Aïnhoa, Ohantzea **132**
Aire-sur-la-Lys, Trois Mousquetaires **79**
Aix-en-Provence, Mas d'Entremont **172**
Aix-en-Provence, Villa Gallici **173**
Aloxe-Corton, Clarion **110**
Amboise, Château de Pray **102**
Les Andelys, Chaîne d'Or **37**
Angles sur l'Anglin, Relais du Lyon D'or **102**
Annecy-le-Vieux, Abbaye **111**
Les Arcs, Logis du Guetteur **202**
Ardenais, Domaine de Vilotte **102**
Argelès-sur-Mer, Cottage **202**
Arnay-le-Duc, Chez Camille **123**
Artzenheim, Artzenheim **86**
Auribeau, Vignette Haute **202**
Auxerre, Parc des Maréchaux **112**
Avallon, Château de Vault-de-Lugny **113**
Avallon, Moulin des Templiers **123**

B

Bagnoles-de-l'Orne, Bois Joli **37**
Bagnoles-de-l'Orne, Manoir du Lys **21**
Bagnols, Château de Bagnols **123**
Baix, Cardinale **202**
Bannegon, Moulin de Chaméron **91**
Barbizon, Bas-Breau **70**
Barbizon, Clé d'Or **70**
Barcaggio, Giraglia **215**
Barfleur, Conquérant **37**
Le Barroux, Géraniums **203**
Bassac, Essille **102**
Les Baux-de-Provence, Benvengudo **203**
Bayeux, Argouges **37**
Beaugency, Abbaye **103**
Les Beaumettes, Moulin Blanc **203**
Le Bec-Hellouin, Abbaye **38**
Belle-Ile-en-Mer, Clos Fleuri **38**
Belle-Ile-en-Mer, Désirade **38**
Beuzeville, Cochon d'Or et Petit Castel **38**
Bléré, Cheval Blanc **103**
Bonnevaux-le-Prieuré, Moulin du Prieuré **123**
La Bouille, St-Pierre **39**
Boulogne-sur-Mer, Métropole **86**
Brantôme, Chatenet **133**
Brantôme, Moulin de l'Abbaye **134**
Brinon-sur-Sauldre, Solognote **103**
Briollay, Château de Noirieux **92**
Le Buisson-de-Cadouin, Manoir de Bellerive **135**
Buzançais, Hermitage **103**

C

Calvi, Signoria **215**
Campigny, Petit Coq aux Champs **22**
Cangey, Fleuray **93**
Cap d'Antibes, Gardiole **203**
Carcassonne, Domaine d'Auriac **204**
Carennac, Fénelon **150**
Castelpers, Château de Castelpers **158**
Caudebec-en-Caux, Normandie **39**
La Celle-Saint-Cyr, Fontaine aux Muses **124**
Céret, Mas Trilles **204**
Céret, Terrasse au Soleil **174**
Chablis, Clos **124**
Chagny, Château de Bellecroix **124**
Chagny, Lameloise **124**
Chamonix, Bois Prin **116**
Chamonix, Jeu de Paume **125**
Champagnac-de-Belair, Moulin du Roc **136**
Charolles, Poste **125**
Chassignelles, Ecluse No. 79 **125**
Château-Arnoux, Bonne Étape **175**
Châteauneuf, Château **125**
Châteauneuf-sur-Sarthe, Sarthe **103**
Châtillon-sur-Seine, Côte d'Or **126**
Chaublanc, Moulin d'Hauterive **114**
Chaumont-sur-Tharonne, Croix Blanche **104**
Chenonceaux, Roseraie **104**
Chinon, Diderot **94**
Chonas-l'Amballan, Domaine de Clairefontaine **126**
Chonas-l'Amballan, Marais Saint-Jean **126**
Clécy, Moulin du Vey **23**
Cloyes-sur-le-Loir, St-Jacques **24**
Cluny, Bourgogne **126**
Coly, Manoir d'Hautegente **137**
Condom, Trois Lys **150**
Condrieu, Beau Rivage **127**
Conques, Ste-Foy **159**
Cordes, Grand Écuyer **160**
Cordes, Vieux Cordes **169**
Cornillon, Vielle Fontaine **176**
Cotignac, Lou Calen **204**
Coulandon, Chalet **161**
Coulon, Marais **104**
Courcelles-sur-Vesle, Château de Courcelles **86**
Crillon-le-Brave, Crillon le Brave **177**
Cuq-Toulza, Cuq en Terrasses **169**
Curtil-Vergy, Manassès **127**

Index of hotel locations

D
Dégagnac, Frontière, Auberge sans **150**
Dieulefit, Hospitaliers **178**
Dinard, Roche Corneille **39**
Domme, Esplanade **150**
Doullens, Château de Remaisnil **80**
Doussard, Marceau **127**
Ducey, Sélune **25**

E
L'Épine, Armes de Champagne **86**
Ermenonville, Prieuré **87**
Escos, Voyageurs **151**
Les Essareaux, La Manescale **179**
Etréaupont, Clos du Montvinage **87**
Etretat, Donjon **26**
Eygalières, Mas de la Brune **204**
Les Eyzies-de-Tayac, Glycines **138**
Les Eyzies-de-Tayac, Moulin de la
   Beune **151**
Eze, Château Eza **205**

F
La Favède, Cévenole **205**
Fayence, Moulin de la Camandoule **180**
Flagy, Moulin **46**
Fleurville, Château de Fleurville **127**
Florent-en-Argonne, Jabloire **87**
Florimont-Gaumiers, Daille **139**
Fondettes, Manoir du
   Grand Martigny **104**
Fontenay-Trésigny, Manoir **70**
Fontgombault, Abbaye **105**
Fontvieille, Régalido **181**
Futeau, Orée du Bois **87**

G
Gémenos, Magdeleine **182**
Gevrey-Chambertin, Grands Crus **115**
Gien, Rivage **105**
Gigondas, Florets **205**
Gisors, Château de la Râpée **27**
Givry, Halle **128**
Gluges, Falaises **151**
Gordes, Ferme de la Huppe **206**
Gordes, Gordos **205**
Goumois, Taillard **128**
Grimaud, Coteau Fleuri **183**
Grimaud, Verger **184**

H
Haut-de-Cagnes, Cagnard **185**
Hennebont, Château de Locguénolé **39**
Hesdin-L'Abbé, Cléry **81**
Honfleur, Chaumière **40**
Honfleur, Ferme St-Siméon **40**
Honfleur, Manoir du Butin **40**
Hossegor, Huitrières du Lac **151**

I
Igé, Château d'Igé **128**

K
Kaysersberg, Chambard **88**

L
Lacabarède, Demeure de Flore **162**
Lacave, Château de la Treyne **140**
Lacave, Pont de l'Ouysse **152**
Lalinde, Château **152**
Lamastre, Château d'Urbilhac **206**
Lamastre, Midi **206**
Lapoutroie, Alisiers **88**
Le Lavandou, Calanque **206**
Lestelle-Bétharram, Vieux Logis **152**
Levernois, Parc **128**
Llo, Atalaya **186**
Loches, Moulin **105**
Louviers, Haye-le-Comte **40**
Lumbres, Moulin de Mombreux **88**

M
Madières, Château de Madières **187**
Mailly-le-Château, Castel **117**
La Malène, Manoir de Montesquiou **169**
Manigod, Croix-Fry **118**
Marans, Porte Verte **105**
Marcigny, Récollets **119**
Marlenheim, Cerf **41**
Martin-Église, Clos Normand **141**
Mauroux, Vert **141**
Maussane-les-Alpilles, Oustaloun **207**
Mercurey, Val d'Or **120**
Meursault, Charmes **129**
Meursault, Magnolias **129**
Mimizan, Bon Coin du Lac **142**
Mirmande, Capitelle **207**
Moëlan-sur-Mer, Moulins du Duc **41**
Le Mont-St-Michel, St-Pierre **41**
Montbron, Ste-Catherine **95**
Montferrat, Calanco **207**
Montfort-en-Chalosse, Tauzins **152**
Monticello, Pasturella **215**
Montreuil-sur-Mer, Château de
   Montreuil **84**
Montreuil-sur-Mer, Grenoullière **83**
Montreuil-sur-Mer, Hauts de
   Montreuil **88**
Montrichard, Château de Chissay **106**
Montrichard, Château de la
   Menaudière **106**
Montsalvy, Fleurie **169**
Mosnac, Moulin de Marcouze **106**
Moudeyres, Pré Bossu **163**
Mougins, Mas Candille **207**
Mougins, Muscadins **188**

Index of hotel locations

N
Najac, Longcol **164**
Najac, Oustal del Barry **170**
Nans-les-Pins, Domaine de
  Chateauneuf **208**
Nieuil, Château de Nieuil **96**
Noves, Noves **208**

O
Olargues, Domaine de Rieumegé **208**
Olivet, Rivage **106**
Ornaisons, Val d'Orbieu **208**
Ouchamps, Landes **107**

P
Paimpol, Repaire de Kerroc'h **41**
Paris, Abbaye **47**
Paris, Angleterre **48**
Paris, Banville **49**
Paris, Beaubourg **70**
Paris, Bersoly's Saint-Germain **71**
Paris, Bretonnerie **50**
Paris, Caron de Beaumarchais **71**
Paris, Chopin **71**
Paris, Christine **61**
Paris, Clos Médicis **71**
Paris, Degrés de Notre-Dame **51**
Paris, Deux Iles **72**
Paris, Duc de St-Simon **52**
Paris, Eber **53**
Paris, Ermitage **54**
Paris, Fleurie **55**
Paris, Globe **72**
Paris, Grandes Écoles **72**
Paris, Grands Hommes **72**
Paris, Jardin des Plantes **73**
Paris, Jeu de Paume **56**
Paris, Lenox **73**
Paris, Lord Byron **73**
Paris, Louvre **62**
Paris, Lys **73**
Paris, Mansart **57**
Paris, Mayflower **74**
Paris, Nice **58**
Paris, Parc Saint-Séverin **59**
Paris, Pavillon de la Reine **60**
Paris, Place des Vosges **74**
Paris, Prima-Lepic **74**
Paris, Prince Albert **74**
Paris, Riboutté Lafayette **75**
Paris, Rives de Notre Dame **75**
Paris, St-Dominique **75**
Paris, St-Germain **63**
Paris, St-Germain-des-Prés **75**
Paris, St Grégoire **64**
Paris, St-Louis **76**
Paris, St-Louis Marais **76**
Paris, St-Merry **65**
Paris, St-Paul **66**

Paris, Ste-Beuve **67**
Paris, Sts-Pères **76**
Paris, Solférino **68**
Paris, Thoumieux **76**
Paris, Tuileries **77**
Paris, Université **77**
Paris, Verneuil-St-Germain **77**
Passenans, Rostaing **121**
Pauillac, Château Cordeillan-Bages **143**
Pégomas, Bosquet **209**
Peillon, Madone **189**
Pérouges, Vieux Pérouges **129**
Perros-Guirec, Sphinx **42**
Plaisance, Ripa Alta **153**
Plan-de-la-Tour, Mas des
  Brugassières **190**
Pléhédel, Château de Coatguélen **42**
Pons, Pontoise **107**
Pont-Audemer, Vieux Puits **28**
Pont-de-L'Arn, Métairie Neuve **170**
Le Pontet, Cassagne **191**
Ile de Port-Cros, Manoir **209**
Poudenas, Belle Gasconne **153**
Puymirol, Loges de l'Aubergade **153**

R
Raguenès-Plage, Chez Pierre **42**
Razac d'Eymet, Petite Auberge **153**
Reillanne, Reillanne **192**
Reims, Château des Crayères **85**
Ribeauvillé, Clos Saint-Vincent **89**
Ribeauvillé, Vosges **89**
Ribérac, France **154**
Rocamadour, Domaine de la Rhue **144**
Rocamadour, Vieilles Tours **154**
La Roche-Bernard, Bretonne **42**
La Roche-Bernard, Deux Magots **43**
La Roche-Bernard, Manoir du Rodoir **43**
La Roche-l'Abeille, Moulin de la
  Gorce **107**
Rochegude, Château de Rochegude **209**
La Rochelle, 33 Rue Thiers **97**
Roquefort-les-Pins, Colombier **193**
Les Rosiers-sur-Loire, Jeanne de
  Laval **99**
Rouen, Cathédrale **43**
Roussillon, Mas de Garrigon **194**

S
Sabres, Pins **154**
St-André-d'Hébertot, Prieuré **29**
St-Chartier, Château de la Vallée
  Bleue **99**
St-Cirq-Lapopie, Pélissaria **145**
St-Clair, Belle-Vue **209**
St-Cyprien, Abbaye **154**
St-Émilion, Plaisance **155**
St-Étienne-de-Baïgorry, Arcé **146**
St-Félix-Lauragais, Poids Public **155**

Index of hotel locations

St-Florentin, Grande Chaumière **129**
St-Hilaire-de-Court, Château de la Beuvrière **107**
St-Jean-Cap-Ferrat, Clair Logis **210**
St-Jean-de-Luz, Fayette **155**
St-Jean-du-Bruel, Midi-Papillon **165**
St-Lattier, Lièvre Amoureux **130**
St-Maixent-l'Ecole, Logis Saint-Martin **108**
St-Malo, Korrigane **30**
St-Martin-Valmeroux, Maronne **166**
St-Martin-du-Fault, Chapelle-Saint-Martin **108**
St-Patrice, Château de Rochecotte **108**
St-Paul-de-Vence, Colombe d'Or **210**
St-Paul-de-Vence, Hameau **195**
St-Paul-de-Vence, Orangers **210**
St-Pierre-dels-Forcats, Mouli del Riu **210**
St-Pierre-du-Vauvray, St-Pierre **31**
St-Rémy-de-Provence, Arts **211**
St-Rémy-de-Provence, Château des Alpilles **211**
St-Rémy-de-Provence, Château de Roussan **196**
St-Rémy-de-Provence, Domaine de Valmouraine **211**
St-Rémy-de-Provence, Mas des Carassins **211**
St-Restitut, Quatres Saisons **212**
St-Saud-Lacoussière, St-Jacques **140**
St-Sernin-sur-Rance, Carayon **170**
St-Tropez, Ponche **197**
St-Tropez, Yaca **212**
St-Vaast-la-Hougue, France et des Fuschias **32**
Ste-Anne-la-Palud, Plage **33**
Les Stes-Maries-de-la-Mer, Mas de la Fouque **198**
Salon-de-Provence, Abbaye de Ste-Croix **212**
Sare, Arraya **148**
Sarlat, Meysset **155**
Séguret, Table du Comtat **212**
Seillans, Deux Rocs **199**
Senlisse, Gros Marronnier **69**
Sept-Saulx, Cheval Blanc **89**
Sourdeval, Maurandière **43**
Soustons, Bergerie **156**
Souvigny-en-Sologne, Croix Blanche **108**

T
Target, Château de Boussac **167**
Tavel, Seigneur **213**
Tavers, Tonnellerie **100**
Tonnay-Boutonne, Prieuré **101**
Tonnerre, Abbaye Saint-Michel **130**
Tourtour, Bastide de Tourtour **213**

Tourtour, St-Pierre **213**
Touzac, Source Bleue **156**
Trébeurden, Manoir de Lan-Kerellec **44**
Trébeurden, Ti Al-Lannec **34**
Tréguier, Kastell Dinec'h **44**
Trégunc, Grandes Roches **44**
Trelly, Verte Campagne **44**
Trémolat, Vieux Logis **149**
Trigance, Château de Trigance **200**

V
Val-Thorens, Fitz Roy **130**
Valence, Pic **213**
Vallon-Pont-d'Arc, Manoir du Raveyron **201**
Vénasque, Fontaine **214**
Vence, Roseraie **214**
Verneuil-sur-Avre, Clos **35**
Vervins, Tour du Roy **89**
Veyrier-du-Lac, Demeure de Chavoire **130**
Vézac, Manoir de Rochecourbe **156**
Vézelay, Pontot **122**
Vieux-Mareuil, Château de Vieux Mareuil **156**
Villeneuve-lès-Avignon, Atelier **214**
Villeneuve-lès-Avignon, Magnaneraie **214**
Villeray, Moulin de Villeray **36**
Vitrac, Tomette **170**

Y
Ydes, Château de Trancis **168**